Penguin Book 2490
Latin American Writing Today

LATIN
AMERICAN
WRITING
TODAY

EDITED BY J. M. COHEN

PENGUIN BOOKS

BALTIMORE · MARYLAND

Penguin Books Ltd, Harmondsworth,
Middlesex, England
Penguin Books Inc., 3300 Clipper Mill Road,
Baltimore, Md 21211, U.S.A.
Penguin Books Australia Ltd, Ringwood,
Victoria, Australia

First published 1967
Copyright © Penguin Books Ltd, 1967

Made and printed in Great Britain by
Hazell Watson & Viney Ltd
Aylesbury, Bucks
Set in Linotype Juliana

To Carlos and Rita

Contents

8 *Contents*

Acknowledgements

For permission to publish or reproduce the material in this anthology, acknowledgement is made to the following:

for BRENO ACCIOLY: 'João Urso' from *João Urso* by Breno Accioly, to Editora Civilizacão Brasileira S.A.;

for MARIO BENEDETTI: 'Los Iriarte' from *Montevideanos* by Mario Benedetti, to Alfa Libreria Editorial and to the author;

for JORGE LUIS BORGES: 'La Escritura de Dios' from *El Aleph* by Jorge Luis Borges, to Emece Editores and the author;

for JOÃO CABRAL DE MELO NETO: extract from 'The Death and Life of a Severino' from *Duas Aguas* by João Cabral de Melo Neto, José Olympio Editora, 1956, to the author;

for G. CABRERA INFANTE: 'En el Gran Ecbo' from *Así en la Paz como en la Guerra* by G. Cabrera Infante, Ediciones R., 1960, to the author;

for ONELIO JORGE CARDOSO: 'Despues de los dias' from *Cuentos Completos* by Onelio Jorge Cardoso, Ediciones A., 1962, to the author;

for ALEJO CARPENTIER: 'Viaja a la semilla' from *Guerra de tiempo* by Alejo Carpentier, 1958, to the author;

for ROSARIO CASTELLANOS: 'La extranjera', to the author;

for ALÍ CHUMACERO: 'Epitafio para una virgen' from *Palabras en Reposo* by Alí Chumacero, Fondo de Cultura Economica, 1956, to the author;

for JULIO CORTÁZAR: 'Bestiario' will soon appear in *End of the Game and Other Stories* by Julio Cortázar, copyright © 1967 Pantheon Books, A Division of Random House, Inc. Used by permission; also to The Harvill Press Ltd who will publish an anthology of Cortázar's short stories in 1968;

for JOSÉ DONOSO: 'Aná-Maria' from *El Charleston* by José Donoso, Nascimento, 1960, to the author;

for CARLOS DRUMMOND DE ANDRADE: 'Viagem na Familia' from *Poesias* by Carlos Drummond de Andrade, Editora José Olympio, 1942, and 'Nao se Mate' from *Brejo das Almas*, Os Amigos do Livro, 1934, both to the author;

for PABLO ARMANDO FERNANDEZ: 'Delación', 'Meditaciones de Abel', and 'Nacimiento de Eggo' from *Libro de los héroes* by Pablo Armando Fernandez, 1963, to the author;

for CARLOS FUENTES: 'Aura' to Farrar, Strauss & Giroux, Inc., and the author;

for GABRIEL GARCÍA MÁRQUEZ: 'The Day after Saturday' translated from

'Un dia despues del Sabado' in *Los Funerales de la Mama Grande* by García Márquez, copyright © 1962. By permission of Harper & Row, Publishers;

for ALBERTO GIRRI: 'Epistola a Hieronymus Bosch', to the author;

for JOÃO GUIMARÃES ROSA: 'A Terceira margem do rio' from *Primeiras Estorias* by João Guimarães Rosa (to be published in an English translation by Alfred A. Knopf, Inc.), to the author;

for ENRIQUE LIHN: 'El bosque en el jardin', 'La invasion', 'Los amigos de la casa', and 'Jonas' from *La pieza oscura* by Enrique Lihn, 1963, to the author;

for RICARDO E. MOLINARI: 'Oda' from *Mundos de la madrugada* by Ricardo Molinari, 1943, to the author;

for MARCO ANTONIO MONTES DE OCA: 'La despedida del bufon' and 'Se agrieta el labio' from *Cantos al sol que no se alcanza* by Marco Antonio Montes de Oca, Fondo de Cultura Economica, to the author;

for VINICIUS DE MORAES: 'Christmas Poem' and 'Sonnet on Separation', to the author;

for PABLO NERUDA: 'Oda a la Magnolia' from *Odas elementales* by Pablo Neruda, 1954, and 'Algunas Bestias' from *Canto general* by Pablo Neruda, 1950, both to the author;

for JUAN CARLOS ONETTI: 'El Infierno tan temido' from *El Infierno tan temido* by J. C. Onetti, Ediciones Asir, 1962, to the author;

for JOSÉ EMILIO PACHECO: 'Los elementos de la noche' from *Los elementos de la noche* by José Emilio Pacheco, Universidad Nacional Autonoma de Mexico, 1963, to the author;

for NICANOR PARRA: 'Autorretrato' and 'El Peregrino' from *Poemas y antipoemas* by Nicanor Parra, 1956 (first published in English in *Antipoems*, City Lights Books, 1959), and 'Solo de Piano', all to the author;

for OCTAVIO PAZ: 'Hymnos entre ruinas' to Fondo de Cultura Economica, to Indiana University Press, who first published the poem in English in *Selected Poems* by Octavio Paz, and to the author; 'Ustica' to Editorial Joaquin Mortiz and to the author; and 'Viento entero' to the author;

for CARLOS PELLICER: 'Esquemas para una oda tropical', to the author;

for JUAN RULFO: 'Nos han dado la tierra' from *El llano en llamas* by Juan Rulfo, Fondo de Cultura Economica, 1953, to the author;

for JAIME SABINES: 'Igual que los cangrejos' and 'Los he visto en el cine' from *Recuento de poemas* by Jaime Sabines, 1962, to the author;

for CÉSAR VALLEJO: 'Four Poems from *Trilce*', to Charles Tomlinson;

for C. VASCONCELOS MAIA: 'Sol' from *O Cavalo e a Rosa* by C. Vasconcelos Maia, Livraria Progresso Editora, 1955, to the author.

The publishers would be interested to hear from any copyright holders not acknowledged here.

Introduction

Around the year 1940, literature in Latin America achieved independence and maturity. Up to that time even the most original writers habitually looked back on a European apprenticeship; and reputations depended very largely on acknowledgement in Paris or Madrid. Isolated in the small and oligarchic literary communities of Buenos Aires, Mexico City, and Rio de Janeiro, the Latin Americans often paid inordinate respect to second-rate European talents, whilst neglecting their own. Lacking self-assurance and an interested public, their novelists and poets either pursued a course of restless experiment, or explained themselves and their situation in excessive detail. The Chilean poet Vicente Huidobro and the first Mexican novelists of the revolution, Mario Azeula and Martín Guzman, typify these two extremes. Not until the last quarter of a century have young writers south of the Río Grande soberly and consistently pursued their own themes, addressing a slowly growing educated middle-class in their own countries.

The new sense of independence which has prompted the wide variety of poems and stories in this book has several causes. The defeat of the Spanish Republic had two beneficial effects on the American republics; it destroyed all deference to Madrid, and also, by exiling so many writers and scholars, greatly contributed to the cultural life of Central and South America. The success of the Mexican revolution also encouraged intellectuals in all these countries by showing them the possibilities of a native-born liberalism, dependent neither on Marxism nor on Yankee plutocracy. Recent events in Cuba have reinforced this tendency. The six years of the war against Hitler also contributed greatly to Latin-American self-sufficiency. Enforced isolation threw writers on their own resources; the journey to Paris, whether physical or spiritual, had become impossible. Moreover, writers of a younger middle-class generation, lacking the inherited wealth of their oligarchic seniors, could not afford either to travel or live abroad.

Some went to the United States on scholarships and returned with a strong admiration for North American writing, but an equally strong distaste for the 'American way of life'. Everything has contributed to the growth of Central and South American nationalism, which is reflected, in its various aspects, by all the contributors to this book.

Literature is vigorously independent in at least half a dozen of the Latin-American republics. But each is independent of the other. Owing to difficulties of communication, customs barriers, and the lack of an international book trade, nothing is harder than for the Mexican writer to discover what is being written in Buenos Aires, Santiago or Rio de Janeiro, and *vice versa*. There is no single Latin-American movement, but a number of vigorous national groups, often in disputatious fission, in the principal countries, the freer and more advanced capitals housing exiles from the smaller dictatorship states where publishing is hampered by repression and censorship. Latin America only seems a unity when viewed from the simplifying distance of London, Paris, or New York; and even so strong national features stand out. The sharply etched realism of the Uruguayan short story writers, represented here by J. C. Onetti and Mario Benedetti, contrasts sharply with the metaphysical fantasy practised by the Argentinians, of whom Jorge Luis Borges and Julio Cortázar are outstanding. The Brazilian modernist poets, Drummond Andrade and João Cabral, owe something to English poets of T. S. Eliot's generation and afterwards, while the Mexicans show more affinities with France, and influences from the greatest modern poet of the whole New World, César Vallejo, are to be seen almost everywhere among the new, post-surrealist generation.

This anthology begins with the half-dozen established giants who made their reputation in the forties and are still widely influential. Borges, Pablo Neruda, Ricardo Molinari, Drummond Andrade, Octavio Paz, and Carlos Pellicer are each represented by characteristic work, not all of it recent, but none of it familiar in English. Vallejo is included too, since, though he died in 1938, he is the greatest and most living Latin-American poet, and still unknown in England. He was the first to write poetry out of hard-bitten life experience, and in language that is raw with the accent of his native Peruvian province; exile in Europe did not *castilianize* him. Posthumously indeed, he has *americanized* some of the best young writers in Franco's Spain, where his collected poetry is still a forbidden book.

Other poetry in this book displays the influence of French surrealism, which was, however, never accepted beyond the Atlantic in its full associative purity. The landscape of Latin America is in itself *surreal*. Molinari's limitless pampas, Pellicer's entangled jungle, Neruda's peaks and slagheaps, are in themselves dreamlandscapes; juxtapositions that are selfconsciously evoked in the streets of Paris take real form in a continent where vegetation swallows houses, and deserts imitate the nightmare vacancy of a landscape by Yves Tanguy. Dream imagery, however, is always applied by these poets to some vision of objective reality; and with the growing influence of Vallejo, reality, in the case of such younger writers as Jaime Sabines and Enrique Lihn, tends to assert itself over dream.

The stories cover a wide field, extending from the metaphysical fantasy of Borges' 'Handwriting of God' to sharply documented incidents like those of the Uruguayans and José Donoso's of the old man and the little girl. Carlos Fuentes, whose *Aura* is a tale of possession in the Henry James tradition, said in a Third Programme interview that the Latin-American novelist must be at the same time a Balzac and a Butor. Circumstantial realism and psychological depth are equally necessary, if this new world is to be revealed both to its own newly educated generations and to the growing number of interested foreigners. In these short stories, the two strands are not often woven together. In 'The Third Bank of the River', Guimarães Rosa presents a man isolated from the life on the other two 'real' banks of his unnamed stream; in 'Journey to the Seed', Alejo Carpentier sets time in reverse, but attempts no social comment. The more accurately documented stories, like García Márquez' economical and objective picture of a decayed town, 'The Day after Saturday', or Onelio Cardoso's gradual uncovering of an old meanness, 'It's a Long Time Ago', contain no metaphysical echoes. A few writers, however, like Julio Cortázar and Carlos Fuentes himself, mingle fantasy and reality : an imagined character takes physical form; a pet puma incarnates the stifled evil of an uncomfortable middle-class house.

The variety is as great as I could make it. One or two major writers, the Brazilian Jorge Amado among the elder and the Peruvian Marío Vargas Llosa among the younger, are excluded only because, being principally novelists, they have written nothing suitable both in length and quality. The choices are entirely my own for the Spanish language countries, though several friends, Carlos Fuentes and Pablo Armando Fernández in particular, have helped me by recommendations and the loan of books. For Brazil on the other hand, I have had able help from R. P. Joscelyne and Elizabeth Bishop. Most of the translations have been made especially for this book. Some of the poetry, however, has appeared in *Translation, The Southern Review, Atlante, Peacock,* and the *Times Literary Supplement;* some has been read in B.B.C. programmes. Borges' 'The Handwriting of God' too has been read in the Third Programme.

December 1964   J.M.C.

Gabriela Mistral

THE LIANA

In the secret of night
my prayer climbs like the liana,
gropes like a blind man,
sees more than the owl.

Up the stalk of night
that you loved, that I love,
creeps my torn prayer,
rent and mended, uncertain and sure.

Here the path breaks it,
here breezes lift it,
wind flurries toss it,
and something I don't know
hurls it to earth again.

Now it creeps like the liana,
now geysers up, at every thrust
received and returned.

My prayer is, and I am not.
It grows, and I perish.
I have only my hard breath,
my reason and my madness.
I cling to the vine of my prayer.
I tend it at the root
of the stalk of night.

Always the same glory
of life, the same death,

you who hear me and I who see you.
The vine tenses, snaps, recoils,
lacerates my flesh.

Grasp the weakening tip
when my prayer reaches you
so that I may know you have it,
sustain it the long night.

Of an instant night hardens,
hard as ipecac, as eucalyptus:
becomes black stretch of road
and frozen hush of river.
My liana climbs and climbs
till tendrils touch your side.

When the vine breaks, you raise it,
and by your touch I know you.
Then my breath catches,
my ardour rekindles, my message flames.

I grow still. I name you. One by one
I tell you all your names.
The liana caresses your throat,
binds you fast, entwines you, and rests.

My poor breath quickens
and words become flood.
My prayer, moored, at last
grows quiet, at last is still.

Then I know the dark vine
of my blood is anchored,
the broken skein of my body
unravelled in prayer;
and I learn that the patient
cry, broken, mends;

climbs again and climbing,
the more it suffers, the more attains.

Gather up my prayer tonight.
Take it and hold it.
Sleep, my love, let my sleep
fall to me in prayer,
and as we were on earth,
so do we remain.

Translated by Doris Dana

Jorge Luis Borges

THE HANDWRITING OF GOD

The prison is high and built of stone; its shape is that of an almost perfect hemisphere. For the floor, which is also of stone, intersects it a little above its greatest possible diameter; which somewhat accentuates the feeling of vastness and oppression. A wall divides it in two and, though very high, does not touch the upper part of the vault. On one side am I, Tzinacán, mage of the pyramid of Qaholom, which was burnt by Pedro de Alvarado; on the other is a jaguar that measures the time and space of its captivity with quiet and even steps. A long barred window pierces the central wall at ground level. At the hour when there are no shadows (midday), a trap is opened in the roof and a jailer, who is decaying with the years, works an iron pulley by which he drops us jars of water and lumps of meat at the end of a rope. Light enters the vault; and at that moment I can see the jaguar.

I have lost reckoning of the years I have lain in darkness. Though I was once young and could walk in this prison, now I do nothing but wait, in the attitude of my death, for the end that the gods have prepared for me. I have opened the breasts of victims with my long flint knife, but now, except by magic, I could not raise myself from the dust.

On the night before the burning of the pyramid, the men who got down from tall horses beat me with red-hot metal to make me reveal the site of a hidden treasure. Before my eyes they threw down the statue of god, but he did not abandon me and I remained silent under their tortures. They tore me, they beat me, they broke my limbs, and then I woke up in this prison which I shall never leave in my mortal life.

Urged by the necessity to do something, to fill time in some way, I decided to remember, in this darkness, all that I knew. I wasted whole nights recalling the order and number of certain stone

serpents or the shape of a medicinal tree. In this way I conquered
the years and took possession of all that belonged to me. One night
I felt that I was drawing near to an exact memory; before he sees
the sea, the traveller feels a disturbance in his blood. Hours later I
began to discern this memory in the distance; it was one of the
traditions concerning god. Foreseeing that much misfortune and
destruction would occur at the end of time, on the first day of
Creation he wrote a magic sentence capable of warding off these
evils. He wrote it in such a way that it would reach the most distant generations and could not be affected by chance. No one
knows in what place he wrote it or in what characters, but we are
certain that it remains secret and will be read by a chosen man. I
reflected that we were, as always, at the end of an age, and that
my fate as the last priest of god might gain me the privilege of
deciphering the writing. The fact that I was immured in prison did
not forbid me this hope. Perhaps I had seen the inscription a
thousand times at Qaholom and merely failed to understand it.

This reflection encouraged me and then made me strangely
dizzy. Within the bounds of the earth exist ancient forms, forms
incorruptible and eternal; one of these might be the symbol I
sought. A mountain might be the word of god; so might a river
or the empire or the configuration of the stars. But in the course of
centuries mountains are levelled, a river will shift its bed, empires
undergo ravages and mutations and the configuration of the stars
alters. In the firmament there is change. Mountain and star are
individuals, and individuals decay. I sought for something firmer,
less vulnerable. I thought of the generations of the grain, of grasses,
of birds, of men. Perhaps the magic formula was written on my
face, perhaps I was myself the object of my search. I was puzzling
over this when I suddenly remembered that the jaguar was one of
the attributes of god.

Then my soul was filled with reverence. I imagined the first
morning of time, I imagined my god confiding the message to the
bright skins of jaguars, who would endlessly couple and engender
in caves and reed-beds and on islands, so that the last man should
receive it. I imagined this chain of jaguars, this hot labyrinth of
jaguars, terrorizing meadows and flocks in order to preserve a

design. In the other cell was a jaguar; I perceived in this presence a confirmation of my guess and a secret favour.

I spent long years learning the order and configuration of its markings. Each blind day allowed me a moment of light, and so I could fix in my mind the black patches on the yellow skin. Some were spots; others took the form of transverse stripes on the inside of the legs, others of repeated rings. Perhaps they meant a single sound or a single word. Many were edged with red.

I will not say how tiring this labour was. More than once I shouted into the vault that it was impossible to decipher that text. Gradually the concrete puzzle engaging me bothered me less than the generic puzzle of a sentence written by a god. What kind of sentence, I asked myself, would be formulated by an absolute mind? I considered that even in human languages there is no proposition that does not involve the whole Universe; to say *the jaguar* is to speak of the jaguars that engendered it, the deer and tortoises it devoured, the pastures on which those deer fed, the earth that produced the pastures, the sky that gave light to the earth. I considered that in a god's language, every word would express this infinite concatenation of facts, and in an explicit, not an implicit way, not gradually but instantaneously. In time the idea of a divine sentence seemed to me puerile or blasphemous. A god, I reflected, has only to say one word, and in that word everything. No spoken word for him can be smaller than the Universe or less than the sum of time. Those poor and ambitious human words, *all*, and *entire world* are shadows or images of that word which is equal to a whole language and all that a language can contain.

One day or night – what difference is there between my days and my nights? – I dreamt that there was a grain of sand on the prison floor. I went to sleep again, unmoved, and dreamt that I had woken up and there were two grains of sand. I went to sleep again, and dreamt that the grains of sand were three. They went on increasing in this way till they filled the cell and I was dying in this hemisphere of sand. I realized that I was dreaming; with a vast effort I woke myself up. Waking was useless; the uncountable sands were choking me. Someone said to me: *You have not woken*

to the waking state but to a previous dream. This dream is within
the other, and so on to infinity, which is the number of the grains
of sand. The road that you will have to retrace is interminable, and
you will die before really waking up.

I felt I was lost. The sand was crushing my mouth, but I shouted:
No grain of sand in a dream can kill me, and there is no such thing
as a dream within a dream. A brightness awoke me. In the upper
darkness appeared a circle of light. I saw the jailer's face and
hands, the pulley, the rope, the meat and the jars.

A man gradually identifies himself with the form of his fate; a
man is, in the long run, his own circumstances. More than a reader
of riddles or an avenger, more than a priest of the god, I was a
prisoner. From the tireless labyrinth I returned to the hard prison,
as if to my home. I blessed its dampness, I blessed its jaguar, I
blessed the hole that let in the light, I blessed my old, painful body,
I blessed the darkness and the stone.

Then came something that I can neither forget nor describe.
There came union with the divinity, with the Universe (I do not
know whether these two words differ). Ecstasy does not repeat its
symbols; some have seen god in a brightness; some have seen him
in a sword, and some in the circlets of a rose. I saw a very tall wheel,
that was not before my eyes or behind them or on either side, but
everywhere at once. This wheel was made of water, and also of fire,
and (though its edges were visible) it was infinite. It was made of
all things future, present and past, woven together, and I was one
of the threads on this total web, and Pedro de Alvarado who tortured me was another. Here were causes and effects, and I had only
to look at this wheel to understand everything limitlessly. Oh, how
much greater is the joy of understanding than of imagining or
feeling! I saw the Universe, and I saw the secret patterns of the
Universe. I saw the origins related in the Book of Counsel. I saw
the mountains that rose from the waters, I saw the first wooden
men, I saw the jars that attacked those men, I saw the dogs that
tore their faces. I saw the faceless gods who are behind the gods. I
saw infinite processes forming a single happiness and, understanding everything, I succeeded also in understanding the writing on
the jaguar.

It is a formula of fourteen casual words (or words that appear casual) and I should only have to speak it out loud to be all-powerful. I should only have to speak it to abolish this stone prison, to let day into my night, to be young, to be immortal, for the tiger to destroy Alvarado, to sink the sacred knife in Spanish breasts, to rebuild the pyramid, to rebuild the empire. Four syllables, fourteen words, and I Tzinacán would rule the lands that Montezuma ruled. But I know that I shall never speak these words because I no longer remember Tzinacán.

Let the mystery that is written on the jaguar's skin die with me. One who has had a glimpse of the Universe, one who has glimpsed the burning patterns of the Universe cannot think about a man and his trivial joys or misfortunes, even if that man is he. This man *has been he,* but now he does not care. Why should he care for the fate of this other, why should he care for this other man's nation, if he is now nobody? For this reason I did not pronounce the formula. For this reason I let the days forget me, stretched out in the dark.

Translated by J. M. Cohen

César Vallejo

FOUR POEMS FROM TRILCE

III

The grown-ups
what time are they coming back?
Blind Santiago is striking six
and already it's very dark.

She'd soon be home, mother said.

Aguedita, Nativa, Miguel,
watch out, don't go there where
griefs that double you up
have just gone by
whining their memories
towards the silent yard
and where the hens are still
getting settled, they were so scared.
Better if we stayed
here : she'd soon be home, mother said.

Besides, we should not
grieve. Let's go on
seeing the boats (mine's
the nicest of the lot !)
with which we play
the whole blessed day without a quarrel
as good children should : they've stayed
in the puddle, ready,
freighted with sweet things for tomorrow.

Obedient and resigned,
let's wait like this
for the return, the excuses
from the grown-ups – they
always the first to abandon
the small ones in the house,
as if it were us were unable to get away.

Aguedita, Nativa, Miguel?
I'm calling, feeling about
In the dark for you. Don't
go out and leave me
and I the only one shut in.

XV

In that corner
          where we slept together
so many nights, I have sat down
to travel now. They have taken away
the bedstead of the dead bridal pair
or who can say
what might have happened!

Early, to other occupations
on you went and now exist
no more. It is the corner where
one night, between your tender punctuations
I read beside you
a tale of Daudet's. It is the beloved
corner. As to that, why argue?

I have set myself to recall
the finished days of summer,
your entrance and your exit,
sufficient and pale and small
through the rooms.

In this night of rain, now far
from both the two, I leap up
suddenly and there are
two doors opening shutting
two doors which go
        and come in the wind
shadow   to   shadow.

LXI

I get down
        from the horse tonight,
before the door of the house, where
at cockcrow I took my leave.
It's shut and nobody answers there.

The stone bench, astraddle on which
Mother gave birth
to my elder brother
so that he might saddle
loins I had ridden bareback
by village lanes
and by garden walls, a child
of the village; the bench on which
I left to yellow in the sun
my painful childhood ... And this
pain that imprints the title page?

A god in the alien peace,
the brute sneezes
as if also calling out;
it noses about
striking the pavement.
Soon, fears
make it hesitate; it neighs,
twitches alert ears.

Father must be awake
praying, and will think perhaps
I have been out late.   My sisters
humming their illusions
simple, ebullient
in their work for the approaching feast
and now, almost nothing
is wanting.   I wait
I wait, my heart
an egg in its moment
that obstructs itself.

Numerous family that we left
not long since,
nobody is keeping
watch today and not one
candle set on the altar
for our homecoming.

I call again ... nothing.
Silent, we begin sobbing and the beast
neighs, neighs all the more.

They are all asleep for ever,
and so soundly
that, in the end, my horse
gets weary in turn
of nodding his head, and between
sleep lets fall
at each nod that it's all
right, everything
is all right.

LXVI

Tolls
                the second day of November.
These chairs are good welcomes.

The bough of presentiment
goes, comes
rises, undulates sweating
weighed down in this drawing-room.   Sad
tolls the second day of November.

Deadmen, what your gone teeth do
cut through below, as you
stitch up blind nerves, unmindful there
of the hard fibre
rotund singing workmen repair
with inexhaustible hemp, the knots
throbbing innumerably
at crossroads.

You, deadmen with shining knees, pure
by dint of yielding yourselves, how you
saw the other heart through
with your white crowns meagre
in cordiality.   Yes.
                    You:
                        the dead.

Sad tolls the second day of November.
And the bough of presentiment is
bitten by a cart, that simply
rolls down the street.

Translated by Charles Tomlinson and Henry Gifford

Ricardo E. Molinari

ODE

Who is it coming through the evening, playing his lute upon the
  clouds as if he were in his own dwelling?
Who is it that with his playing turns the leaves over on the trees?

I have filled my heart with the shadows of words;
with the dream of certain voices.
And they sound within me disconnectedly, bringing no relief: *you,
  no one, tomorrow, space, solitude, tenderness, air, emptiness, sea-
  wave*, and *never*. With them I solace my being, the sky's anguish,
  and the obdurate loneliness
of the blood.
I refresh my mouth with their absence, and call on myself by day
  and by night,
and raise them, naked, to my head, that I may tell their names to
  oblivion, facing the high zenith
of the plains.
I have placed their gods and bodies between my lips, to be praised
  for ever;
they support the air before me – yes, and the impenetrable height
  of death;
no one sees them, as the breath that stirs and harshly steers them
  is not seen.
(Angels scatter and travel through space; some carry sheaves of
  corn, others choose red poppies,
and the rest bring seed for the birds that are among the naked trees.

No one sees them; but the light they scatter from their ancient
  robes parches my throat.
I see them lift their heads, unharmed by the air, and disappear
  rapidly, bathed in clear light, before the night's fury.

I am used to seeing them, within me, as in the days whose smoke
    has blown away
and whose kingdoms, laid beneath the ashes,
undespairingly await their lilies.)
I long to tear joy from my heart, to open my eyes so very wide
    that they hurt,
and to gaze, to gaze at the horizon till I see beyond the void of
    nostalgia, to where my shadow,
like a tree, changes its leaves in winter.

O love – time lost beyond recall !

Translated by J. M. Cohen

Pablo Neruda

SOME ANIMALS

It was the twilight of the iguana.
From his rainbow-arched battlements
his tongue plunged like a lance
into the vegetation,
the monkish ant-eater
trod the forest making music with his feet,
the guanaco, light as oxygen
in his golden shoes
trod the wide brown uplands,
while the llama opened his candid eyes
on the fineness
of a world full of dew.
The monkeys formed an endlessly
erotic chain
on the banks of the dawn,
knocking down walls of pollen
and scaring the Muzo butterflies
into violent flight.
It was the alligators' night,
the pure and quivering night
of snouts emerging from the slime,
and from the sleeping swamps
a dull noise of skeletons
returned to the earth whence they began.

The jaguar touched the leaves
with the gleam of his absence,
the puma runs through the branches,
a devouring fire;
in him like alcohol

the forest's eyes burn.
The badgers scratch the river's
feet, sniffing a nest
whose throbbing weakness
they will attack with red teeth.

And deep in the great waters
like the circle of the earth
lies the giant anaconda,
covered with mud,
devouring and devout.

ODE TO THE MAGNOLIA

Here in the depths
of dense Brazil
a magnolia.
They rose up
like
black boas
the roots,
the trunks of the trees
were
inexplicable
thorny pillars.
Around
the tops
of the mangoes
were broad
cities,
with balconies
peopled by
birds
and stars.
Between

the ashen
leaves fell
ancient heads of hair
terrible flowers
with devouring mouths.
All around rose
the silent
terror
of animals, of teeth
that bit;
despairing country
of blood and green shade !
A pure
magnolia,
round as a circle
of snow,
rose to my window
and reconciled me to its beauty.
Between the smooth leaves
– ochre and green –
closed,
it was perfect
as a celestial
egg,
open
it was the moon
stone,
sweet-smelling aphrodite
platinum planet.
Its great petals reminded me
of the sheets
of the first month
of love,
and its erect
pistil
was the wedding tower
of the bees.

O whiteness
among
all whitenesses,
immaculate magnolia
resplendent love,
odour of white snow
with lemons,
secret secretary
of the dawn,
cupola
of the swans,
radiant apparition !
How
can I sing of you without
touching
your
purest skin,
love you
only
at the foot
of your beauty,
and carry you
asleep
to the tree of my soul,
resplendent, open,
dazzling,
above the dark wood
of dreams !

Translated by J. M. Cohen

Juan Carlos Onetti

DREADED HELL

The first letter with the first photograph reached him at the newspaper between midnight and the deadline. He was hitting the typewriter, feeling rather hungry and ill because of the coffee and
tobacco; and he had a familiar feeling of happiness at being
absorbed in the movement of the sentence and the docile appearances of the words. He was writing 'it must be emphasized that
the Race Course Officials found nothing strange or extraordinary
in the crowning triumph of Play Boy, who was able to take advantage of the winter turf and shoot into the lead like an arrow at the
decisive moment', when he saw the red, ink-stained hand of Political Column between his face and the typewriter, offering him an
envelope.

'It's for you. They always mix up the letters. Not a damned line
from the local branches and then they come and moan; when the
elections are near, no space is too big for them. It's midnight
already and tell me what you want the column filled up with.'

The envelope bore his address, 'Racing Column: *El Liberal*'. The
only odd thing was a pair of green stamps and the Bahía postmark.
He finished the article as they came up from the printers to ask for
it. He was weak and happy, almost alone in the vast space of the
newspaper office, thinking of his last sentence: 'We repeat this
statement with the impartiality which for many years we have
maintained in all our allegations. We owe it to the racing public.'
In the background, the Negro was turning over envelopes from the
file and the middle-aged woman – 'Social Column' – was slowly
taking off her gloves in her glass cabin when Risso carelessly
opened the envelope.

There was a postcard-sized photo inside; it was a dark photo
poorly lit, one in which hate and sordidness gathered in the sombre
margins, forming gross, indistinct edges as in a relief, like drops of

sweat on an anguished face. He was taken by surprise, did not fully understand, knew that he would give anything to forget what he had seen.

He put the photograph in his pocket and was putting on his overcoat when Social Column came out of her glass cubby-hole smoking and with a sheaf of papers in her hand.

'Hullo,' she said, 'What a time of night for me to come here! The party's just over.'

Risso looked down at her. Fair, dyed hair, wrinkled neck, double chin which drooped, round and pointed, like a tiny belly, small, excessive attempts to liven up her clothes. 'She's a woman, too. Now I see the red scarf round her throat, the violent nails on old-tobacco-stained fingers, the rings and bracelets, the dress given to her as payment by a dress-designer not by a lover, very high, perhaps twisted heels, the sad curve of her mouth, the almost frantic enthusiasm she puts into a smile. It will all be easier if I can convince myself that she is a woman too.'

'It looks as if you do it on purpose. You always go away just as I arrive, as if you were trying to avoid me. It's freezing outside. They leave me the copy as they promised but not so much as a name or a headline. Guess, make a mistake, publish some fantastic howler! I don't know any names except those of the couple and that's sheer luck. What they had plenty of was luxury and bad taste. They held a brilliant reception for their friends at the home of the bride's parents. Nobody these days gets married on a Saturday. Wrap yourself up. There's a freezing blast coming off the avenue.'

When Risso married Gracia César, there had been a conspiracy of silence amongst us, we suppressed gloomy forecasts. At that time, she was staring at the inhabitants of Santa María from the billboards of 'The Basement' theatre, from walls which were shabby at the end of autumn. Sometimes intact, sometimes with pencilled moustaches, the poster torn by rancorous fingers or soaked by the first rains, she turned her head sideways to look at the street, with a wide-awake rather defiant air as if she cherished the hope of succeeding and of being understood. Her face looked wider because of the shine on the tear ducts which the Orloff studios had put into their photographic enlargement and underneath the comedy of undying love (something of which was expressed in her face), there lay her own determined and single-minded search for happiness.

This was good, Risso must have thought. It was desirable and necessary and coincided with the accumulated results of the months of his widowhood, with the sum of innumerable identical Saturday dawns on which he had successfully reproduced polite attitudes of expectation and familiarity in the brothel on the coast. A shining – that of the eyes on the poster – was connected with his frustrated skill in tying his always gaudy if sober mourning tie in front of the oval, swinging mirror of the brothel bedroom.

They married and Risso thought that it was enough to go on living as he always had done, but devoting his life to her without thinking about it, almost without thinking of her, of the fury of his body and the crazy need for absolutes which possessed him during their prolonged nights.

She thought of Risso as a bridge, as an exit, as a beginning. She had remained a virgin through two engagements – one to a producer and another to an actor – perhaps because the theatre was a career as well as a hobby for her and she felt that love should be born and kept apart, uncontaminated by what is done for money and for oblivion. With first one and then the other, on their dates in the squares, avenues and cafés, she had been condemned to feel the boredom of rehearsals, the strain of adapting to a part, the attention to voice and gesture. She always anticipated any expression on her own face a second beforehand as if she could look at it and touch it. She acted bravely, involuntarily, and without belief, she analysed her performance and that of the other, weighed up the sweat and dust of the theatre which covered them both, those two inseparable signs of the age.

When the second photograph arrived from Asunción and with an obviously different man, Risso feared more than anything that he would not be able to bear a strange feeling which was neither hatred nor love, which would die nameless with him, which was bound up with injustice and fate, and with the first fear of the first man on earth, with nihilism and the beginning of faith.

The second photograph was handed to him by Police Court

News on Wednesday night. Thursdays were days when he could have his daughter to himself from ten in the morning till ten at night. He decided to tear up the envelope without opening it; he kept it and early on Thursday morning, while his daughter was waiting for him in the drawing-room of the boarding-house, he allowed himself a rapid glance at the card before tearing it up in the lavatory; on this one too the man had his back turned to the camera.

But he had looked at the photo from Brazil many times. He had kept it for an entire day and by dawn imagined it to be a joke, a mistake, a passing absurdity. It had happened to him now; he had often awakened from a nightmare smiling humbly and thankfully at the flowers on the bedroom walls.

He was lying on his bed when he took the envelope from his jacket and the photo from the envelope.

'Good,' he said aloud, 'that's fine; it's certain and true. It isn't important; even if I hadn't seen it, I should know that it was happening.'

When she took the photograph, using an automatic shutter release, when she developed it in the dark room under the encouraging red glow of the lamp, she probably foresaw this reaction of Risso's, this defiance, this refusal to let himself go in rage. She had also foreseen (or perhaps faintly desired though scarcely acknowledging her hope), that he would discover a message of love in the obvious insult, in the dreadful indignity.

He protected himself again before looking: 'I am alone, and dying of cold in a Piedras street boarding-house in Santa María on any dawn, alone and regretting my loneliness as if I had sought it, proud as if I had deserved it.'

In the photograph, the headless woman dug her heels ostentatiously into the edge of the divan and awaited the impatient desire of the dark man, gigantic in the inevitable foreground. She would be sure that it was not necessary to show her face in order to be recognized. On the back in her calm handwriting was written 'Greetings from Bahía'.

On the night of the second photograph, he thought he could understand and even accept the completeness of the disgrace. But he knew that the deliberation, persistence and the organized passion with which vengeance was pursued was beyond his reach. He measured the disproportion, felt unworthy of such hatred, such love, such will to make him suffer.

When Gracia met Risso, she could imagine many present and future things. She guessed his loneliness as she looked at his chin and at a button on his waistcoat; she guessed that he was bitter and not defeated and that he needed some solace but did not want to admit it. On many Sundays in the square, before the performance, she had watched with careful calculation his sullen and impassioned face, the dirty hat abandoned on his head, his big, indolent body that was running to fat. The first time that they were alone together, she thought of love or desire or of her desire to stroke away the sadness in the man's face and cheeks. She also thought of the city in which the only possible wisdom was that of resigning oneself in time. She was twenty and Risso was forty. She began to believe in him and discovered depths of curiosity; she told herself that one only really lives when each day brings its own surprise.

During the first few weeks, she would shut herself in her room and laugh to herself; she compelled herself to fetishistic adorations and learned to distinguish states of mind through smell. She was learning to discover what lay behind the voice, the silences, the tastes and attitudes of the man's body. She loved Risso's daughter and transformed her face by insisting upon her resemblance to her father. She did not leave the theatre because the Town Council had just subsidized it and in 'The Basement' she now had a steady wage and a world that was separate from her home, from her bedroom and from the passionate and indestructible man. She did not attempt to escape from lust; she wished to rest and forget it, to allow lust to rest and forget. She made plans and kept to them; she was certain that the universe of love was infinite and certain that each night would offer them a different and newly-created marvel.

'Anything,' Risso insisted, 'absolutely anything can happen to us and we shall always be happy and in love. Anything – whether God invents it or we do.'

He had never really had a woman before and he believed that he was creating what was now being imposed upon him. But it was not she who imposed, Gracia César, Risso's creation, separated from him in order to complete him like the air in the lung or wheat in winter.

The third photograph did not arrive for another three weeks. It, too, came from Paraguay and it did not arrive at the newspaper office but at the boarding-house; it was brought to him by the maid at the end of an afternoon on which he had awakened from a dream; in it he had been warned to guard himself from fear and madness by keeping any future photograph in his wallet, thus rendering it trivial, impersonal and inoffensive by exposing it to a hundred nonchalant, daily glances.

The maid knocked on his door and he saw the envelope dangling from the slats of the blind and began to perceive how it distilled its noxious condition, its vibrating menace into the shadows and the dirty air. He lay watching it from the bed as if it were an insect, a poisonous creature which would lie in wait for a moment of negligence, for the propitious mistake.

In the third photograph, she was alone, her whiteness pressing against the shadows of a badly-lit room, her head painfully thrown backwards towards the camera, her shoulders half-covered by her loose black hair – a vigorous quadruped. She was as unmistakable now as if she had been photographed in a studio and had posed with the tenderest, the most significant and oblique of her smiles.

Risso now felt only a hopeless pity for her, for himself and for all lovers who had loved in the world, for the truth and error of their beliefs, for the simple absurdity of love and for the complex absurdity of man-created love.

But he tore up this photograph too and he knew that it would be impossible to look at another one and go on living. But on the magic plane on which they had begun to understand one another and communicate, Gracia must realize that he was going to tear up the photos with ever-decreasing curiosity and remorse as soon as they arrived.

On the magic plane, all the coarse or timid, lusting men were no more than obstacles, unavoidable postergations of the ritual act of choosing (in the street, in the restaurant or in the café), the most credulous and inexpert, the one who would lend himself unsuspectingly and with comic pride to the exhibition in front of the camera and the shutter, the least unpleasant of those who might believe her memorized commercial-traveller's patter :

'Really, I've never had a man like you, someone so unique and different. In this life of the theatre I never know where I'll be next or if I'll ever see you again. I'd at least like to look at you in a photograph when we're apart and I miss you.'

And after the almost always easy persuasion, as she thought of Risso or put off thinking of him till next day, she would perform the duty she had imposed upon herself, would arrange the lights, prepare the camera and arouse the man. If she thought of Risso, she would conjure up an old incident, would again reproach him for not having beaten her, and for having sent her away for ever with a stale insult, a knowing smile and a remark which identified her with all other women. And he had not understood; he had shown that despite the nights and the words, he had never understood.

Without any great hopes, she trailed sweating about the always sordid and hot hotel room, measuring distances and lights and correcting the position of the man's stiff body. Using any method, any suggestion, any filthy lie, she would force him to turn his cynical and distrustful face towards her, the face of the next man in the queue. She would try to smile and tempt him; she would imitate the endearing clucks that are made to small babies, and she would be measuring the passing of the seconds and at the same time measuring the intensity with which the photo would express her love for Risso.

But as she could never know this, as she did not even know whether the photographs would arrive into Risso's hands or not, she began to add to the evidence of the photos and made them into documents which had very little to do with the two of them, with Risso and Gracia.

Eventually she permitted and so arranged it that the faces, sharpened by desire, stupefied by the old masculine dream of possession, should turn with a hard smile, with shamefaced insolence towards the camera eye. She thought it necessary to slide on to her back and appear in the photographs herself so that her head, her short nose, her great fearless eyes came down from the space outside the photo and entered into the filthiness of the world, into the clumsy, erroneous photographic vision, into the satire of love which she had sworn to send regularly to Santa María. But her real mistake was to change the addresses on the envelopes.

*

After six months of marriage, their first separation was welcome and excessively painful. 'The Basement' – now Santa María Civic Theatre – went up to Rosario. She there continued the old, fascinating game of being an actress among actors and of believing what happened on the stage. The audience were enthusiastic, applauded or did not allow themselves to be carried away. Programmes and criticisms duly appeared; and people accepted the game and prolonged it far into the night. They talked of what they had seen and heard, of what they had paid to see and hear, and talked with some passion, with somewhat forced enthusiasm of performances, décor, speeches and plots.

So that the game, the alternatively sad and intoxicating mockery which she began when she moved slowly towards the window that looked on to the fjord, when she shivered and murmured for the whole theatre: 'Perhaps . . . but I too have a life full of memories which other people do not know', was also accepted in Rosario. Cards always fell in response to those which she threw down, the game became serious and it was now impossible to amuse herself by watching it from outside.

The first separation lasted exactly fifty-two days and in them Risso tried to reproduce the life he had lived during his six months of marriage to Gracia César. He went to the same café and the same restaurant at the same times; he saw the same friends, reenacted their silences and solitudes along the avenues and walked back to the boarding-house obsessively anticipating their reunion, feeling on his brow and in his mouth immoderate sensations which arose from heightened memories and from unattainable aspirations.

In the unsettled interval between winter and spring, on nights disturbed by warm or chilling winds, he would walk the ten or twelve blocks more slowly now and alone. The distance served to measure the extent of his necessity and isolation and to make him realize that the madness which they shared at least had the grandeur of having no future and of not being a means towards anything else.

She, for her part, had believed that Risso set the seal on their mutual love when, lying on the bed, overwhelmed, he whispered to her with fresh surprise:

'Anything can happen and we shall always be happy and in love.'

The words were no longer a conviction or an opinion; they did not express a desire. They were prescribed and imposed upon them; they represented a confirmation, an old truth. Nothing that they did or thought could reduce the strength of their folly, their endless and unchanging love. Every human potentiality could be brought into play and everything was bound to nourish it.

She believed that outside the two of them, outside their room lay a world devoid of meaning; inhabited by beings who did not matter and full of trifling events.

So that when the man began to wait for her at the stage-entrance, when he solicited and escorted her, when she took off her clothes, she was only thinking of Risso and of the two of them.

It had happened during her last week in Rosario and she thought it unnecessary to mention it in her letters to Risso; because the event was not something apart from the two of them and yet, at the same time, it had nothing to do with them; because she acted like a curious and lucid animal, feeling rather sorry for the man and somewhat contemptuous of the inferiority of what he was adding to her love for Risso. When she returned to Santa María, she chose to wait for a Wednesday night – because on Thursdays Risso did not go to the newspaper office – for a timeless night and a dawn exactly like the other twenty-five they had lived together.

Before getting undressed, she began to tell the story with pride and tenderness as if she had simply created a new embrace. He leaned on the table in his shirt-sleeves and shut his eyes and smiled. Then he made her undress and asked her to repeat the story; she was standing up now, moving barefooted on the carpet; almost without shifting from the spot, she faced him, stood sideways and turned her back to him, balanced her body and leaned first on one foot and then on the other. At times, she would see Risso's long, sweating face, his heavy body leaning on the table, his shoulders rounded as if protecting the glass of wine; at other times, she only imagined these things, she was carried away by her eagerness to repeat the story faithfully and by the happiness of living again that especially intense love she had felt for Risso in Rosario when she was with the man whose face she had forgotten, with nobody, with Risso.

'Good, now get dressed again,' he said in the same surprised, hoarse voice in which he had declared that anything was possible and that everything would be for them.

She examined his smile and put on her clothes again. For a while, they both stood looking at the patterns on the table-cloth, at the stains and at the ash-tray with the bird with a broken beak. Then he finished dressing and went out; he devoted his Thursday, his day off to talking to Dr Guiñazu and persuading him of the urgency of the divorce, frustrating in advance any meetings of reconciliation.

There followed a long, unhealthy period in which Risso wanted to have her again and at the same time hated the difficulties and disgust of any conceivable reunion. Afterwards, he decided that he now needed Gracia even more than before; that a reconciliation was necessary and that he was prepared to pay any price as long as his will did not come into it, as long as it was possible to have her again without saying yes, even with his silences.

He again spent his Thursdays taking his daughter out and listening over the dessert to the grandmother going over the list of predictions that had been fulfilled. Of Gracia he had vague, evasive reports and he began to think of her as if she were an unknown woman whose looks and reactions must be guessed at or deduced, as if she were a woman who kept alone and apart among persons and places, who was destined for him and whom he would have to love, perhaps from their first meeting.

Almost a month after the beginning of their separation, Gracia gave out conflicting addresses and left Santa María.

'Don't worry,' Guiñazu said, 'I know what women are like and I was waiting for something of the sort. That confirms the desertion and it simplifies the case which can't be harmed by obvious delaying tactics which only prove that the accused party is in the wrong.'

There was a damp beginning to that spring and on many nights Risso walked home from the newspaper or the café, cursing the rain and reviving his suffering as if blowing on a live coal, standing apart from it so that he could see it in a clearer and more incredible light, and imagining acts of love which he had never experienced only to start immediately remembering them with desperate cupidity.

Risso had destroyed the last three messages without looking at them. Now and for ever more, he sat in the newspaper office or in the boarding-house like an animal in its lair, like a beast which could hear the shots of the huntsmen at the mouth of its cave. He could save himself from death and from the idea of death only by forcing quietude and ignorance upon himself. He crouched down and shook his whiskers, his snout and his paws. He could only await the spending of the alien fury. Without admitting it in words or thoughts, he was forced to begin to understand and to identify the Gracia who picked up men and chose the positions for the photos, with the girl who many months ago had planned her clothes, conversations, make-up, endearing expressions for his daughter in order to conquer a widower who had devoted himself to grief, a man who earned a slender salary and who could offer women only a surprised and loyal lack of understanding.

He had begun to believe that the girl who had written him long, intense letters during the brief, summer separations of their engagement was the same girl who was procuring his desperation and destruction by sending him the photographs. And eventually he came to believe that the lover who has once breathed the dark smell of death in the endless striving on the bed is obliged to pursue destruction and the definitive peace of nothingness – both for himself and for the woman.

He thought about the girl who used to stroll arm in arm with two of her friends along the avenue in the afternoons, wearing the wide check dresses of stiff cloth which his memory created and imposed, the girl who had glanced across the overture to the *Barber* (which was the crowning item of the Sunday Band Concert) to look at him for a second. He thought of that brief lightning flash into which she had concentrated a passionate expression of challenge and surrender, and in which she had displayed the full almost masculine beauty of her thoughtful and intelligent face, and in which she had chosen him, a man pining away in his widowhood. And gradually he began to admit that this was the same naked woman (though a bit fatter and with a rather mature and settled look) who sent him the photographs from Lima, Santiago and Buenos Aires.

And why not?, he finally thought; why not accept the fact that the photographs and their careful preparation and regular transmission had their origin in the same love, the same capacity for nostalgia, the same congenital fidelity.

*

The next photograph came from Montevideo and arrived neither at the newspaper office nor at the boarding-house. And he never managed to see it. He was leaving *El Liberal* one night when he heard old Lanza limping downstairs after him, heard the shaking cough behind him and the deceptively innocent introductory sentence. They went to eat at the Baviera and Risso could have sworn afterwards that he had known all the time that this slovenly, sick, bearded man who all the way through dessert kept putting a damp cigarette into his sunken mouth, who did not want to look him in the eyes and who reeled off obvious comments on the news which UP had sent in to the newspaper during the day, that this man was impregnated with Gracia and with the passionate, absurd aroma distilled by love.

'Man to man,' Lanza said resignedly. 'Or rather, speaking as an old man who has no happiness in life other than the questionable one of still being alive. Speaking as an old man to you and I don't know who you are since no one ever knows. I know one or two things and I've heard rumours. But I am no longer interested in wasting time in conjecture and suspicion. It's all the same. Every morning I register the fact that I'm still alive without feeling either

bitterness or gratitude. I drag my bad leg and my arteriosclerosis
around the newspaper office and around Santa María. I remember
Spain, correct proofs, write and sometimes I talk too much. Like
tonight I received a dirty photograph and there is no possible doubt
as to who sent it. I can't guess why they chose me, either. On the
back, it says "To be donated to the Risso collection" or something
of the sort. It arrived on Saturday and I spent two days wondering
whether I should give it to you or not. Finally I thought that it
was better to tell you about it because sending it to me is sheer
madness and perhaps it'll do you good to know that she is mad.
Now you know; I simply want to ask you to let me tear up the
photograph without showing it to you.'

Risso agreed and that night he watched until daylight the glow
of the street lamp on the ceiling of his room and he realized that
the second disaster, the revenge was basically less serious than the
first – the betrayal – but it was much less bearable. He felt as if
his long body were exposed like a nerve to the pain of the air
without protection and unable to find any relief.

The second photograph which was not addressed to him was
thrown on to the table by his daughter's grandmother on the following Thursday. The child had gone to bed and the photograph
was once more in the envelope. It fell between the syphon and the
preserve jar where it lay full-length, crossed and darkened by the
reflection of a bottle, exposing the ardent letters in blue ink.

'You understand that after this . . .' the grandmother stam-
mered. She stirred her coffee and looked at Risso's face, seeking in
its profile the secret of the impurity of the world, the cause of her
daughter's death and the explanation of so many things that she
had suspected without having the courage to believe. 'You understand,' she repeated furiously in her funny, aged voice.

But she did not know what it was necessary to understand and
Risso himself understood nothing although he made an effort as
he stared at the envelope which lay confronting him with a corner
resting on the edge of the plate.

Outside the night was oppressive and the open windows of the
city blended the mysteries of men's lives, their habits and preoccu-
pations into the cloudy mystery of the sky. Lying on his bed, Risso

thought that he was beginning to understand, that like sickness or health, understanding was happening inside him and was freed from his will and intelligence. It was happening, quite simply, from the point where his shoes touched his feet to the tears which reached his cheeks and neck. Understanding was happening inside him and he was not interested in knowing what it was that he understood whilst he was remembering or whilst he was seeing his tears and his quietude, the passivity of his body stretched upon the bed, the curve of the clouds in the window or past and future scenes. He saw death and love of death and proud contempt for the rules which all men had agreed to observe and genuine aston-ishment at freedom. Slowly and skilfully, afraid of making a noise or of interrupting, he tore the photograph into pieces upon his chest without taking his eyes away from the window. Afterwards he felt a fresh breeze blowing in, one which he had perhaps breathed in childhood and which began filling the room and ex-panding with clumsy torpor through the streets and unsuspecting buildings in order to wait for him and protect him tomorrow and on the following days.

Until dawn he went on learning about disinterestedness, about happiness without cause and the acceptance of loneliness as if they were cities which had seemed unattainable to him. And when he awoke at midday, when he loosened his tie, his belt and his wrist-watch and as he walked sweating towards the window at which there was the putrid smell of a storm, he was pierced for the first time by a feeling of paternal affection for men and for what they had achieved and constructed. He had made up his mind to find out Gracia's address and phone her or go and live with her.

That night in the newspaper office, he was a slow, happy man who acted with the awkwardness of a new-born child. He com-pleted his quota of lines, but made slips and errors that would normally only be excused in a foreigner. The big news was Ribereña scratching at San Isidro; 'we are now able to inform our readers that the star of "El Gorrión" stable was found today to be suffering from pains in one of the forelegs, a symptom of inflammation of the tendons which clearly indicates the gravity of his complaint.'

*

'Bearing in mind that he was a Racing Columnist,' Lanza declared, 'one is tempted to explain that discomposure by comparing him to a man who had gambled his salary on a tip which had come to him from the trainer, the jockey, the owner and the horse itself and which they had all confirmed. Because, as you know, though he had the best of motives for feeling upset and for swallowing the whole stock of sleeping-pills from all the chemist shops in Santa María without further ado – yet what he demonstrated half an hour before doing this was nothing more nor less than the reasoning and attitudes of a man who has been cheated. He was like a man who had been safe and secure and is so no longer, and who cannot explain how it came about and what error of judgement brought about the disaster. Because he never once called the bitch who was sending filthy photographs all over the town a bitch and he didn't even agree to take the way out I offered him when I insinuated (without believing it) the possibility that the bitch – stark naked and in the position that she liked everyone to see her in, or acting out on the stage the ovarian problems of other famous bitches of world drama – that she was raving mad. He had made a mistake and not when he married her but at some other time that he did not care to mention. It was his fault and our meeting was unbelievable and frightening. Because he had already told me that he was going to kill himself so that it was both useless and grotesque and useless twice over to try and argue with him in order to save him. And he spoke to me coldly, refusing my pleas that he should go and get drunk. He had made a mistake, he insisted; it was his fault and not that of the damned whore who sent the photograph to the little girl in the convent school, perhaps thinking that the Mother Superior would open the envelope, perhaps wanting the envelope to reach the hands of Risso's daughter unopened, but sure that this time she had found Risso's vulnerable spot.'

Translated by Jean Franco

Carlos Pellicer

SKETCHES FOR A TROPICAL ODE

A tropical ode for four voices
must come seated on a swing
that is moored by the wreath of an orchid.
It will come from the South, the East and the West
from the aeroplane North, and from the Centre that is crowned
by the blunted pyramid of my life

I will burn my feet on the braziers
of the most solitary anguish,
to emerge naked to the poem
on airy sandals that will give it
new, innocent pores.

The young oils of moonlit nights
on the swamps will run
to the torrid belt of day.
The svelteness of that day
will be the dance's escape into it,
the measured will at the instant
of monumental repose,
the water of thirst broken in the jar.
Then I would be able to
bear the integument
of the spiral life of the palm,
take advantage of its shade that the breezes mutilate,
be faithful to its beauty,
without a pedestal, erect in itself,
alone, so much alone that all the trees
gaze on it night and day.
So my voice at the centre of the four

elemental voices
would support the weight
of the birds of paradise on its shoulders.
The ocean
would bathe in gulps of gold
and in the floating spray that breaks
be heard, spray upon spray, gigantic.

The desire to travel
might always be a desire.
Between the green fruit and the ripe fruit
distances ripen in partial shadows
then suddenly break out afresh in primary colours.

In the city, among mechanical forces,
there is a faint smell of vitreous custard-apple.
It is the seed-pod of the tropics
that smells of blue sky on early morning flesh
in the gloomy enchantment of the wood.
The land tortoise
carries on his back a great slice
that fell when the sun became tongues.
And so it smells of custard-apple
from the ferns to the silk-cotton tree.

A divine triangle
pounds its quietness in the forests
of the Ganges. Passions
grow and decay. Then rises
the time of the lotus, and the forest
now has a smile in its power.
From the tigers to the boa-constrictor
swarms the voice of spiritual
adventure. And the Himalayas
have taken in their arms the silence
born beside the green mechanism of the Tropics.

Lemon-tree breezes
circle over the backwaters of the rivers.
And the ancient nostalgic iguana
on the long contours of its time
was, is and will be.

One evening in Chichén I was among
the underground waters that suddenly
turn to sky. On the walls of the pool
a vertical garden closed the flight
of my eyes. Silence after silence
strangled my voice, and in every muscle
I felt my nakedness born of fear.
A snake barely
unknotted that spell
and through my blood there passed a great shadow
that was now a day-star on the horizon.
Was it the hands of fate
lighting the bonfire of my body?
On the ponds of Brazil ten leaves
beside another ten leaves, beside another ten leaves
a metre across
flower for one day each year,
one flower only, white when it opens,
which as the great sun of the Amazon
rises
slowly colours through a gamut of rose
to the reds that perforate the blood of death;
and then it is shipwrecked when the sun sets
and with its decay nourishes the next spring.
The devoted Tropics
sustain with their living flesh
the beauty of God. Earth, water, air, fire
to the South, the North, the East and the West
concentrate the essential seeds,
the heaven of surprises,

the intact nakedness of the hours
and the noise of vast solitudes.

A tropical ode for four voices
will reach me, word by word,
to drink from my lips,
to moor itself to my arms,
to strike my chest,
to seat itself on my legs,
to give me such health that it kills me,
and to place me within itself
so that I shall be contained in the words
palm and antelope,
silk-cotton tree and alligator,
fern and lyre-bird,
tarantula and orchid,
zenzontle and anaconda.
Then I shall be a cry
a single clear cry
that will project with my voice
the words themselves
and raise from mountain to mountain
the voice of the sea that drags down
cities, O Tropic,
and the cry of the night
that puts the horizon on its guard.

Translated by J. M. Cohen

Alejo Carpentier

JOURNEY TO THE SEED

I

'What do you want, old 'un?'

The question fell several times from the top of the scaffolding. But the old man did not reply. He went from one spot to another, poking about, a long monologue of incomprehensible phrases issuing from his throat. They had already brought down the roof-tiles which covered the faded pavings with their earthenware mosaic. Up above, the picks were loosening the masonry, sending the stones rolling down wooden channels in a great cloud of lime and chalk. And through each one of the embrasures which had been cut into the battlements appeared (their secret uncovered) smooth oval or square ceilings, cornices, garlands, denticles, mouldings and wall-paper which hung down from the friezes like old, cast-off snake skins. Watching the demolition, a Ceres with a broken nose, a discoloured robe and with a blackened crown of maize upon her head stood in her back court upon her fountain of faded masks. Visited by the sun in the dusky hours, the grey fish in her basin yawned in mossy, warm water, their round eyes watching those black workmen in the gap in the sky-line who were gradually reducing the age-old height of the house. The old man had seated himself at the foot of the statue with his stick pointing at his chin. He watched the raising and lowering of buckets in which valuable remains were carried away. There was the sound of muffled street noises and, up above, the pulleys harmonized their disagreeable and grating bird-songs in a rhythm of iron upon stone.

Five o'clock struck. The cornices and entablatures emptied of people. There only remained the hand-ladders ready for the next day's assault. The breeze turned fresher, now that it was relieved of its load of sweat, curses, rope-creakings, axles shrieking for the oil-can, and the slapping of greasy bodies. Twilight arrived earlier for the denuded house. It was clothed in shadows at an hour when the now-fallen upper parapets had been wont to regale the façade with a sparkle of sunlight. Ceres tightened her lips. For the first time, the rooms slept without window-blinds, open on to a landscape of ruins.

Contrary to their wishes, several capitals lay in the grass. Their acanthus leaves revealed their vegetable condition. A climbing plant, attracted by the family resemblance, ventured to stretch its tendrils towards the ionic scrolls. When night fell, the house was nearer the ground. A door-frame still stood on high with planks of shade hanging from its bewildered hinges.

II

Then the dark old man who had not moved from that place, gestured strangely and waved his stick over a cemetery of tiles.

The black and white marble squares flew back and covered the floors again. With sure leaps, stones closed the gaps in the battlements. The walnut panels, garnished with nails, fitted themselves into their frames whilst, with rapid rotations, the screws of the hinges buried themselves in their holes. Raised up by an effort from the flowers, the tiles on the faded pavings put together their broken fragments and in a noisy whirlwind of clay fell like rain upon the roof-tree. The house grew, returned again to its usual proportions, clothed and modest. Ceres was less grey. There were more fish in the fountain. And the murmur of water invoked forgotten begonias.

The old man put a key into the lock of the main door and began to open windows. His heels sounded hollow. When he lit the brass lamps, a yellow tremor ran along the oil of the family portraits and black-robed people murmured in all the galleries to the rhythm of spoons stirred in chocolate bowls.

Don Marcial, Marquis of Capellanías lay on his deathbed, his breast clad in medals, and with an escort of four candles with long beards of melted wax.

III

The candles grew slowly and lost their beads of sweat. When they regained their full height, a nun put them out and drew away her taper. The wicks became white and threw off their snuff. The house emptied of visitors and the carriages departed into the night. Don Marcial played on an invisible keyboard and opened his eyes.

The blurred and jumbled roof-beams fell gradually back into place. The flasks of medicine, the damask tassels, the scapulary over the head of the bed, the daguerrotypes and the palms of the balcony grille emerged from the mists. Whilst the doctor shook his head with professional condolence, the sick man felt better. He slept for a few hours and awoke with the black beetle-browed regard of Father Anastasio upon him. The confession changed from being frank, detailed and full of sins to being reticent, halting and full of concealments. And after all, what right had that Carmelite friar to interfere in his life? Suddenly Don Marcial felt himself drawn into the middle of the room. The weight on his forehead lifted and he got up with surprising speed. The naked woman who was lounging upon the brocade of the bed searched for her petticoats and bodices and took away with her, soon afterwards, the sound of crushed silk and perfume. Below, in the closed carriage, covering the seat studs, there was an envelope containing gold coins.

Don Marcial did not feel well. As he arranged his tie in front of the pier-glass he found that he looked bloated. He went down to the office where legal men, solicitors and notaries were waiting for him to settle the auctioning of the house. It had all been useless. His belongings would go bit by bit to the highest bidder to the rhythm of hammer-blows upon the table. He greeted them and they left him alone. He thought of the mysteries of the written word, of those black threads which, ravelling and unravelling over wide, filigrained balance sheets, had ravelled and unravelled agreements, oaths, covenants, testimonies, declarations, surnames, titles, dates, lands, trees and stones – a web of threads extracted from the inkwell, threads in which a man's legs became fouled and which formed barriers across the paths, access to which was denied by law; they formed a noose pressing at his throat and muffling his voice as he perceived the dreadful sound of words which floated free. His signature had betrayed him, getting involved in knots and tangles of parchments. Bound by it, the man of flesh became a man of paper.

It was dawn. The dining-room clock had just struck six in the afternoon.

IV

Months of mourning passed, overshadowed by a growing feeling of remorse. At first the idea of bringing another woman into that bedroom seemed almost reasonable to him. But, little by little, the need for a new body was replaced by increasing scruples which reached the point of flagellation. One night, Don Marcial drew blood from his flesh with a strap and immediately felt a more intense desire, though of short duration. It was then that the Marchioness returned, one afternoon, from her ride along the banks of the Almendares. The horses of the calash had no moisture on their manes other than that of their own sweat. But all the rest of the day, they kicked at the panels of the stable as if irritated by the stillness of the low clouds.

At twilight, a basin full of water fell in the Marchioness' bath and broke. Then the May rains made the tank overflow. And the dark old woman who had a touch of the tar-brush and who kept doves under her bed walked through the yard muttering: 'Beware of rivers, child, beware of the running green.' There wasn't a day on which water did not betray its presence. But this presence was finally nothing more than a bowlful spilled upon a Paris gown when they came back from the anniversary ball given by the Captain General of the colony.

Many relatives reappeared. Many friends returned. The chandeliers of the great drawing-room now sparkled very brightly. The cracks in the façades gradually closed. The piano again became a clavichord. The palm trees lost some rings. The climbing plants let go of the first cornice. The rings under Ceres' eyes grew whiter and the capitals seemed newly-carved. Marcial grew livelier and would spend whole afternoons embracing the Marchioness. Crows-feet, frowns and double chins were erased and the flesh regained its firmness. One day the smell of fresh paint filled the house.

V

The blushes were genuine. Every night the leaves of screens opened wider, skirts fell in the darker corners and there were new barriers of lace. Finally the Marchioness blew out the lamps. Only he spoke in the darkness.

They left for the sugar-mill in a great train of calashes – a shin-ing of sorrel croups, of silver bits and of varnish in the sun. But in the shade of the poinsettias which made the inner portico of the house glow red, they realized that they hardly knew one another. Marcial gave permission for Negro tribal dances and drums in order to divert them a little on those days which were odorous with Cologne perfume, baths of benzoin, with loosened hair and sheets taken from the cupboards which, when opened, spilled out bunches of vetiver herb on to the tiles. A whiff of cane liquor whirled in the breeze with the prayer-bell. The low breezes wafted tidings of reluctant rains whose first, big, noisy drops were sucked in by roofs so dry that they gave out the sound of copper. After a dawn lengthened by an awkward embrace, their disagreements made up, the wound healed, they both went back to the city. The Mar-chioness changed her travelling dress for a bridal gown and as usual, the couple went to church to recover their liberty. They gave the presents back to relatives and friends and in a flurry of bronze bells, a parade of harnesses, each one took the road back to his own home. Marcial went on visiting María de las Mercedes for some time until the day when the rings were taken to the gold-smith's to be disengraved. There began a new life for Marcial. In the house with the high balconies, Ceres was replaced by an Italian Venus and the masks of the fountain almost imperceptibly pushed out their reliefs on seeing the flames of the oil-lamps still alight when dawn already dappled the sky.

VI

One night when he had been doing a lot of drinking and felt dizzied by the smell of stale tobacco left by his friends, Marcial had the strange sensation that all the clocks in the house were striking five, then half-past four, then half-past three. It was like a distant recognition of other possibilities. Just as one imagines oneself during the lassitude of a sleepless night able to walk on the smooth ceiling among furniture placed amidst the roof-beams and with the floor as a smooth ceiling above. It was a fleeting impression that left not the slightest trace in his mind which was now little inclined to meditation.

And there was a big party in the music-room on the day when he reached his minority. He was happy when he thought that his signature no longer had any legal value and that the moth-eaten registers and the notaries were erased from his world. He was reaching the stage where law courts were no longer to be feared by those whose persons were not held in any regard by the law codes. After getting tipsy on full-bodied wines, the young men took down from the wall a guitar encrusted with mother-of-pearl, a psaltery and a trombone. Someone wound up the clock which played the Tyrolean Cow Song and the Ballad of the Scottish Lakes. Another blew on the hunting horn that had lain coiled in its copper case upon the scarlet felt of a show-case alongside the transverse flute brought from Aránjuez. Marcial who was boldly courting the Campoflorido girl joined in the din and picked out the tune of Trípili-Trápala on the bass notes of the keyboard. Then they all went up into the attic, suddenly remembering that there, under the beams which were once again covered with plaster, were hoarded the dresses and liveries of the House of Capellanías. Along shelves frosted with camphor lay court-gowns, an Ambassador's sword, several braided military jackets, the cloak of a Prince of the Church and long dress-coats with damask buttons and with damp marks in the folds. The shadows were tinted with amaranth ribbons, yellow crinolines, faded tunics and velvet flowers. A tinker's costume with a tasselled hair-net made for a Carnival masquerade

won applause. The Campoflorido rounded her shoulders underneath a shawl which was the colour of creole flesh and which had
been used by a certain grandmother on a night of momentous
family decision, in order to receive the waning fires of a rich
treasurer of the Order of St Clare.

The young people returned to the music-room in fancy dress.
Wearing an alderman's tricorne hat on his head, Marcial struck
the floor three times with his stick, and started off the waltz which
the mothers found terribly improper for young ladies with that
clasping around the waist and the man's hand touching the whale-
bone supports of their corsets which they had all made from the
latest pattern in the 'Garden of Fashion'. The doors were obscured
by maidservants, stable-boys, servants who came from their far-off
outbuildings and from stifling basements to marvel at such a
riotous party. Later, they played blind man's buff and hide-and-
seek. Marcial hid with the Campoflorido girl behind the Chinese
screen and imprinted a kiss on her neck and in return received a
perfumed handkerchief whose Brussels lace still held the soft
warmth from her décolleté. And when, in the twilight, the girls
went off to the watchtowers and fortresses which were silhouetted
grey-black against the sea, the young men left for the Dance Hall
where mulatto girls with huge bracelets swayed so gracefully without ever losing their little high-heeled shoes however agitated the
dance. And from behind a neighbouring wall in a yard full of
pomegranate trees the men of the Cabildo Arará Tres Ojos band
beat out a drum roll just as if it were carnival time. Standing on
tables and stools, Marcial and his friends applauded the grace of
a Negress with greyish kinky hair who was beautiful, almost desirable again when she looked over her shoulder and danced with a
proud gesture of defiance.

VII

The visits of Don Abundio, the family notary and executor, grew
more frequent. He sat down gravely at the head of Marcial's bed,
letting his stick of acana wood fall to the floor in order to wake
him up before time. When he opened his eyes, they met an alpaca

coat covered with dandruff, a coat whose shining sleeves gathered up titles and rents. There was finally only a small allowance left, one designed to put a check on any folly. It was then that Marcial resolved to enter the Royal Seminary of San Carlos.

After passing his examinations indifferently, he began to frequent the cloisters where he understood less and less of the teachers' explanations. The world of ideas was slowly becoming empty. What had first been a universal assembly of togas, doublets, ruffs and wigs, debaters and sophists took on the immobility of a waxworks museum. Marcial was now content with the scholastic exposition of system and accepted as true what was said in the text book. Over the copper engravings of Natural History were inscribed Lion, Ostrich, Whale, Jaguar. In the same way, Aristotle, Saint Thomas, Bacon and Descartes headed the black pages on which boring catalogues of interpretations of the universe appeared in the margins of the lengthy chapters. Little by little, Marcial left off studying them and found that a great weight was lifted from him. His mind became light and happy when he accepted only an instinctive knowledge of things. Why think of the prism when the clear winter light gave added detail to the fortress of the door? An apple falling from the tree was only an incitement to the teeth. A foot in a bathtub was only a foot in a bathtub. The day on which he left the Seminary, he forgot his books. The gnomon recovered its fairy character; the spectrum became synonymous with the word spectre; the octander was an armour-plated insect with spines on its back.

Several times, he had walked quickly with an anxious heart to visit women who whispered behind blue doors at the foot of the battlements. The memory of one of them who wore embroidered shoes and basil leaves over her ear pursued him like a toothache on hot afternoons. But one day, the anger and threats of his confessor made him weep with fear. He fell for the last time between the sheets of hell and renounced forever his wanderings along quiet streets, and his last-minute cowardice which made him return home angrily after turning his back on a certain cracked pavement (the sign, when he was walking with his eyes lowered, of the half-turn he must make in order to enter the perfumed threshold).

Now he was living his religious crisis, full of amulets, paschal lambs and china doves, Virgins in sky-blue cloaks, angels with swan's wings, the Ass, the Ox and a terrible Saint Dionysius who appeared to him in dreams with a big hollow between his shoulders and the hesitant walk of one who seeks for something he has lost. He stumbled against the bed and Marcial awoke in fear, grasping the rosary of muffled beads. The wicks in their oil vessels gave a sad light to the images which were recovering their pristine colours.

VIII

The furniture grew. It became more and more difficult to keep his arms on the edge of the dining-room table. The cupboards with carved cornices became wider at the front. Stretching their bodies, the Moors on the staircase brought their torches up to the balustrades of the landing. The armchairs were deeper and the rocking-chairs tended to go over backwards. He no longer needed to bend his legs when he lay down at the bottom of the bathtub which had marble rings.

One morning, whilst reading a licentious book, Marcial suddenly felt like playing with the lead soldiers which lay in their wooden boxes. He hid the book again under the wash-basin and opened a drawer covered with spiders' webs. The study table was too small to fit so many persons. For this reason, Marcial sat on the floor. He placed the grenadiers in lines of eight, then the officers on horseback, clustered round the standard-bearer and behind, the artillery with their cannons, gunwads and matchstaffs. Bringing up the rear came fifes and kettledrums and an escort of drummers. The mortars were provided with a spring which enabled them to shoot glass marbles from a yard away.

Bang ! Bang ! Bang !

Horses fell, standard-bearers fell, drums fell. He had to be called three times by the Negro Eligio before he made up his mind to wash his hands and go down to the dining-room.

From then on, Marcial retained the habit of sitting on the tile floor. When he realized the advantages, he was surprised at not having thought of it before. Grown-ups with their addiction to

velvet cushions sweat too much. Some smell of notary – like Don
Abundio – because they know nothing of the coolness of marble
(whatever the temperature) when one is lying full-length on the
floor. It is only from the floor that all the angles and perspectives
of a room can be appreciated. There are beauties of wood, mysterious insect paths, shadowy corners which are unknown from a
man's height. When it rained, Marcial hid under the clavichord.
Each roll of thunder made the box tremble and all the notes sang.
From the sky fell thunderbolts which created a cavern full of im-
provisations – the sounds of an organ, of a pine grove in the wind,
of a cricket's mandoline.

IX

That morning, they shut him in his room. He heard murmurs all
over the house and the lunch they served him was too succulent for
a weekday. There were six cakes from the confectioner's shop on
the Alameda when only two could be eaten on Sundays after mass.
He amused himself by looking at the travel engravings until the
rising buzz which came from under the doors caused him to peep
out between the Venetian blinds. Men dressed in black were arriving, carrying a box with bronze handles. He felt like crying but at
that moment, Melchor the coachman appeared, displaying a toothy
smile over his squeaky boots. They began to play chess. Melchor
was knight. He was King. With the floor-tiles as the board, he could
advance one at a time whilst Melchor had to jump one to the front
and two sideways or vice versa. The game went on until nightfall
when the Chamber of Commerce's Fire Brigade went past.

When he got up, he went to kiss the hand of his father who lay
on his sick-bed. The Marquis was feeling better and spoke to his
son with his normal looks and phrases. His 'Yes, father' and 'No,
father' were fitted in between each bead in the rosary of questions
like the responses of the acolyte in mass. Marcial respected the
Marquis but for reasons which nobody would have guessed. He
respected him because of his great height and because he appeared
on ball nights with decorations sparkling across his breast; because
he envied his sabre and his militia officer's epaulets, because at

Christmas he had eaten a whole turkey stuffed with almonds and raisins to win a bet; because, on one occasion, perhaps because he wanted to beat her, he seized one of the mulatto girls who was sweeping in the rotunda and carried her in his arms to his room. Hidden behind a curtain, Marcial saw her emerge a short time later weeping and with her dress unbuttoned, and he was glad she had been punished because she was the one who always emptied the jam-pots that were returned to the larder.

His father was a terrible, magnanimous being whom he ought to love first after God. Marcial felt that he was more God than God because his gifts were daily and tangible. But he preferred the God of heaven because he interfered with him less.

X

When the furniture grew taller and Marcial knew better than anyone else what there was underneath beds, cupboards and escritoires, he had a big secret; life held no charm away from Melchor, the coachman. Neither God nor his father, nor the gilded bishop in the Corpus processions were as important as Melchor.

Melchor came from far away. He was the grandson of conquered princes. In his kingdom, there were elephants, hippopotamus, tigers and giraffes. There men did not work in dark rooms full of parchments like Don Abundio. They lived by being cleverer than the animals. One of them had caught a great crocodile in a blue lake by piercing it with a hook concealed in the tightly-packed bodies of twelve roast geese. Melchor knew songs that were easy to learn because the words had no meaning and were repeated a great deal. He stole sweets from the kitchen, got out at night through the stable door and on one occasion had thrown stones at the police and then had disappeared into the shadows of Amargura street.

On rainy days, his boots were put to dry in front of the kitchen fire. Marcial would have liked to have had feet to fill such boots. The right-hand one was called Calambín. The left-hand one was called Calambán. The man who tamed unbroken horses just by putting his fingers on their lips, this lord of velvet and spurs who wore such tall top hats also knew how cool the marble floor was in

summer and hid under the furniture a fruit or cake snatched from
the trays which were destined for the big drawing-room. Marcial
and Melchor had a secret store full of fruit and almonds which
they held in common and called Urí, urí, urá, with understanding
laughs. Both of them had explored the house from top to bottom
and were the only ones who knew of the existence of a small basement full of Dutch flasks underneath the stables and of twelve
dusty butterflies which had just lost their wings in a broken glass
box in a disused attic over the maids' rooms.

XI

When Marcial acquired the habit of breaking things, he forgot about
Melchor and drew closer to the dogs. There were several of them
in the house. There was a big, striped one, a hound with dragging
teats, a greyhound who was too old to play with, a woolly dog
which the rest chased at certain periods and which the housemaids
had to lock up.

Marcial liked Canelo best because he took shoes from out of the
bedrooms and dug up the rose-bushes in the garden. He was always
black from charcoal or covered with red earth and he used to devour
the other dogs' meals, whine without reason and hide stolen bones
by the fountain. Occasionally he would finish off a newly-laid egg
after sending the hen flying into the air with a swift levering
movement of the muzzle. Everyone would kick Canelo. But Marcial
fell ill when they took him away. And the dog returned in triumph,
wagging its tail after having been abandoned at the other side of
the Charity Hospital and recovered a position in the house which
the other dogs with their skill at hunting or their alertness as
watchdogs never occupied.

Canelo and Marcial used to pee together. Sometimes, they chose
the Persian carpet in the drawing-room and upon the wool pile, they
outlined the shapes of clouds which would grow slowly bigger. For
this they were given the strap. But the beating did not hurt as
much as the grown-ups thought. On the contrary, it was an excellent excuse for setting up a concert of howls and of arousing the
sympathy of the neighbours. When the cross-eyed woman in the

attic called his father a 'savage', Marcial looked at Canelo and laughed with his eyes. They cried a bit more to get a biscuit and all was forgotten. Both of them used to eat earth, roll in the sun, drink from the fish-pond and look for shade and perfume under the sweet basil. In hours of the greatest heat, the damp paving-stones were crowded. There was a grey goose with a bag hanging between its bow-legs; there was the old hen with a bare behind and the lizard that croaked and shot out a tongue like a pink tie issuing from its throat; there was the juba snake born in a city without females and the mouse which walled up its hole with the seed of the carey bush. One day they showed Marcial a dog.

'Bow, wow,' he said.

He spoke his own language. He had attained the supreme freedom. He already wanted to reach with his hands things which were out of reach of his hands.

XII

Hunger, thirst, heat, pain, cold. When Marcial had reduced his perception to these essential realities, he renounced light which was now incidental to him. He did not know his name. The baptism with its unpleasant salt was taken away from him and he did not now need smell, hearing or sight. His hands brushed against pleasing forms. He was a totally sentient and tactile being. The universe entered him through all his pores. Then he closed his eyes which only perceived nebulous giants and penetrated into a warm, damp body full of shadows in which he died. The body, on feeling him wrapped in its own substance, slipped towards life.

But now time sped more rapidly and lessened its last hours. The minutes sounded like the slipping of cards under a gambler's thumb.

The birds returned to the egg in a rush of feathers. The fish coagulated into spawn leaving a snowstorm of scales at the bottom of the tank. The palms folded their fronds and disappeared into the earth like closed fans. Stalks sucked in the leaves and the ground drew in all that belonged to it. Thunder resounded in the corridors. Hair grew on the suède of gloves. Woollen shawls lost their dye and plumped out the fleece of distant sheep. Cupboards, escritoires, beds, crucifixes, tables, blinds flew into the night seeking their ancient roots in the jungles. Everything which had nails in it crumbled. A brig anchored (heaven knows where) hurriedly took the marble of the floor-tiles and the fountain back to Italy. The collection of arms, ironwork, the keys, copper-pans, horse-bits from the stables melted, swelling the river of metal which was channelled along roofless galleries into the earth. All was metamorphosed and went back to its primitive condition. The clay became clay again leaving a desert in place of a house.

XIII

When the workmen came at daybreak to continue the demolition, they found their work finished. Someone had taken away the statue of Ceres which had been sold the day before to an antique-dealer. After lodging a complaint with the Union, the men went and sat on the benches of the city park. Then one of them recalled the very vague story of a Marchioness of Capellanías who had been drowned one May afternoon among the lilies of the Almendares. But nobody paid any attention to the tale, because the sun was travelling from East to West and the hours which grow on the right-hand of clocks must become longer out of laziness since they are those which lead most surely to death.

Translated by Jean Franco

Carlos Drummond de Andrade

TRAVELLING IN THE FAMILY

To Rodrigo M. F. de Andrade

In the desert of Itabira
the shadow of my father
took me by the hand.
So much time lost.
But he didn't say anything.
It was neither day nor night.
A sigh? A passing bird?
But he didn't say anything.

We have come a long way.
Here there was a house.
The mountain used to be bigger.
So many heaped-up dead,
and time gnawing the dead.
And in the ruined houses,
cold disdain and damp.
But he didn't say anything.

The street he used to cross
on horseback, at a gallop.
His watch. His clothes.
His legal documents.
His tales of love-affairs.
Opening of tin trunks
and violent memories.
But he didn't say anything.

In the desert of Itabira
things come back to life,
stiflingly, suddenly.
The market of desires
displays its sad treasures;
my urge to run away;
naked women; remorse.
But he didn't say anything.

Stepping on books and letters
we travel in the family.
Marriages; mortgages;
the consumptive cousins;
the mad aunt; my grandmother
betrayed among the slave-girls,
rustling silks in the bedroom.
But he didn't say anything.

What cruel, obscure instinct
moved his pallid hand
subtly pushing us
into the forbidden
time, forbidden places?
I looked in his white eyes.
I cried to him : Speak ! My voice
shook in the air a moment,
beat on the stones. The shadow
proceeded slowly on
with that pathetic travelling
across the lost kingdom.
But he didn't say anything.

I saw grief, misunderstanding
and more than one old revolt
dividing us in the dark.
The hand I wouldn't kiss,

the crumb that they denied me,
refusal to ask pardon.
Pride. Terror at night.
But he didn't say anything.

Speak   speak   speak   speak.
I pulled him by his coat
that was turning into clay.
By the hands, by the boots
I caught at his strict shadow
and the shadow released itself
with neither haste nor anger.
But he remained silent.

And there were separate silences
deep within his silence.
There was my deaf grandfather
hearing the painted birds
on the ceiling of the church;
my own lack of friends;
and your lack of kisses;
there were our difficult lives
and a great separation
in the little space of the room.

The narrow space of life
crowds me up against you,
and in this ghostly embrace
it's as if I were being burned
completely, with poignant love.
Only now do we know each other !
Eye-glasses, memories, portraits
flow in the river of blood.
Now the waters won't let me
make out your distant face,
distant by seventy years . . .

I felt that he pardoned me
but he didn't say anything.
The waters cover his moustache,
the family, Itabira, all.

DON'T KILL YOURSELF

Carlos, keep calm, love
is what you're seeing now :
today a kiss, tomorrow no kiss,
day after tomorrow's Sunday
and nobody knows what will happen
Monday.

It's useless to resist
or to commit suicide.
Don't kill yourself. Don't kill yourself !
Keep all of yourself for the nuptials
coming nobody knows when,
that is, if they ever come.

Love, Carlos, tellurion,
spent the night with you,
and now your insides are raising
an ineffable racket,
prayers,
victrolas,
saints crossing themselves,
ads for better soap,·
a racket of which nobody
knows the why or wherefore.

In the meantime you go on your way
vertical, melancholy.
You're the palm tree, you're the cry
nobody heard in the theatre

and all the lights went out.
Love in the dark, no, love
in the daylight, is always sad,
sad, Carlos, my boy,
but tell it to nobody,
nobody knows nor shall know.

Translated by Elizabeth Bishop

Julio Cortázar

BESTIARY

Between the last spoonful of rice pudding (a pity there was too little cinnamon) and the kisses before going to bed, the bell in the phone-room rang, and Isabel lingered until Inés came from answering it and whispered something in her mother's ear. They looked at one another and then the two of them looked at Isabel – who thought about the broken cage, the multiplication beads, and a little bit about Miss Lucera being angry because she had rung her doorbell on her way home from school. She was not very worried; her mother and Inés were looking beyond her, almost using her as a pretext. All the same, they were looking at her.

'Believe me, I don't like the idea of her going,' Inés said. 'It's not the tiger so much because after all they are very careful about it. But that sad house and that lonely kid to play with her . . .'

'I'm not keen on it either,' her mother said, and Isabel knew with overwhelming certainty that they would send her to spend the summer at the Funes place. She plunged into the news as into an enormous green wave – the Funes place, the Funes place, of course they were sending her there. They didn't like it but it was desirable. Delicate chest, Mar de Plata very expensive, the difficulty of controlling a spoilt child, a silly child, conduct fair despite the fact that Miss Tania is very good, not a good sleeper, toys everywhere, questions, buttons, dirty knees. She felt fear, delight, the scent of willow-trees; and the *u* of Funes was mixed up with rice pudding and very late, off to bed and go to sleep this minute.

In bed, without a light and covered in kisses and sad looks from Inés and her mother who had not quite decided to send her away and yet were fully decided to do so. She savoured in anticipation her arrival in the station wagon, the first breakfast, the happiness of Nino the cockroach hunter, Nino toad, Nino fish (a memory from three years ago – Nino showing her some little pictures pasted in an album and telling her seriously, 'This is a toad, and this a f-f-fish'). Then Nino in the garden waiting for her with his butterfly net. And she saw Rema's soft hands too, rising out of the darkness; her eyes were open and instead of Nino's face, hey presto, the hands of Rema, the youngest of the Funes. 'Aunt Rema loves me so much,' Nino's eyes grew big and wet; again she saw Nino detach himself and float in the blurred air of the bedroom, looking at her happily. Nino fish. She went to sleep wishing that the week would pass in that one night and the goodbyes and the train journey, the mile in the station wagon, the gate and the eucalyptus trees along the drive. Before she went to sleep, she felt a momentary terror thinking that she might have been dreaming. All at once as she stretched herself, she knocked her feet against the bronze rails; they hurt her through the coverlets and she heard her mother and Inés talking in the big dining-room – luggage, see the doctor about her rash, cod-liver oil, witch hazel. It wasn't a dream. It wasn't a dream.

No, it wasn't a dream. They took her to Constitución Square one windy morning, and there were little flags on the hawkers' carts in the market, sandwiches on the stopping train, and a lot of people going on to number fourteen platform. Between Inés and her mother, she was kissed so much that her face felt as if it had been walked over, felt soft, and smelt of rouge and Coty Rachel face powder, damp around the mouth and disgust that the wind swept away. She wasn't afraid of travelling alone because she was a big girl with no less than twenty pesos in her wallet; a sweet waft from the Sansinena Ice Cream Company blew in through the window, then the Little Yellow River and Isabel who had already recovered from her enforced bout of weeping was happy, dead with apprehension, energetically using the whole of her seat and her window. She was almost the only passenger in her part of the coach and she could try all the seats and look at herself in the mirrors. She thought of her mother and Inés once or twice – they would already be in the 97 leaving Constitución Square. She read smoking prohibited, spitting prohibited, seating capacity – 42; they went through Banfield at top speed, whee . . . country, more country, more country mixed up with the taste of Milky Way and menthol pastilles. Inés had advised her to pass her time knitting the green bed-jacket and so Isabel had put it into the deepest corner of her suit-case. Poor Inés, such corny ideas.

In the station she felt a bit afraid in case the station-wagon . . . But it was there with don Nicanor flowery and respectful, Miss this . . . Miss that . . . if a good journey, if doña Elisa as beautiful as ever, yes, of course it had rained. – Oh, the motion of the station-wagon, the trouble there had been carrying the whole of the aquarium from her previous visit to Los Horneros. Everything tinier, more glass and pink and without the tiger in those days and don Nicanor had not been so grey only three years ago. Nino a toad, Nino a fish, and Rema's hands which made her want to cry and feel them eternally against her head in an embrace almost like death and vanilla with cream, the two best things in life.

They gave her a very pretty room upstairs all to herself, a grown-up's room (it was Nino's idea; he was all black, curly hair and big eyes, sweet in his blue jeans; of course Luis made him dress very well in the evenings in slate grey with a coloured tie) and inside there was another tiny room with an enormous, fierce red cardinal bird. The bathroom was only two doors away (but they were inside doors so that she could go out without first finding out where the tiger was), full of faucets and metal although Isabel was not easily taken in and even in the bathroom, it was obviously the country; things were not so perfect as in a city bathroom. It smelt old and on the second morning she found a little damp grub walking round the wash-basin. She hardly touched it and it rolled into a frightened little ball, slipped and went down the gurgling drain.

Dear Mummy, I am writing to . . . They ate in the glass dining-room where it was cooler. Babe was always complaining because of the heat. Luis would say nothing but little by little drops of water would appear on his brow and chin. Only Rema remained calm; she would pass the dishes slowly and always as if the meal were a birthday occasion, rather solemn and exciting. (Isabel learned in secret her way of serving and of giving orders to the maids.) Luis would nearly always read with his head on his hands and the book propped against the syphon. Rema would touch his arm before passing him a dish and sometimes Babe would interrupt him and call him a philosopher. Isabel was sorry that Luis was a philosopher, not because he was but because it gave Babe an excuse for teasing him and calling him one.

They would eat in this way: Luis at the head of the table, Rema and Nino on one side and Babe and Isabel on the other so that there was a grown-up at the end and a child and a grown-up on each side. When Nino wanted to tell her something properly he would kick her on the shin. Once Isabel cried out and Babe got mad and called her a naughty child. Rema stared at her until Isabel was comforted by her look and by the julienne soup.

Mummy, before you go to eat just as at every other time, you have to see whether . . . Usually it was Rema who went to see if they could go into the mirror dining-room. On the second day, she came into the main drawing-room and told them to wait. A long time passed before a peon announced that the tiger was in the clover garden, then Rema took the children by the hand and they all went in to eat. That day the potatoes were very dry though only Babe and Nino complained.

You told me that I mustn't go and . . .

For Rema with her pure goodness seemed to prevent any questioning. There was so much space that there was no need to worry about rooms. It was a huge house and at the very worst there was just one room you hadn't to go into: never more than one, so that it didn't matter. Within two days, Isabel was as used to it as Nino. They played from morning till night in the willow grove and if they couldn't play in the willow grove, there was the clover garden, the hammock paddock and the bank of the stream. In the house it was the same, they had their bedrooms, the corridor on the middle floor, the lower library (except for one Thursday when they couldn't go into the library) and the mirror dining-room. They did not go into Luis's study because he was always reading; sometimes he called his son and gave him picture-books but Nino would take them away and they would go and look at them in the drawing-room or in the front garden. They never went into Babe's study because they were afraid of his tempers. Rema said it was better that way, she said it as if warning them. They already knew how to read her silences.

Taking everything into account, it was a sad life. Isabel wondered one night why the Funes had invited her to spend the summer there. She wasn't old enough to understand that it wasn't for her but for Nino, a summer toy to cheer Nino up. She only noticed the sad house, the fact that Rema seemed tired and that it scarcely rained and yet, despite this, that things looked damp and deserted. After a few days, she got used to the routine of the house and not very hard discipline of that summer in Los Horneros. Nino began to understand the microscope that Luis had given him; they spent a wonderful week breeding grubs in a tank full of stagnant water and lily leaves and putting drops on the glass in order to look at the microbes. 'They are mosquito larvae; you can't see microbes through this microscope,' Luis told them with his dry, faraway smile. They couldn't believe that this moving horror was not a microbe. Rema brought them a kaleidoscope which they kept in a cupboard but they always preferred discovering microbes and counting their feet. Isabel kept a notebook with notes of the experiments and combined biology with chemistry and the preparation of a small pharmacy. They made the pharmacy in Nino's room after searching the house to provision themselves with things. Isabel told Luis about it: 'We want everything – things.' Luis gave them cough tablets, pink bandage and a test tube; Babe a hot-water bottle and a bottle of little green pills with the label scratched off. Rema came to see the pharmacy, read the inventory in the notebook and said that they were learning useful things. It was either she or Nino (who always got excited and tried to show off in front of Rema) who thought of starting a herbarium. As they were able to go into the clover garden that morning, they went picking samples and by nightfall had filled their bedroom floors with leaves and flowers on pieces of paper; there was almost no room to walk. Before going to sleep, Isabel wrote down: 'Leaf No. 74: green, heart-shaped with brown spots.' She was rather bored by the fact that nearly all the leaves were green, nearly all smooth and nearly all were spotted.

On the day they went to catch ants, she saw the farm labourers. She knew the overseer and the estate manager because they came to the house with information. But these other younger labourers stayed by the side of the sheds with a casual air, yawning from time to time and watching the children play. One of them said to Nino: 'Whatya collecting all those insects for?' and he smacked him with two fingers on his curls. Isabel would have liked Nino to get mad and show he was the boss's son. They already had the bottle swarming with ants and on the bank of the stream they came upon an enormous armour-plated one and they threw it in as well to see what happened. The idea of a formicarium had been taken from the Children's Encyclopedia and Luis lent them a long, deep glass box. As they were going away, carrying it between the two of them, Isabel heard him say to Rema: 'It's better for them to be playing quietly in the house like this.' And she also thought that Rema sighed. She remembered it before going to sleep, at the time when faces appeared to her in the dark. She saw Babe again going out on to the porch for a smoke; he was slim, humming to himself; she saw Rema bringing him his coffee and saw him take the cup very clumsily squeezing Rema's fingers by mistake as he grasped the cup. Isabel from the dining-room had watched Rema draw her hand back and Babe only just stopped the cup from falling and he was laughing at the confusion. Black ants better than red ones: bigger, fiercer. Afterwards they would let loose a lot of red ones, watch the war from behind the glass, safe and sound. Unless they wouldn't fight. Two ant-hills one at each end of the glass case. As a consolation they would study the different habits with a special notebook for each type of ant. But it was almost certain that they would fight, war with *no quarter given* which they would watch through the glass; and only one notebook.

Rema did not like spying on them; sometimes she went past one of the bedrooms and saw them with the ant-hill by the side of the window, looking enthusiastic and important. Nino was an expert at finding any new galleries at once, and Isabel would enlarge the plan which was traced in ink across a double page. On Luis's advice, they finally took only black ants and the ant-hill was already enormous; the ants looked furious and worked till nightfall, digging and moving about in a thousand groups and making a thousand evolutions; there were cautious rubbings of legs and antennae, sudden bursts of anger or energy, and concentration and dispersals for no visible reason. Isabel no longer knew what to write down; she gradually abandoned the notebook and spent hours studying her discoveries and then forgetting them. Nino began to want to return to the garden; he talked about the hammocks and the ponies. Isabel despised him a little. The ant-hill was worth more than the whole of Los Horneros and she loved to think that the ants came and went without fear of any tiger; sometimes she liked imagining a tiny little tiger the size of an india-rubber prowling round the corridors of the ant-hill. Perhaps that was why there were the dispersals and concentrations. And she liked to see the adult world reflected in the glass one now that she felt rather trapped, now that it was forbidden to go down to the dining-room until Rema told them.

She brought her nose close to one of the glass panes, suddenly alert because she liked them to take notice of her; she heard Rema pause in the doorway and watch her without speaking. These things she heard with such clear distinctness when it was Rema.

'Why all alone?'

'Nino went to the hammocks. I think this must be a queen. It's very big.'

Rema's apron was reflected in the glass. Isabel saw her hand slightly raised; because of the reflection in the glass, it looked as if it were inside the ant-hill. She suddenly thought of the same hand giving a cup of coffee to Babe but now there were ants walking along the fingers, ants instead of the cup and Babe's hand squeezing the finger-tips.

'Take your hand away, Rema,' she asked.

'My hand?'

'Now it's all right. The reflection was frightening the ants.'

'Oh, I see. You can go down to the dining-room now.'

'Afterwards. Is Babe cross with you, Rema?'

The hand passed over the glass like a bird through a window. It seemed to Isabel that the ants were really frightened and that they fled from the reflection. Now you couldn't see anything any more. Rema had gone away and was rushing down the corridor as if running away from something. Isabel felt fear because of her question, a dull, senseless fear, perhaps not because of the question but because of seeing Rema go away like that from the glass case which was now clear again where the galleries emerged; and they were twisted like clenched fingers inside the earth.

One afternoon there was a siesta, watermelon, bat and ball against the wall which faced the stream and Nino was marvellous hitting back shots which seemed impossible and climbing up the wistaria on to the roof to dislodge a ball wedged between two tiles. A young labourer came from beside the willow trees and played with them but he was slow and missed shots. Isabel smelt the aguaribay leaves and at one moment, as with a backhand she was returning a treacherous shot which Nino had sent low down, she felt deep within her the happiness of summer. For the first time she understood her presence in Los Horneros, the holidays, Nino. She thought of the ant-hill upstairs and it was a dead, smelly thing, a horror of feet trying to escape and stuffy, poisonous air. She hit the ball angrily, cut off a stem of aguaribay with her teeth and spat it out in disgust, but happy, really happy at last in the country sunshine.

The window-panes fell like hail. It was Babe's study. They saw him looking out in his shirt-sleeves with his wide, black glasses.

'Filthy kids !'

The young labourer ran away. Nino stood at Isabel's side. She felt him trembling in the same wind as the willow trees.

'We didn't do it on purpose, uncle.'

'It's true, Babe. We didn't do it on purpose.'

He was no longer there.

She had asked Rema to take away the ant-hill and Rema had promised to. Later, they forgot because they were chatting as Rema helped her hang up her things and put her pyjamas on. Isabel felt the nearness of the ants when Rema put out the light and went down the corridor to say goodnight to Nino who was still tearful and hurt, but she did not have the heart to call her back again. She decided to go to sleep right away and she stayed awake more than ever. At the time when faces appeared to her in the dark, she saw her mother and Inés looking at one another with a smiling, conspiratorial air and putting on yellow, phosphorescent gloves. She saw Nino crying and her mother and Inés with their gloves which now were violet caps which whirled round and round upon their heads. She saw Nino with huge, hollow eyes – perhaps from so much crying – and she foresaw that now she would see Rema and Luis. She wanted to see them and not Babe, but she saw Babe without his glasses and with the same distorted expression as when he had begun to smack Nino. Nino was slowly moving backwards until he was against the wall and he was looking at him as if hoping that it would all be over and Babe was smacking his face again with a light, soft smack which sounded damp until Rema put herself in front of him and then Luis could be heard coming back and saying from the distance that they could now go into the inside dining-room. It had all happened so quickly, all because Nino was there and Rema had come to tell them not to go out of the drawing-room until Luis found out which room the tiger was in and she had stayed to watch them play draughts. Nino had won and Rema congratulated him. Then Nino had been so happy that he had put his arms round her waist and tried to kiss her. Rema had bent down laughing and Nino had kissed her on the eyes and nose. They were both laughing and so was Isabel, they were so happy playing like that. They didn't see Babe approaching. When he was close to them, he dragged Nino out, said something about the window-pane in his room and began to smack him. He was watching Rema as he did it. He seemed mad at Rema and she defied him for a moment with her eyes. Isabel was terrified seeing her stand up to Babe and put herself in front to protect Nino. The whole of supper was a pretence, a lie. Luis thought Nino was crying because of a bump, Babe looked at Rema as if ordering her to be silent. Isabel could see him now with his hard, beautiful mouth and the very red lips; his lips seemed even more scarlet in the twilight and she could just see the shining tips of his teeth. From his teeth emerged a spongy cloud, a green triangle. Isabel blinked to erase the images and once again Inés and her mother emerged with their yellow gloves; she watched them for a short time and thought about the ant-hill. The ant-hill was really there and you couldn't see it; the yellow gloves were not really there and yet she could see them as clear as daylight. It seemed rather strange to her that she couldn't make the ant-hill appear but perceived it more as if it were a weight or a piece of dense, living space. She felt it so distinctly that she began to look for the matches and the night-light. The ant-hill leapt out of nothingness enveloped in a wavering darkness. Isabel carried the candle up to it. Poor ants! they would think that the sun was rising. When she was able to see one of the corners, she felt afraid; the ants had been working in pitch darkness. She saw them running busily to and fro in a silence that was quite visible and palpable. Inside there, they were working away as if they had not yet lost the hope of getting out.

It was nearly always the overseer who reported the tiger's movements. Luis had the greatest confidence in him and as he spent nearly all day working in his study, he would never go out or allow those who had been on the top floor to move until don Roberto had sent his report. But they also had to trust one another. Rema who was busy with housework knew quite well what was going on downstairs and up above. On other occasions the youngsters brought information to Babe or Luis, not because they had seen anything – but if don Roberto met them outside, he would show them the whereabouts of the tiger and they would go back to report. They believed Nino completely but Isabel less because she was new and might make a mistake. Later, as she and Nino were inseparable, they finally believed her as well. That was in the morning and afternoon; at night it was Babe who went out to make sure that the dogs were tied up and to see if any smouldering ashes had been left near the house. Isabel noticed that he carried a revolver and sometimes a silver-handled stick.

She didn't like to ask Rema questions because Rema seemed to find the arrangements so necessary and obvious; she would have appeared stupid if she had asked her and she was careful of her dignity in front of another woman. With Nino it was easier; he would talk and explain things. It was all so clear and obvious when he explained. But at night when she tried to repeat this clarity and obviousness, Isabel realized that the important reasons were still missing. She quickly learned the thing that really mattered which was to find out first of all if she could leave the house or go down into the glass dining-room, to Luis's study or to the library. 'You must trust don Roberto,' Rema had said. And she must trust Nino and her. You didn't ask Luis because he rarely knew. Babe, who always knew, you never asked. And so it was all very easy. Life fell into a pattern for Isabel with a few more responsibilities with regard to her movements and a few less with regard to her clothes, meals and bedtime. A real summer holiday, just as it ought to be all the year round.

. . . see you soon. They are all well. Nino and I have an ant-hill and we play and we have a very big herbarium. Rema sends kisses, she is well. I think she's sad, also Luis who is very well. I think Luis has something the matter with him and he studies all the time. Rema gave me some lovely, coloured handkerchiefs. Inés will like them. Mummy, this is lovely and I am enjoying myself with Nino and don Roberto. He is the overseer and he tells us when we can go out and where, one afternoon he nearly made a mistake and he sent us to the stream, then a labourer came to tell us not to go there and you should have seen how upset don Roberto was and afterwards Rema picked Nino up and was kissing him and she squeezed me very hard. Luis was saying that the house was not for youngsters and Nino asked him who the youngsters were and they all laughed, even Babe laughed. Don Roberto is the overseer.

If you came to fetch me, you could stay for a few days you could be with Rema and cheer her up. I think that she . . .

But how could she tell her mother that Rema cried at night, that she had heard her cry as she went down the corridor with faltering steps, as she stopped in front of Nino's door and then went on downstairs (she would be drying her eyes) and then came Luis's distant voice: 'What's the matter, Rema? Aren't you well?' A silence in which the whole house was like a huge ear and then Luis's voice again, 'He's a wretch, a wretch . . .' as if he were coldly confirming a fact, a deduction, a destiny.

. . . is a little unwell, it would do her good if you came to stay with her. I want to show you the herbarium and some pebbles from the stream which the labourers brought. Tell Inés . . .

It was the sort of night she liked with insects, damp, toasted bread and semolina pudding with currants in it. The dogs kept on barking by the river bank and an enormous mamboretá insect flew down and landed on the tablecloth. Nino went to look for a magnifying-glass and they put a wide glass over it and made it get so angry that it would show the colour of its wings.

'Throw that insect away,' Rema begged them, 'I have a horror of them.'

'It's a fine specimen,' Luis admitted. 'Look how it follows my hand with its eyes. It's the only insect that turns its head.'

'What a beastly night,' Babe said from behind his newspaper.

Isabel would have liked to behead the mamboretá, to slice off its head with a pair of scissors to see what happened.

'Leave it in the glass,' she begged Nino. 'Tomorrow we can put it into the ant-hill to see what happens.'

The heat increased and by half past ten it was impossible to breathe. The youngsters stayed with Rema in the inside dining-room and the men were in their studies. Nino was the first to say that he was sleepy.

'Go upstairs by yourself. I'll come up and see you later. It's all right upstairs.' And Rema put her arm around his waist in a way which he liked so much.

'Will you tell us a story, Aunt Rema?'

'Some other night.'

They were left alone with the mamboretá looking at them. Luis came to say goodnight, muttered something about the time children ought to be in bed. Rema smiled as she kissed him.

'Bear with a sore head,' she said and Isabel bending over the glass with the mamboretá in it realized that she had never seen Rema kissing Babe or a mamboretá that was such a green green. She moved the glass a little and the mamboretá got angry. Rema came up and asked her to go to bed.

'Throw away that insect, it's horrible.'

'Tomorrow, Rema.'

She asked her to come up and say goodnight. Babe had the door of his study ajar and was walking about in his shirt-sleeves with his neck unbuttoned. He whistled to her as she went past.

'I'm going to bed, Babe.'

'Listen. Tell Rema to make me some nice, cool lemonade and bring it up to me. Afterwards go right up to your room.'

Of course she would go up to her room; she didn't see why he had to tell her to do it. She went back to the dining-room to tell Rema and saw that she hesitated.

'Don't go up yet. I'll make the lemonade and you can take it yourself.'

'He said that . . .'

'Please.'

Isabel sat by the table. Please. There were clouds of insects whirling about under the carbon lamp. She could have stayed for hours watching nothing and repeating. Please, please, please. Rema, Rema. Anything she wanted . . . and that endlessly sad voice, sad without any possible reason, the very epitome of sadness. Please Rema, Rema . . . Fever heat flooded her face and she wanted to throw herself at Rema's feet and let Rema carry her; she felt willing to die looking at her and wanted Rema to be sorry for her, to stroke her hair and eyelids with her slender fingers.

Now she handed her a green jug full of sliced lemons and ice.

'Take it to him.'

'Rema . . .'

It seemed to her that she was trembling and that she had turned her back to the table so that she should not see her eyes.

'I threw away the mamboretá, Rema.'

You sleep badly in the sticky heat and with such a buzzing of mosquitoes. Twice she was on the point of getting up and going into the corridor or into the bathroom to wet her wrists and face. But she could hear someone walking about downstairs, someone pacing from one end of the dining-room to the other. It was not Luis's long, gloomy step nor Rema's walk. How hot Babe was that night! he must have swallowed the lemonade in long gulps. Isabel could see him drinking out of the jug, his hands holding the green jug with yellow slices wavering in the water under the lamp; and at the same time she was sure that Babe had not drunk the lemonade and that he was still looking at the jug which she had taken up to the table as if he were witnessing an act of infinite perversity. She did not want to think about Babe's smile and the way he went to the door as if to look into the dining-room, and his slow return.

'She was supposed to bring it to me. I told you to go up to your room.'

And she could only think of a stupid reply.

'It's very cool, Babe.'

The jug was green like the mamboretá.

Nino was the first to get up and he suggested that they should go and look for snails in the stream. Isabel had hardly slept. She had remembered drawing-rooms with flowers, bells, hospital corridors, sisters of mercy, thermometers in jars of disinfectant, first communion impressions, Inés, the broken bicycle, the stopping train, a gipsy fancy-dress costume she had when she was eight. In the midst of all this, like a slight breeze ruffling the pages of an album, she was also awake and thinking of many things that were not flowers, bells, hospital corridors. She got up reluctantly, and washed her ears very hard. Nino said that it was ten o'clock and the tiger was in the music-room so that they could go to the stream right away. They went down together, hardly greeting Luis and Babe who were reading with their doors open. The snails were left in the wheat-fields by the river bank. Nino went about complaining of Isabel's absent-mindedness, he called her a spoil-sport and said she wasn't helping to make the collection. She suddenly found him very small, such a little boy amongst his snails and leaves.

She was the first to return when they put the flag out at the house for lunch. Don Roberto returned from his inspection and as usual Isabel asked him about it. Nino was approaching slowly, carrying the box of snails and the rakes. Isabel helped him to put the rakes in the porch and they went in together. Rema was there, white and silent. Nino put a blue snail into her hand.

'The prettiest is for you . . .'

Babe was eating already with his newspaper at his side. There was hardly any room left for Isabel to put her arm. Luis came down from his room last, happy as he always was at midday. They ate, Nino talked of his shells, of snails' eggs in the reeds, of his collection which he was classifying according to size and colour. He would kill them by himself because Isabel did not like doing it and he would put them out to dry on a zinc tray. Afterwards the coffee arrived and Luis looked at them with the usual question.

Isabel then got up first to look for don Roberto although don Roberto had already told her previously. At the porch she turned back and went inside again. Rema and Nino had their heads together over the snails as if they were in a family portrait. Only Luis looked at her and she said: 'It's in Babe's study' and she saw Babe shrug his shoulders in annoyance and watched Rema touching a snail so delicately that her finger seemed to have something of a snail about it. Then Rema went to get more sugar and Isabel followed, talking to her and they came back laughing at a joke they had exchanged in the kitchen. Luis had no tobacco and he sent Nino to his study for it. Isabel bet him that she would be the first to find the cigarettes and they went out together. They came back running and pushing one another and almost bumped into Babe who was going to the library to read his newspaper and complaining at not being able to use his study. Isabel went to look at the snails and Luis, who was waiting for her to light his cigarette as usual, saw that she was absorbed in studying the snails which had slowly begun to emerge and move about. She looked suddenly at Rema but looked away again in a flash, so absorbed by the snails that she did not move at Babe's first shout. They were all running now and she was standing over the snails as if she had not heard Babe's second muffled cry or Luis banging on the library door or don Roberto who came in with the dogs or Babe's moans in between the furious barking of the dogs, or Luis who kept saying: 'But it was in his study. She said that it was in his study.' She bent over the snails which were slim as fingers, slim as Rema's fingers perhaps or Rema's hands which took her by the shoulders, forced her to raise her head and look at her and to remain looking at her for an age. Then she was weeping furiously against Rema's skirt, feeling an uneasy happiness and Rema was stroking her hair with her hand, calming her with a soft pressure of her fingers and a murmur in her ear, an incoherent murmur as if she were expressing gratitude and unutterable acquiescence.

Translated by Jean Franco

Octavio Paz

HYMN AMONG RUINS, 1948

Donde espumoso el mar siciliano.
GÓNGORA

Day crowned with its own crown displays its plumage.
Tall shout of yellow,
hot gusher in the centre of à kindly
impartial sky !
The outward show is lovely beneath this, its momentary truth.
Sea climbs the shore,
clings in between the rocks, a dazzling spider;
the livid wound on the mountain glistens;
a handful of goats may be a flock of stones;
sun lays its golden egg and spills on the sea;
Everything's god.
A statue, broken-limbed,
columns gnawed by the light,
ruins alive in a world of living dead !

Night falls on Teotihuacán.
On the pyramid top the youths smoke marijuana,
the guitars throb hoarsely.
What herb, what water of life will life give to us,
where can we unearth the word,
the measure that gives laws to hymn and speech,
to dances, cities, scales?
Mexican song explodes in an imprecation,
a many-coloured star whose light is quenched,
a stone that blocks our doorways of communion.
Earth tastes of earth, of earth that has grown old.

Eyes see, hands touch.
Here few things are enough :
prickly pear and the spiny coral cactus,
figs in their hood of leaves,
grapes with a taste that is a resurrection,
clams, stubborn maidenheads,
salt, cheese, wine and the bread of sun.
From her dusky height an island girl looks down on me,
a slim cathedral in a robe of light.
Towers of salt, the white sails of the ships
stand out against the green pines of the shore.
Light is creating temples on the sea.

New York, London, Moscow.
Darkness covers the plain with its ghostly ivy,
with the swaying and shivering of its vegetation,
its scanty down, its pad and scamper of rats.
There shudders now and then an anaemic sun.
Elbow on mounds that yesterday were cities, yawns Polyphemus.
Below, among craters, crawls a horde of men.
(Domestic bipeds, flesh of whom
– despite recent prohibitions by the Church –
is greatly relished by the wealthier classes,
though till lately the masses reckoned them unclean.)

To see, to touch each new day's lovely forms.
The light pulsates, all darts and wings.
The stain of wine on the tablecloth smells of blood.
As the coral stretches its branches in the water,
I stretch my senses in this living hour :
the moment fulfils itself in a yellow harmony.
Noon, wheat-ear heavy with minutes,
eternity's brimming cup !

My thoughts divide, meander, grow confused,
then start again,

and finally lose motion, mouthless rivers,
delta of blood beneath an unwinking sun.
Must everything end in this spatter of stagnant water?

Day, round-faced day,
day, shining orange with four-and-twenty segments,
pierced through and through with a single yellow sweetness !
Intellect finally incarnates in forms,
the two hostile halves are reconciled,
and the conscience mirror dissolves,
becomes once more a fountain, a spring of legends.
Man, image-laden tree,
words that are flowers, that are fruit, that are deeds.

Translated by J. M. Cohen

USTICA

*(Author's note: Ustica is a volcanic desert island in the
Sicilian sea. It was a Saracen graveyard.)*

The successive suns of summer,
The succession of the sun and of its summers,
All the suns,
The sole, the sol of sols
Now become
Obstinate and tawny bone,
Darkness-before-the-storm
Of matter cooled.

Fist of stone,
Pinecone of lava,
Ossuary,
Not earth
Nor island either,
Rock off a rockface,
Hard peach,
Sun-drop petrified.

Through the nights one hears
The breathing of the cisterns,
The panting of fresh water
Troubled by the sea.
The hour is late and the light, greening.
The obscure body of the wine
Asleep in jars
Is a darker and cooler sun.

Here the rose of the depths
Is a candelabrum of pinkish veins
Kindled on the sea-bed,
Ashore, the sun extinguishes it,
Pale, chalky lace
As if desire were worked by death.

Cliffs the colour of sulphur,
High austere stones.
You are beside me.
Your thoughts are black and golden.
To extend a hand
Is to gather a cluster of truths intact.
Below, between sparkling rocks
Goes and comes
A sea full of arms.
Vertigos. The light hurls itself headlong.
I looked you in the face,
I saw into the abyss :
Mortality is transparency.

Ossuary, paradise garden :
Our roots,
Knotted in sex, in the undone mouth
Of the buried Mother.
Incestuous trees
That mountain
A garden on the dead's domain.

Translated by Charles Tomlinson and Henry Gifford

WIND FROM ALL COMPASS POINTS

To Marie José

The present is motionless
The mountains are of bone and of snow
They have been here since the beginning
The wind has just been born
                                        Ageless
As the light and the dust
                              A windmill of sounds
The bazaar spins its colours
                              Bells   motors   radios
The stony trot of dark donkeys
Songs and complaints entangled
Among the beards of the merchants
The tall light chiselled with hammer-strokes

In the clearings of silence
                              Boys' cries
            Explode
Princes in tattered clothes
On the banks of the tortured river
Pray pee meditate
                              The present is motionless
The flood-gates of the year open
                              Day flashes out
            Agate
            The fallen bird
Between rue Montalambert and rue de Bac
Is a girl
            Held back
At the edge of a precipice of looks
If water is fire

Flame
Dazzled
In the centre of the spherical hour
A sorrel filly
A marching batallion of sparks
A real girl
Among wraithlike houses and people
Presence a fountain of reality
I looked out through my own unrealities
I took her hand
Together we crossed
The four quadrants the three times
Floating tribes of reflections
And we returned to the day of beginning
The present is motionless
June 21st
Today is the beginning of summer
Two or three birds
Invent a garden
You read and eat a peach
On the red couch
Naked
Like the wine in the glass pitcher
A great flock of crows
Our brothers are dying in Santo Domingo
If we had the munitions you people would not be here
We chew our nails down to the elbow
In the gardens of his summer fortress
Tipoo Sultan planted the Jacobin tree
Then distributed glass shards among
The imprisoned English officials
And ordered them to cut their foreskins
And eat them
The century
Has caught fire in our lands
From that blaze
With scorched hands

The cathedral and pyramid-builders
Will raise their transparent houses
                    The present is motionless
The sun has fallen asleep between your breasts
The red covering is black and heaves
Not planet and not jewel
                    Fruit
You are named
          Date
              Datia
Castle of Leave-If-You-Can
                    Scarlet stain
Upon the obdurate stone
Corridors terraces stairways
Dismantled nuptial chambers
Of the scorpion
              Echoes   repetitions
The intricate and erotic works of a watch
                    Beyond time
                              You cross
Taciturn patios under the pitiless afternoon
A cloak of needles on your untouched shoulders
If fire is water
                    You are a diaphanous drop
The real girl
              Transparency of the world
The present is motionless
                    The mountains
                    Quartered suns
Petrified storm earth-yellow
                    The wind whips
                              It hurts to see
The sky is another deeper abyss
Gorge of the Salang Pass
Black cloud over black rock
Fist of blood strikes
                    Gates of stone

Only the water is human
In these precipitous solitudes
Only your eyes of human water
                              Down there
In the cleft place
Desire covers you with its two black wings
Your eyes flash open and close
                              Phosphorescent animals
Down there
                The hot canyon
The wave that stretches and breaks
                              Your legs apart
The plunging whiteness
The foam of our bodies abandoned
                              The present is motionless
The hermit watered the saint's tomb
His beard was whiter than the clouds
Facing the mulberry
                On the flank of the rushing stream
You repeat my name
                Dispersion of syllables
A young man with green eyes presented you
With a pomegranate
                On the other bank of the Amu-Darya
Smoke rose from Russian cottages
The sound of an Usbek flute
Was another river   invisible   clearer
The boatman
                On the barge was strangling chickens
The countryside is an open hand
                              Its lines
                Marks of a broken alphabet
Cow skeletons on the prairie
Bactria
                A shattered statue
I scraped a few names out of the dust
By these fallen syllables

Seeds of a charred pomegranate
I swear to be earth and wind
                         Whirling
Over your bones
                    The present is motionless
Night comes down with its trees
Night of electric insects and silken beasts
Night of grasses which cover the dead
Meeting of waters which come from far off
Rustlings
                    Universes are strewn about
A world falls
                    A seed flares up
Each word beats
                         I hear you throb in the shadow
A riddle shaped like an hour-glass
                              Woman asleep
Space   living spaces
Anima mundi
                    Maternal substance
Always torn from itself
Always falling into your empty womb
                              Anima mundi
Mother of the nomadic tribes
                              Of suns and men
The spaces turn
                              The present is motionless
At the top of the world
Shiva and Parvati caress
                    Each caress lasts a century
For the god and for the man
                         An identical time
An equivalent hurling headlong
                         Lahore
                    Red river   black boats
A barefoot girl between two tamarinds
And her timeless gaze

An identical throbbing

Death and birth
A group of poplars
Suspended between sky and earth
They are a quiver of light more than a trembling of leaves
Do they rise or fall?
The present is motionless
It rains on my childhood
It rains on the feverish garden
Flint flowers   trees of smoke
In a figleaf you sail on my brow
The rain does not wet you
You are flame of water
The diaphanous drop of fire
Spilling upon my eyelids
I look out through my own unrealities
The same day is beginning
Space wheels
The world wrenches up its roots
Our bodies
Stretched out
Weigh no more than dawn

Cabul and Kunduz
21 June – 6 July 1965

Translated by Paul Blackburn

João Guimarães Rosa

THE THIRD BANK OF THE RIVER

My father was an honest, orderly, and reliable man; he had
been so ever since his youth and boyhood, as several trustworthy
people told me when I asked them. From what I remember of him,
he was neither gayer nor sadder than the other men we knew.
But he was quiet. Mother was the one who ruled at home and
gave us our daily scolding – my sister, my brother and me. But
there came a day when my father ordered a canoe to be made for
him.

It was no joke. He ordered a special canoe, made of yellow-
wood, and small, with just a ledge at the prow for the paddler to
sit on. It had to be all hand built, of picked timber bent in the solid,
and capable of lasting twenty or thirty years in the water. Mother
was set against the idea. Did he, who had never wasted his time
on these arts, now propose to take up hunting and fishing? My
father didn't say anything. Our house at that time was even nearer
the river, about a quarter of a mile away; the river at this point
stretched wide, deep and silent as ever. It was so broad that you
could hardly make out the shape of the opposite bank. And I shall
always remember the day when the canoe was ready.

With neither joy nor care, Father pulled on his hat and made
his farewells. He said nothing more, took nothing with him, gave
us no advice. We thought Mother would make a scene but she just
stood pale as a ghost and bit her lips.

'You're going,' she said. 'You're stopping there. You're never
coming back.'

Father gave no reply. He looked at me tenderly, pleading for
me to go with him for a few steps. I was afraid that Mother would
be angry, but I followed him anyhow. An idea struck me and I
asked him: 'Father, can I come with you, in your canoe?' He
turned to look at me, gave me his blessing and sent me back with

a wave of his hand. I pretended to go, but turned round at the
entrance to the woods, to see if he really meant it. Father got into
the canoe, untied it and began paddling. And the canoe moved
away, its shape reflected in the water like an alligator, long and
narrow.

My father didn't come back. He went nowhere at all. He just
carried out his idea of staying right out in the river, half-way between the banks, always in the canoe, which he was never again
to leave. The strangeness of this action alarmed the neighbourhood.
The unheard of had happened. The family, neighbours and friends
met together to talk it over.

Our poor mother was ashamed and took it very quietly. So
people thought, though nobody cared to say so, that my father was
mad. A few of them suggested that he must be keeping a vow, or
that maybe, thinking that he had some horrible disease, leprosy
perhaps, my father had banished himself to another kind of existence, both near and far from his family. Various people – passers-
by, people who lived on the banks of the river, even the opposite
shore – brought the news that, night and day, my father never
landed on point or creek, but he paddled the river in utter solitude.
Well, Mother and our relatives agreed: the supply of food that
he had hidden in the canoe would soon run out and he would either
have to land and go right away for ever, which would be a good
thing at present, or he would repent and return home once and for
all.

They were wrong. I took on the job of getting him a bit of stolen
food each day – an idea I came to on the night after he left, while
everybody else was lighting fires on the banks of the river, and
praying and shouting to him in the light of them. On the very
next day I went down to the bank with some scraps, a hunk of
bread and a bunch of bananas. An hour slowly passed; then I was
just able to make out my father, sitting in the bottom of his canoe,
motionless on the smooth river. He saw me, but made no approach
or sign. I showed him the food and left it in a hollow in the bank,
safe from animals and sheltered from the rain and the dew. This I
did time and again for months on end. I was surprised to discover
some while later that Mother knew what I was doing, though she

pretended not to. She would put the leavings in places where I would find them. Mother was never one to show her feelings.

She sent for our uncle, her brother, to help with the farm and put the business in order. She sent for the schoolmaster to look after us boys. She got the priest one day to put on his robes and go to the river bank to chase away the evil spirits and try to persuade my father of his duty to stop his tragic obstinacy. Later there were the two soldiers who came at her request to try to frighten him. All of which did no good at all. Sometimes clearly, sometimes dimly, my father would pass in the distance, floating by in his canoe, but he would never let anybody get near enough to touch or to talk to him. It was the same when, not so long ago, two reporters hired a launch and tried without success to take his photograph: my father disappeared towards the other bank, steering his canoe among the shallows which stretch for miles among tall grass and rushes where only he could have known his way, they were so dark.

We just had to get used to it. But to be truthful, we never really did get used to it. Judging by my own case, I was always thinking of Father whether I wanted to or not; and that always made me think of the past with regret. It was hard for anybody to understand how he could bear it out there: day and night, sun, rain, heat, mist; the terrible spells of cold in the middle of the year; nowhere to go; only an old hat on his head for all those weeks, months, years: and life slipping by unnoticed. He touched neither of the shores, nor the islands and mud banks in the river. He never stepped on ground or grass again. Clearly he must, at least, have tied the canoe to some corner of an island out of sight to get a bit of sleep. But not a fire was lit, nor torch flashed, nor match struck.

As for food, he ate almost nothing. Even of what we left for him between the roots of the fig tree, or in the stony hollow of the bank, he touched little, hardly enough. Was he never ill? And the constant strain of his arms steering his canoe, resisting the river at full flood, the rising water, when in the rushing torrent everything brings danger, bodies of dead animals, drifting tree trunks – the danger of capsizing? And he never spoke again. Nor did we ever speak of him. We only thought of him. Father could never be forgotten. If we pretended to forget it was only suddenly to wake up again, the memory still with us, mixed up with all our other fears.

My sister got married. Mother didn't want a party. We used to think of him if there was something good to eat; so too, sheltered from the night, from those relentless nights of cold, fierce rain : Father with only his hands and a small bowl to bale the storm water from the canoe. Sometimes an acquaintance would tell me that I was looking more like my father every day. But I knew that he was all hairy and unshaven, with long nails, ill and thin and blackened by the sun. I knew that he looked like an animal with his long hair, and was almost naked, in spite of the bits of clothing which we left for him now and then.

And he did not want anything to do with us; was there no affection? But it was from affection and respect that whenever somebody praised me for some good deed I would say, 'Father taught me to do that' : which was not the whole truth, but a lie on behalf of the truth. If he really no longer remembered us and wanted no more to do with us, why then did he not move upstream or down, to other parts, far away, where he could never be found? Only he knew. When my sister had a child, she insisted that she must show him his grandson. We all went down to the river bank. It was a beautiful day. My sister wore the white dress she had been married in. She lifted the little baby in her arms while her husband held the sunshade over them both. We called and waited. Father was nowhere to be seen. My sister cried. Then we all cried, embracing one another.

My sister moved, with her husband, some way away. My brother decided to go and live in a town. Times changed with the slow swiftness of time. Finally mother went too, to live for good with my sister. She had aged considerably. I stayed on, all that was left. I could never think of marrying. I remained with the burden of life. My father needed me I know – in his wanderings, in the solitude of the river – but he never explained his reasons. When I really wanted to know and started to ask, the know-alls said it appeared my father had once explained himself to the person who had made the canoe for him. But the man had died by then.

Nobody knew, nobody remembered anything any more. There were only false rumours that meant nothing: such as the one, early on, when the first floods came, and it seemed as though the rain would never stop and everybody was fearing the end of the world. My father, they said, had been chosen, like Noah, and had had his canoe made providentially; it all comes back to me now. I could never condemn my father. And the first grey hairs had appeared on my head.

I am a man of sad words. Why did I feel so much the guilt was mine? It was only my father's absence lasting on and on, and the river-river-river, flowing for ever and ever. I was already suffering from the onset of old age – this life is just a time of waiting. Even I had my illnesses, my fits of depression, my weariness and my bouts of rheumatism. What of him? Why? He must have suffered so much. He was an old man now: sooner or later wouldn't he lose his strength, capsize the canoe, or let it drift unguided on the river currents to be hurled, miles down, in the roar and fall of the mighty cataract, down into the boiling water and his death? One's heart went out to him. There he was, without my peace of mind. I am guilty of I don't know what, an open sore within me, in my conscience. I would have known – if things had been different. I was forming an idea.

Without delay. Am I mad? No: the word mad wasn't used at home: it had never been used again for all those years. We never accused anybody of being mad. Nobody is mad – or else everybody is. What I did was to go there. I took a handkerchief so that he could see me waving. I was very much in possession of my senses. I waited. At last, a fleeting shadow, he appeared, sitting in the stern, within shouting distance. I called out several times, saying what I had to say, my heart bursting, my voice straining.

'Father, you're an old man now. You've done what you had to do. Come back now, there's no need to go on. Come back, and right now, whenever you want, if we both want it, I will take your place in the canoe.'

My heart beat with relief when I had finished.

He heard me, stood up and, putting the paddle in the water, moved towards me as if in agreement. Suddenly I shuddered deeply: before moving he had lifted his arm in a gesture of greeting – the first after the passing of so many years. And I couldn't . . . in terror, my hair on end, I ran, fled, rushed away like a madman. Because he seemed to be coming: from the Beyond. And I ask profoundly to be forgiven.

The coldness of fear possessed me: I became ill. I knew that no more was heard of him. Can I be called a man after that failure? I am something that never was before, that must remain silent. It is too late now, I know, and I am afraid to cut short this life, in the waste of the world. But I would wish, then, at least, at the moment of death, to be taken and laid in a small canoe on the water which runs for ever past the long banks: and I, down the river, up the river, through the river – the river.

Translated by R. P. Joscelyne

Rosario Castellanos

FOREIGN WOMAN

I come from far away. I have forgotten my country.
I no longer understand the words
they use there for money or implements.
I have attained the mineral silence of a statue.
For sloth and contempt and something
that I cannot make out have defended me
from this language, from this heavy
jewel-studded velvet, with which the people
among whom I live cover their rags.

This land, like the other land of my childhood,
still bears on its face
the brand of fire, injustice and crime,
its scars of slavery.
Alas, as a girl I slept to the hoarse cooing
of a black dove : a conquered race.
I hid beneath the sheets
because a great beast
was crouching in the shadows, ravenous and yet
hard and patient as a stone.
Compared with it, what is the sea or disaster
or love's thunderbolt
or annihilating happiness?
What I mean is then
that I had to grow up quickly
(before terror devoured me)
and go away and put a firm hand
on the rudder and steer my life.

Too early
I spat in those places
that the common people consecrate for worship.
And among the crowd I was like a dog
that offends with its scabs and copulations,
and its sudden barking in the middle
of the rite, and the important ceremony.

And yet. Youth
– although serious – was not quite mortal.
I recovered, I got well. With a skilful pulse
I learnt to assess success, renown,
honour and riches.
I had what the mediocre envy, what the
triumphant dispute, and only one attains.
I had it, and it was like eating spray,
like stroking the back of the wind.

Supreme pride is supreme
renunciation. I did not want
to be the dead star
that absorbs borrowed light to revive itself.
Nameless, without memories,
naked as a ghost I turn
in a narrow domestic orbit.

But even so I ferment
in the dull imagination of others.

My presence has brought
to this sleepy inland city
a salty breath of adventure.

When they look at me, men remember
that fate is the great hurricane
that splits boughs and fells firm trees,
and confirms in its dominion –

over human poverty –
the pitiless cosmic law.
The women smell me from afar, and dream
like beasts of burden when they sniff
the brutal gust of the storm.

Before the elder, however,
I perform a passive rôle
as the caller-up of legends.

And when at midnight
I open the windows wide, it is so that
the sleepless man, the man who is brooding on death,
and the man who is suffering on the bed of his remorse,
and the youth too
(beneath whose head the pillow burns)
may question the dark through me.

Enough. I have concealed more than I have said.

The upland sun burnt my hand,
and on the finger that is called here the heart-finger
I wear a gold ring with an incised seal.

The ring that serves
to identify corpses.

Translated by J. M. Cohen

Alí Chumacero

EPITAPH FOR A VIRGIN

Her body threw no shadow on evil, none,
perhaps because, struck rigid by the splendour
of sudden disaster, from a sound she passed
to be evident only as spray.
The wind dispersed her hair
on a light storm, and in her features
the world extended its appearances.

There was no birth in her, the psalm did not
swoop down to overthrow her. Anger never
opposed her wakefulness with doubt:
she was silence itself, and ignorance
of the threatening invocation, the fish
and the snake that suddenly glisten
like the rapid death leap of a lightning-flash.

Hidden between her eyes, and dazzling under
the liquid odour of her quietness,
there sang the promise of the girl herself
leaving the expectation as desire.
Bed nor asylum, fever nor truth
knew her breath, she did not demand
an answer to the question she never asked.

She went to cafés, she took a seat at the theatre
always in haste, and in the distance was
the arsenic's temptation to suicide.
Now her soul pursues glory
still talking in its mansion
ignorant of terror, but the memory of her
drops evil on our clay.

Translated by J. M. Cohen

Carlos Fuentes

AURA

Man hunts and struggles. Woman intrigues and dreams; she is the mother of fantasy, the mother of the gods. She has second sight, the wings that enable her to fly to the infinite of desire and the imagination. . . The gods are like men: they are born and they die on a woman's breast. . . .

JULES MICHELET

I

You're reading the advertisement: an offer like this isn't made every day. You read it and reread it. It seems to be addressed to you and nobody else. You don't even notice when the ash from your cigarette falls into the cup of tea you ordered in this cheap, dirty café. You read it again. 'Wanted, young historian, conscientious, neat. Perfect knowledge of colloquial French. Youth . . . knowledge of French, preferably after living in France for a while . . . Four thousand pesos a month, all meals, comfortable bedroom-study.' All that's missing is your name. The advertisement should have two more words, in bigger, blacker type: Felipe Montero. Wanted, Felipe Montero, formerly on scholarship at the Sorbonne, historian full of useless facts, accustomed to digging among yellowed documents, part-time teacher in private schools, nine hundred pesos a month. But if you read that, you'd be suspicious, and take it as a joke. 'Address, Donceles 815.' No telephone; come in person.

You leave a tip, reach for your briefcase, get up. You wonder if another young historian, in the same situation you are, has seen this same advertisement, has got ahead of you and taken the job already. You walk down to the corner, trying to forget this idea. As you wait for the bus, you run over the dates you must have on the tip of your tongue so that your sleepy pupils will respect you. The bus is coming now, and you're staring at the tips of your black shoes. You've got to be prepared. You put your hand in your pocket, search among the coins, and finally take out thirty centavos. You've got to be prepared. You grab the hand-rail – the bus slows down but doesn't stop – and jump aboard. Then you shove your way forward, pay the driver the thirty centavos, squeeze yourself in among the passengers already standing in the aisle, hang on to the overhead rail, press your briefcase tighter under your left arm, and automatically put your left hand over the back pocket where you keep your billfold.

This day is just like any other day, and you don't remember the advertisement until the next morning, when you sit down in the same café and order breakfast and open your newspaper. You come to the advertising section and there it is again: *young historian.* The job is still open. You reread the advertisement, lingering over the final words: four thousand pesos.

It's surprising to know that anyone lives on Donceles Street. You always thought that nobody lived in the old centre of the city. You walk slowly, trying to pick out the number 815 in that conglomeration of old colonial mansions, all of them converted into repair shops, jewellery shops, shoe stores, drugstores. The numbers have been changed, painted over, confused. A 13 next to a 200. An old plaque reading 47 over a scrawl in blurred charcoal: Now 924. You look up at the second storeys. Up there, everything is the same as it was. The jukeboxes don't disturb them. The mercury streetlights don't shine in. The cheap merchandise on sale along the street doesn't have any effect on that upper level . . . on the Baroque harmony of the carved stones; on the battered stone saints with pigeons clustering on their shoulders; on the latticed balconies, the copper gutters, the sandstone gargoyles; on the greenish curtains that darken the long windows; on that window from which someone draws back when you look at it. You gaze at the fanciful vines carved over the doorway, then lower your eyes to the peeling wall and discover 815, *formerly* 69.

You rap vainly with the knocker, that copper head of a dog, so worn and smooth that it resembles the head of a canine foetus in a museum of natural science. It seems as if the dog is grinning at you and you let go of the cold metal. The door opens at the first light push of your fingers, but before going in you give a last look over your shoulder, frowning at the long line of stalled cars that growl, honk, and belch out the unhealthy fumes of their impatience. You try to retain some single image of that indifferent outside world.

You close the door behind you and peer into the darkness of a roofed alleyway. It must be a patio of some sort, because you can smell the mould, the dampness of the plants, the rotting roots, the thick drowsy aroma. There isn't any light to guide you, and you're searching in your coat pocket for the box of matches when a sharp, thin voice tells you, from a distance: 'No, it isn't necessary. Please. Walk thirteen steps forward and you'll come to a stairway at your right. Come up, please. There are twenty-two steps. Count them.'

Thirteen. To the right. Twenty-two.

The dank smell of the plants is all around you as you count out your steps, first on the paving-stones, then on the creaking wood, spongy from the dampness. You count to twenty-two in a low voice and then stop, with the matchbox in your hand, the briefcase under your arm. You knock on a door that smells of old pine. There isn't any knocker. Finally you push it open. Now you can feel a carpet under your feet, a thin carpet, badly laid. It makes you trip and almost fall. Then you notice the greyish, filtered light that reveals some of the humps.

'Señora,' you say, because you seem to remember a woman's voice. 'Señora . . .'

'Now turn to the left. The first door. Please be so kind.'

You push the door open: you don't expect any of them to be latched, you know they all open at a push. The scattered lights are braided in your eyelashes, as if you were seeing them through a silken net. All you can make out are the dozens of flickering lights. At last you can see that they're votive-lights, all set on brackets or hung between unevenly-spaced panels. They cast a faint glow on the silver objects, the crystal flasks, the gilt-framed mirrors. Then you see the bed in the shadows beyond, and the feeble movement of a hand that seems to be beckoning to you.

But you can't see her face until you turn your back on that galaxy of religious lights. You stumble to the foot of the bed, and have to go around it in order to get to the head of it. A tiny figure is almost lost in its immensity. When you reach out your hand, you don't touch another hand, you touch the ears and thick fur of a creature that's chewing silently and steadily, looking up at you with its glowing red eyes. You smile and stroke the rabbit that's crouched beside her hand. Finally you shake hands, and her cold fingers remain for a long while in your sweating palm.

'I'm Felipe Montero. I read your advertisement.'

'Yes, I know. I'm sorry, there aren't any chairs.'

'That's all right. Don't worry about it.'

'Good. Please let me see your profile. No, I can't see it well enough. Turn towards the light. That's right. Excellent.'

'I read your advertisement . . .'

'Yes, of course. Do you think you're qualified? *Avez-vous fait des études?*'

'*À Paris, Madame.*'

'*Ah, oui, ça me fait plaisir, toujours, toujours, d'entendre . . . oui . . . vous savez . . . on était tellement habitué . . . et après . . .*'

You move aside so that the light from the candles and the reflections from the silver and crystal show you the silk coif that must cover a head of very white hair, and that frames a face so old it's almost childlike. Her whole body is covered by the sheets and the feather-pillows and the high, tightly-buttoned white collar, all except for her arms, which are wrapped in a shawl, and her pallid hands resting on her stomach. You can only stare at her face until a movement of the rabbit lets you glance furtively at the crusts and bits of bread scattered on the worn-out red silk of the pillows.

'I'll come directly to the point. I don't have many years ahead of me, Señor Montero, and therefore I decided to break a lifelong rule and place an advertisement in the newspaper . . .'

'Yes, that's why I'm here.'

'Of course. So you accept.'

'Well, I'd like to know a little more . . .'

'Yes. You're wondering.'

She sees you glance at the night-table, the different-coloured bottles, the glasses, the aluminium spoons, the row of pillboxes, the other glasses – all stained with whitish liquids – on the floor within reach of her hand. Then you notice that the bed is hardly raised above the level of the floor. Suddenly the rabbit jumps down and disappears in the shadows.

'I can offer you four thousand pesos.'

'Yes, that's what the advertisement said today.'

'Ah, then it came out.'

'Yes, it came out.'

'It has to do with the memoirs of my husband, General Llorente. They must be put in order before I die. I want them to be published. I decided that a short time ago.'

'But the General himself? Wouldn't he be able to ...'

'He died sixty years ago, Señor. They're his unfinished memoirs. They have to be completed before I die.'

'But ...'

'I can tell you everything. You'll learn to write in my husband's own style. You'll only have to arrange and read his manuscripts to become fascinated by his style ... his clarity ... his ...'

'Yes, I understand.'

'Saga, Saga. Where are you? *Ici*, Saga ...'

'Who?'

'My companion.'

'The rabbit?'

'Yes. She'll come back.'

When you raise your eyes, which you've been keeping lowered, her lips are closed but you can hear her words again – 'She'll come back' – as if the old lady were pronouncing them at that instant. Her lips remain still. You look in back of you and you're almost blinded by the gleam from the religious objects. When you look at her again you see that her eyes have opened very wide, and that they're clear, liquid, enormous, almost the same colour as the yellowish whites around them, so that only the black dots of the pupils mar that clarity. It's lost a moment later in the heavy folds of her lowered eyelids, as if she wanted to protect that glance which is now hiding at the back of its dry cave.

'Then you'll stay here. Your room is upstairs. It's sunny there.'

'It might be better if I didn't trouble you, Señora. I can go on living where I am and work on the manuscripts there.'

'My conditions are that you have to live here. There isn't much time left.'

'I don't know if . . .'

'Aura . . .'

The old woman moves for the first time since you entered her room. As she reaches out her hand again you sense that agitated breathing beside you, and another hand reaches out to touch the Señora's fingers. You look around and a girl is standing there, a girl whose whole body you can't see because she's standing so close to you and her arrival was so unexpected, without the slightest sound – not even those sounds that can't be heard but are real anyway because they're remembered immediately afterwards, because in spite of everything they're louder than the silence that accompanies them.

'I told you she'd come back.'

'Who?'

'Aura. My companion. My niece.'

'Good afternoon.'

The girl nods and at the same instant the old lady imitates her gesture.

'This is Señor Montero. He's going to live with us.'

You move a few steps so that the light from the candles won't blind you. The girl keeps her eyes closed, her hands folded at her side. She doesn't look at you at first, then little by little she opens her eyes as if she were afraid of the light. Finally you can see that those eyes are sea-green and that they surge, break to foam, grow calm again, then surge again like a wave. You look into them and tell yourself it isn't true, because they're beautiful green eyes just like all the beautiful green eyes you've ever known. But you can't deceive yourself: those eyes do surge, do change, as if offering you a landscape that only you can see and desire.

'Yes. I'm going to live with you.'

II

The old woman laughs sharply and tells you that she is grateful for your kindness and that the girl will show you to your room. You're thinking about the salary of four thousand pesos, and how the work should be pleasant because you like these jobs of careful research that don't include physical effort or going from one place to another or meeting people you don't want to meet. You're thinking about this as you follow her out of the room, and you discover that you've got to follow her with your ears instead of your eyes : you follow the rustle of her skirt, the rustle of taffeta, and you're anxious now to look into her eyes again. You climb the stairs behind that sound in the darkness, and you're still unused to the obscurity. You remember it must be about six in the afternoon, and the flood of light surprises you when Aura opens the door to your bedroom – another door without a latch – and steps aside to tell you : 'This is your room. We'll expect you for supper in an hour.'

She moves away with that same faint rustle of taffeta, and you weren't able to see her face again.

You close the door and look up at the skylight that serves as a roof. You smile when you find that the evening light is blinding compared with the darkness in the rest of the house, and smile again when you try out the mattress on the gilded metal bed. Then you glance around the room : a red wool rug, olive and gold wallpaper, an easy-chair covered in red velvet, an old walnut desk with a green leather top, an old Argand lamp with its soft glow for your nights of research, and a bookshelf over the desk in reach of your hand. You walk over to the other door, and on pushing it open you discover an outmoded bathroom : a four-legged bathtub with little flowers painted on the porcelain, a blue hand-basin, an old-fashioned toilet. You look at yourself in the large oval mirror on the door of the wardrobe – it's also walnut – in the bathroom hallway. You move your heavy eyebrows and wide thick lips, and your breath fogs the mirror. You close your black eyes, and when you open them again the mirror has cleared. You stop holding your breath and run your hand through your dark, limp hair; you touch your fine profile, your lean cheeks; and when your breath hides your face again you're repeating her name : 'Aura.'

After smoking two cigarettes while lying on the bed, you get up, put on your jacket, and comb your hair. You push the door open and try to remember the route you followed coming up. You'd like to leave the door open so that the lamplight could guide you, but that's impossible because the springs close it behind you. You could enjoy playing with that door, swinging it back and forth. You don't do it. You could take the lamp down with you. You don't do it. This house will always be in darkness, and you've got to learn it and relearn it by touch. You grope your way like a blind man, with your arms stretched out wide, feeling your way along the wall, and by accident you turn on the light-switch. You stop and blink in the bright middle of that long, empty hall. At the end of it you can see the banister and the spiral staircase.

You count the stairs as you go down: another custom you've got to learn in Señora Llorente's house. You take a step backward when you see the reddish eyes of the rabbit, which turns its back on you and goes hopping away.

You don't have time to stop in the lower hallway because Aura is waiting for you at a half-open stained-glass door, with a candelabra in her hand. You walk towards her, smiling, but you stop when you hear the painful yowling of a number of cats – yes, you stop to listen, next to Aura, to be sure that they're cats – and then follow her to the parlour.

'It's the cats,' Aura tells you. 'There's lots of rats in this part of the city.'

You go through the parlour: furniture upholstered in faded silk; glass-fronted cabinets containing porcelain figurines, musical clocks, medals, glass balls; carpets with Persian designs; pictures of rustic scenes; green velvet curtains. Aura is dressed in green.

'Is your room comfortable?'

'Yes. But I have to get my things from the place where . . .'

'It won't be necessary. The servant has already gone for them.'

'You shouldn't have bothered.'

You follow her into the dining-room. She places the candelabra in the middle of the table. The room feels damp and cold. The four walls are panelled in dark wood, carved in Gothic style, with fretwork arches and large rosettes. The cats have stopped yowling. When you sit down, you notice that four places have been set. There are two large, covered plates and an old, grimy bottle.

Aura lifts the cover from one of the plates. You breathe in the pungent odour of the liver and onions she serves you, then you pick up the old bottle and fill the cut-glass goblets with that thick red liquid. Out of curiosity you try to read the label on the wine-bottle, but the grime has obscured it. Aura serves you some whole broiled tomatoes from the other plate.

'Excuse me,' you say, looking at the two extra places, the two empty chairs, 'but are you expecting someone else?'

Aura goes on serving the tomatoes. 'No. Señora Consuelo feels a little ill tonight. She won't be joining us.'

'Señora Consuelo? Your aunt?'

'Yes. She'd like you to go in and see her after supper.'

You eat in silence. You drink that thick wine, occasionally shifting your glance so that Aura won't catch you in the hypnotized stare that you can't control. You'd like to fix the girl's features in your mind. Every time you glance away you forget them again, and an irresistible urge forces you to look at her once more. As usual, she has her eyes lowered. While you're searching for the pack of cigarettes in your coat pocket, you run across that big key, and remember, and say to Aura: 'Ah! I forgot that one of the drawers in my desk is locked. I've got my papers in it.'

And she murmurs: 'Then you want to go out?' She says it as a reproach.

You feel confused, and reach out your hand to her with the key dangling from one finger.

'It isn't important. The servants can go for them tomorrow.'

But she avoids touching your hand, keeping her own hands on her lap. Finally she looks up, and once again you question your senses, blaming the wine for your bewilderment, for the dizziness brought on by those shining, clear green eyes, and you stand up after Aura does, running your hand over the wooden back of the Gothic chair, without daring to touch her bare shoulder or her motionless head.

You make an effort to control yourself, diverting your attention away from her by listening to the imperceptible movement of a door behind you – it must lead to the kitchen – or by separating the two different elements that make up the room: the compact circle of light around the candelabra, illuminating the table and one carved wall, and the larger circle of darkness surrounding it. Finally you have the courage to go up to her, take her hand, open it, and place your key-ring in her smooth palm as a token.

She closes her hand, looks up at you, and murmurs, 'Thank you.' Then she rises and walks quickly out of the room.

You sit down in Aura's chair, stretch your legs, and light a cigarette, feeling a pleasure you've never felt before, one that you knew was part of you but that only now you're experiencing fully, setting it free, bringing it out because this time you know it'll be answered and won't be lost . . . And Señora Consuelo is waiting for you, as Aura said. She's waiting for you after supper . . .

You leave the dining-room, and with the candelabra in your hand you walk through the parlour and the hallway. The first door you come to is the old lady's. You rap on it with your knuckles, but there isn't any answer. You knock again. Then you push the door open because she's waiting for you. You enter cautiously, murmuring: 'Señora . . . Señora . . .'

She doesn't hear you, for she's kneeling in front of that wall of religious objects, with her head resting on her clenched fists. You see her from a distance: she's kneeling there in her coarse woollen nightgown, with her head sunk into her narrow shoulders; she's thin, even emaciated, like a medieval sculpture; her legs are like two sticks, and they're inflamed with erysipelas. While you're thinking of the continual rubbing of that rough wool against her skin, she suddenly raises her fists and strikes feebly at the air, as if she were doing battle against the images you can make out as you tiptoe closer: Christ, the Virgin, St Sebastian, St Lucia, the Archangel Michael, and the grinning demons in an old print, the only happy figures in that iconography of sorrow and wrath, happy because they're jabbing their pitchforks into the flesh of the damned, pouring cauldrons of boiling water on them, violating the women, getting drunk, enjoying all the liberties forbidden to the saints. You approach that central image, which is surrounded by the tears of Our Lady of Sorrows, the blood of Our Crucified Lord, the delight of Lucifer, the anger of the Archangel, the viscera preserved in bottles of alcohol, the silver heart: Señora Consuelo, kneeling, threatens them with her fists, stammering the words you can hear as you move even closer : 'Come, City of God ! Gabriel, sound your trumpet ! Ah, how long the world takes to die !'

She beats her breast until she collapses in front of the images and candles in a spasm of coughing. You raise her by the elbow, and as you gently help her to the bed you're surprised at her small-ness : she's almost a little girl, bent over almost double. You realize that without your assistance she'd have had to get back to bed on her hands and knees. You help her into that wide bed with its bread-crumbs and old feather-pillows, and cover her up, and wait till her breathing is back to normal, while the involuntary tears run down her parchment cheeks.

'Excuse me . . . excuse me, Señor Montero . . . Old ladies have nothing left but . . . the pleasures of devotion . . . Give me my hand-kerchief, please.'

'Señorita Aura told me . . .'

'Yes, of course. I don't want to lose any time. We should . . . we should begin working as soon as possible . . . Thank you . . .'

'You should try to rest.'

'Thank you . . . Here . . .'

The old lady raises her hand to her collar, unbuttons it, and lowers her head to remove the frayed purple ribbon that she hands to you. It's heavy because there's a copper key hanging from it.

'Over in that corner . . . Open that trunk and bring me the papers at the right, on top of the others . . . They're tied with a yellow ribbon . . .'

'I can't see very well . . .'

'Ah, yes . . . it's just that I'm so accustomed to the darkness. To my right . . . keep going till you come to the trunk . . . They've walled us in, Señor Montero. They've built up all around us and blocked off the light. They've tried to force me to sell, but I'll die first. This house is full of memories for us. They won't take us out of here till I'm dead . . . Yes, that's it. Thank you. You can begin reading this part. I'll give you the others later. Goodnight, Señor Montero. Thank you. Look, the candelabra has gone out. Light it outside the door, please. No, no, you can keep the key. I trust you.'

'Señora, there's a rat's nest in that corner . . .'

'Rats? I never go over there . . .'

'You should bring the cats in here.'

'The cats? What cats? Goodnight. I'm going to sleep. I'm very tired.'

'Goodnight.'

III

That same evening you read those yellow papers written in mustard-coloured ink, some of them with holes where a careless ash had fallen, others heavily fly-specked. General Llorente's French doesn't have the merits his wife attributed to it. You tell yourself you can make considerable improvements in the style, can tighten up his rambling account of past events: his childhood on an hacienda in Oaxaca, his military studies in France, his friendship with the Duke of Morny and the intimates of Napoleon III, his return to Mexico on the staff of Maximilian, the imperial ceremonies and gatherings, the battles, the defeat in 1867, his exile in France. Nothing that hasn't been described before. As you undress you think of the old lady's distorted notions, the value she attributes to these memoirs. You smile as you get into bed, thinking of the four thousand pesos.

You sleep soundly until a flood of light wakes you up at six in the morning; that glass roof doesn't have any curtain. You bury your head under the pillow and try to go back to sleep. Ten minutes later you give it up and walk into the bathroom, where you find all your things neatly arranged on a table and your few clothes hanging in the wardrobe. Just as you finish shaving the early morning silence is broken by that painful, desperate yowling.

You try to find out where it's coming from: you open the door to the hallway, but you can't hear anything from there: those cries are coming from up above, from the skylight. You jump up on the chair, from the chair on to the desk, and by supporting yourself on the bookshelf you can reach the skylight. You open one of the windows and pull yourself up to look out at that side garden, that square of yew-trees and brambles where five, six, seven cats – you can't count them, can't hold yourself up there for more than a second – are all twined together, all writhing in flames and giving off a dense smoke that reeks of burnt fur. As you get down again you wonder if you really saw it: perhaps you only imagined it from those dreadful cries that continue, grow less, and finally stop.

You put on your shirt, brush off your shoes with a piece of paper, and listen to the sound of a bell that seems to run through the passageways of the house until it arrives at your door. You look out into the hallway: Aura is walking along it with a bell in her hand. She turns her head to look at you and tells you that breakfast is ready. You try to detain her but she goes down the spiral staircase, still ringing that black-painted bell as if she were trying to wake up a whole asylum, a whole boarding-school.

You follow her in your shirt-sleeves, but when you reach the downstairs hallway you can't find her. The door of the old lady's bedroom opens behind you and you see a hand that reaches out from behind the partly-opened door, sets a chamberpot in the hallway and disappears again, closing the door.

In the dining-room your breakfast is already on the table, but this time only one place has been set. You eat quickly, return to the hallway, and knock at Señora Consuelo's door. Her sharp, weak voice tells you to come in. Nothing has changed: the perpetual shadows, the glow of the votive lights and the silver objects.

'Good morning, Señor Montero. Did you sleep well?'

'Yes. I read till quite late.'

The old lady waves her hand as if in a gesture of dismissal. 'No, no, no. Don't give me your opinion. Work on those pages and when you've finished I'll give you the others.'

'Very well. Señora, would I be able to go into the garden?'

'What garden, Señor Montero?'

'The one that's outside my room.'

'This house doesn't have any garden. We lost our garden when they built up all around us.'

'I think I could work better outdoors.'

'This house has only got that dark patio where you came in. My niece is growing some shade-plants there. But that's all.'

'It's all right, Señora.'

'I'd like to rest during the day. But come to see me tonight.'

'Very well, Señora.'

You spend all morning working on the papers, copying out the passages you intend to keep, rewriting the ones you think are especially bad, smoking one cigarette after another and reflecting that you ought to space your work so that the job lasts as long as possible. If you can manage to save at least twelve thousand pesos, you can spend a year on nothing but your own work, which you've postponed and almost forgotten. Your great, inclusive work on the Spanish discoveries and conquests in the New World. A work that sums up all the scattered chronicles, makes them intelligible, and discovers the resemblances among all the undertakings and adventures of Spain's Golden Age and all the human prototypes and major accomplishments of the Renaissance. You end up by putting aside the General's tedious pages and starting to compile the dates and summaries of your own work. Time passes and you don't look at your watch until you hear the bell again. Then you put on your coat and go down to the dining-room.

Aura is already seated. This time Señora Llorente is at the head of the table, wrapped in her shawl and nightgown and coif, hunching over her plate. But the fourth place has also been set. You note it in passing: it doesn't bother you any more. If the price of your future creative liberty is to put up with all the manias of this old woman, you can pay it easily. As you watch her eating her soup you try to figure out her age. There's a time after which it's impossible to detect the passing of the years, and Señora Consuelo crossed that frontier a long time ago. The General hasn't mentioned her in what you've already read of the memoirs. But if the General was 42 at the time of the French invasion, and died in 1901, forty years later, he must have died at the age of 82. He must have married the Señora after the defeat at Querétaro and his exile. But she would only have been a girl at that time . . .

The dates escape you because now the Señora is talking in that thin, sharp voice of hers, that bird-like chirping. She's talking to Aura and you listen to her as you eat, hearing her long list of complaints, pains, suspected illnesses, more complaints about the cost of medicines, the dampness of the house and so forth. You'd like to break in on this domestic conversation to ask about the servant who went for your things yesterday, the servant you've never even glimpsed and who never waits on table. You're about to ask about him but you're suddenly surprised to realize that up to this moment Aura hasn't said a word and is eating with a sort of mechanical fatality, as if she were waiting for some outside impulse before picking up her knife and fork, cutting a piece of liver – yes, it's liver again, apparently the favourite dish in this house – and carrying it to her mouth. You glance quickly from the aunt to the niece, but at that moment the Señora becomes motionless and at the same moment Aura puts her knife on her plate and also becomes motionless, and you remember that the Señora had put down her knife only a fraction of a second earlier.

There are several minutes of silence: you finish eating while they sit there rigid as statues, watching you. At last the Señora says, 'I'm very tired. I ought not to eat at the table. Come, Aura, help me to my room.'

The Señora tries to hold your attention: she looks directly at you so that you'll keep looking at her, although what she's saying is aimed at Aura. You have to make an effort in order to evade that look, which once again is wide, clear, and yellowish, free of the veils and wrinkles that usually obscure it. Then you glance at Aura, who is staring fixedly at nothing and silently moving her lips. She gets up with a motion like those you associate with dreaming, takes the arm of the bent old lady, and slowly helps her from the dining-room.

Alone now, you help yourself to the coffee that has been there since the beginning of the meal, the cold coffee you sip as you wrinkle your brow and ask yourself if the Señora doesn't have some secret power over her niece: if the girl, your beautiful Aura in her green dress, isn't kept in this dark old house against her will. But it would be so easy for her to escape while the Señora was asleep in her shadowy room. You tell yourself that her hold over the girl must be terrible. And you consider the way out that occurs to your imagination: perhaps Aura is waiting for you to release her from the chains in which the perverse, insane old lady, for some unknown reason, has bound her. You remember Aura as she was a few moments ago, spiritless, hypnotized by her terror, incapable of speaking in front of the tyrant, moving her lips in silence as if she were silently begging you to set her free; so enslaved that she imitated every gesture of the Señora, as if she were permitted to do only what the Señora did.

You rebel against this tyranny: you walk towards the other door, the one at the foot of the staircase, the one next to the old lady's room: that's where Aura must live, because there's no other room in the house. You push the door open and go in. This room is dark also, with whitewashed walls, and the only decoration is an enormous black Christ. At the left there's a door that must lead into the widow's bedroom. You go up to it on tiptoes, put your hands against it, then decide not to open it: you should talk with Aura alone.

And if Aura wants your help she'll come to your room. You go up there for a while, forgetting the yellowed manuscripts and your own notebooks, thinking only about the beauty of your Aura. And the more you think about her, the more you make her yours, not only because of her beauty and your desire, but also because you want to set her free: you've found a moral basis for your desire, and you feel innocent and self-satisfied. When you hear the bell again you don't go down to supper because you can't bear another scene like the one at the middle of the day. Perhaps Aura will realize it and come up to look for you after supper.

You force yourself to go on working on the papers. When you're bored with them you undress slowly, get into bed, and fall asleep at once, and for the first time in years you dream, dream of only one thing, of a fleshless hand that comes towards you with a bell, screaming that you should go away, everyone should go away; and when that face with its empty eye-sockets comes close to yours, you wake up with a muffled cry, sweating, and feel those gentle hands caressing your face, those lips murmuring in a low voice, consoling you and asking you for affection. You reach out your hands to find that other body, that naked body with a key dangling from its neck, and when you recognize the key you recognize the woman who is lying over you, kissing you, kissing your whole body. You can't see her in the black of the starless night, but you can smell the fragrance of the patio plants in her hair, can feel her smooth, eager body in your arms: you kiss her again and don't ask her to speak.

When you free yourself, exhausted, from her embrace, you hear her first whisper: 'You're my husband.' You agree. She tells you it's daybreak, then leaves you, saying that she'll wait for you that night in her room. You agree again and then fall asleep, relieved, unburdened, emptied of desire, still feeling the touch of Aura's body, her trembling, her surrender.

It's hard for you to wake up. There are several knocks on the door, and at last you get out of bed, groaning and still half-asleep. Aura, on the other side of the door, tells you not to open it: she says that Señora Consuelo wants to talk with you, is waiting for you in her room.

Ten minutes later you enter the widow's sanctuary. She's propped up against the pillows, motionless, her eyes hidden by those drooping, wrinkled, dead-white lids; you notice the puffy wrinkles under her eyes, the utter weariness of her skin.

Without opening her eyes she asks you, 'Did you bring the key to the trunk?'

'Yes, I think so . . . Yes, here it is.'

'You can read the second part. It's in the same place. It's tied with a blue ribbon.'

You go over to the trunk, this time with a certain disgust: the rats are swarming around it, peering at you with their glittering eyes from the cracks in the rotted floorboards, galloping towards the holes in the rotted walls. You open the trunk and take out the second batch of papers, then return to the foot of the bed. Señora Consuelo is petting her white rabbit. A sort of croaking laugh emerges from her buttoned-up throat, and she asks you, 'Do you like animals?'

'No, not especially. Perhaps because I've never had any.'

'They're good friends. Good companions. Above all when you're old and lonely.'

'Yes, they must be.'

'They're always themselves, Señor Montero. They don't have any pretensions.'

'What did you say his name is?'

'The rabbit? She's Saga. She's very intelligent. She follows her instincts. She's natural and free.'

'I thought it was a male rabbit.'

'Oh? Then you still can't tell the difference.'

'Well, the important thing is that you don't feel all alone.'

'They want us to be alone, Señor Montero, because they tell us that solitude is the only way to achieve saintliness. They forget that in solitude the temptation is even greater.'

'I don't understand, Señora.'

'Ah, it's better that you don't. Get back to work now, please.'

You turn your back on her, walk to the door, leave her room. In the hallway you clench your teeth. Why don't you have courage enough to tell her that you love the girl? Why don't you go back and tell her, once and for all, that you're planning to take Aura away with you when you finish the job? You approach the door again and start pushing it open, still uncertain, and through the crack you see Señora Consuelo standing up, erect, transformed, with a military tunic in her arms: a blue tunic with gold buttons, red epaulettes, bright medals with crowned eagles – a tunic the old lady bites ferociously, kisses tenderly, drapes over her shoulders as she performs a few teetering dance-steps. You close the door.

Yes: 'She was fifteen years old when I met her,' you read in the second part of the memoirs. '*Elle avait quinze ans lorsque je l'ai connue et, si j'ose le dire, ce sont ses yeux verts qui ont fait ma perdition.*' Consuelo's green eyes, Consuelo who was only fifteen in 1867, when General Llorente married her and took her with him into exile in Paris. '*Ma jeune poupée,*' he wrote in a moment of inspiration, '*ma jeune poupée aux yeux verts; je t'ai comblée d'amour.*' He described the house they lived in, the outings, the dances, the carriages, the world of the Second Empire, but all in a dull enough way. '*J'ai même supporté ta haine des chats, moi qui aimais tellement les jolies bêtes . . .*' One day he found her torturing a cat: she had it clasped between her legs, with her crinoline skirt pulled up, and he didn't know how to attract her attention because it seemed to him that '*tu faisais ça d'une façon si innocente, par pur enfantillage,*' and in fact it excited him so much that if you can believe what he wrote, he made love to her that night with extraordinary passion, 'parce que tu m'avais dit que torturer les chats était ta manière à toi de rendre notre amour favorable, par un sacrifice symbolique . . .' You've figured it up: Señora Consuelo must be 109. Her husband died fifty-nine years ago. 'Tu sais si bien t'habiller, ma douce Consuelo, toujours drappée dans de velours verts, verts comme tes yeux. Je pense que tu seras toujours belle, même dans cent ans . . .' Always dressed in green. Always beautiful, even after a hundred years. 'Tu es si fière de ta beauté; que ne ferais tu pas pour rester toujours jeune?'

IV

Now you know why Aura is living in this house: to perpetuate the illusion of youth and beauty in that poor, crazed old lady. Aura, kept here like a mirror, like one more icon on that votive wall with its clustered offerings, preserved hearts, imagined saints and demons.

You put the manuscript aside and go downstairs, suspecting there's only one place Aura could be in the morning: the place that greedy old woman has assigned to her.

Yes, you find her in the kitchen, at the moment she's beheading a kid: the vapour that rises from the open throat, the smell of spilt blood, the animal's glazed eyes, all give you nausea. Aura is wearing a ragged, blood-stained dress and her hair is dishevelled; she looks at you without recognition and goes on with her butchering.

You leave the kitchen: this time you'll really speak to the old lady, really throw her greed and tyranny in her face. When you push open the door she's standing behind the veil of lights, performing a ritual with the empty air: one hand stretched out and clenched, as if holding something up, and the other clasped around an invisible object, striking again and again at the same place. Then she wipes her hands against her breast, sighs, and starts cutting the air again, as if – yes, you can see it clearly – as if she were skinning an animal . . .

You run through the hallway, the parlour, the dining-room, to where Aura is slowly skinning the kid, absorbed in her work, heedless of your entrance or your words, looking at you as if you were made of air.

You climb up to your room, go in, and brace yourself against the door as if you were afraid someone would follow you : panting, sweating, victim of your horror, of your certainty. If something or someone should try to enter, you wouldn't be able to resist, you'd move away from the door, you'd let it happen. Frantically you drag the armchair over to that latchless door, push the bed up against it, then fall on to the bed, exhausted, drained of your will-power, with your eyes closed and your arms wrapped around your pillow . . . the pillow that isn't yours . . . nothing is yours.

You fall into a stupor, into the depths of a dream that's your only escape, your only means of saying No to insanity. 'She's crazy, she's crazy,' you repeat again and again to make yourself sleepy, and you can see her again as she skins the imaginary kid with an imaginary knife. 'She's crazy, she's crazy . . .'

in the depths of the dark abyss, in your silent dream with its mouths opening in silence, you see her coming towards you from the blackness of the abyss, you see her crawling towards you,

in silence,

moving her fleshless hand, coming towards you until her face touches yours and you see the old lady's bloody gums, her toothless gums, and you scream and she goes away again, moving her hand, sowing the abyss with the yellow teeth she carries in her blood-stained apron :

your scream is an echo of Aura's, she is standing in front of you in your dream, and she's screaming because someone's hands have ripped her green taffeta skirt in two, and then

she turns her head towards you

with the torn folds of the skirt in her hands, turns towards you and laughs silently, with the old lady's teeth superimposed on her own, while her legs, her naked legs, shatter into bits and fly towards the abyss . . .

There's a knock at the door, then the sound of the bell, the supper bell. Your head aches so much that you can't make out the hands on the clock, but you know it must be late : above your head you can see the night clouds beyond the skylight. You get up painfully, dazed and hungry. You hold the glass pitcher under the faucet, wait for the water to run, fill the pitcher, then pour it into the basin. You wash your face, brush your teeth with your worn toothbrush that's clogged with greenish paste, dampen hair – you don't notice you're doing all this in the wrong order – and comb it meticulously in front of the oval mirror on the walnut wardrobe. Then you tie your tie, put on your jacket and go down to the empty dining-room, where only one place has been set: yours.

Beside your plate, under your napkin, there's an object you start caressing with your fingers: a clumsy little rag doll, filled with a powder that trickles from its badly-sewn shoulder; its face is drawn with indian ink, and its body is naked, sketched with a few brushstrokes. You eat the cold supper – liver, tomatoes, wine – with your right hand while holding the doll in your left.

You eat mechanically, without noticing at first your own hypnotized attitude, but later you glimpse a reason for your oppressive sleep, your nightmare, and finally identify your sleep-walking movements with those of Aura and the old lady. You're suddenly disgusted by that horrible little doll, in which you begin to suspect a secret illness, a contagion. You let it fall to the floor. You wipe your lips with the napkin, look at your watch, and remember that Aura is waiting for you in her room.

You go cautiously up to Señora Consuelo's door, but there isn't a sound from within. You look at your watch again: it's barely nine o'clock. You decide to feel your way down to that dark, roofed patio you haven't been in since you came through it, without seeing anything, on the day you arrived here.

You touch the damp, mossy walls, breathe the perfumed air, and try to isolate the different elements you're breathing, to recognize the heavy, sumptuous aromas that surround you. The flicker of your match lights up the narrow, empty patio, where various plants are growing on each side in the loose, reddish earth. You can make out the tall, leafy forms that cast their shadows on the walls in the light of the match; but it burns down, singeing your fingers, and you have to light another one to finish seeing the flowers, fruits and plants you remember reading about in old chronicles, the forgotten herbs that are growing here so fragrantly and drowsily: the long, broad, downy leaves of the henbane; the twining stems with flowers that are yellow outside, red inside; the pointed, heart-shaped leaves of the nightshade; the ash-coloured down of the grape-mullein with its clustered flowers; the bushy gatheridge with its white blossoms; the belladonna. They come to life in the flare of your match, swaying gently with their shadows, while you recall the uses of these herbs that dilate the pupils, alleviate pain, reduce the pangs of childbirth, bring consolation, weaken the will, induce a voluptuous calm.

You're all alone with the perfumes when the third match burns out. You go up to the hallway slowly, listen again at Señora Consuelo's door, then tiptoe on to Aura's. You push it open without knocking and go into that bare room, where a circle of light reveals the bed, the huge Mexican crucifix, and the woman who comes towards you when the door is closed. Aura is dressed in green, in a green taffeta robe from which, as she approaches, her moon-pale thighs reveal themselves. The woman, you repeat as she comes close, the woman, not the girl of yesterday: the girl of yesterday – you touch Aura's fingers, her waist – couldn't have been more than 20; the woman of today – you caress her loose black hair, her pallid cheeks – seems to be 40. Between yesterday and today, something about her green eyes has turned hard; the red of her lips has strayed beyond their former outlines, as if she wanted to fix them in a happy grimace, a troubled smile: as if, like that plant in the patio, her smile combined the taste of honey and the taste of gall. You don't have time to think of anything more.

'Sit down on the bed, Felipe.'

'Yes.'

'We're going to play. You don't have to do anything. Let me do everything myself.'

Sitting on the bed, you try to make out the source of that diffuse, opaline light that hardly lets you distinguish the objects in the room, and the presence of Aura, from the golden atmosphere that surrounds them. She sees you looking up, trying to find where it comes from. You can tell from her voice that she's kneeling down in front of you.

'The sky is neither high nor low. It's over us and under us at the same time.'

She takes off your shoes and socks and caresses your bare feet.

You feel the warm water that bathes the soles of your feet, while she washes them with a heavy cloth, now and then casting furtive glances at that Christ carved from black wood. Then she dries your feet, takes you by the hand, fastens a few violets in her loose hair, and begins to hum a melody, a waltz, to which you dance with her, held by the murmur of her voice, gliding around to the slow, solemn rhythm she's setting, very different from the light movements of her hands, which unbutton your shirt, caress your chest, reach around to your back and grasp it. You also murmur that wordless song, that melody rising naturally from your throat: you glide around together, each time closer to the bed, until you muffle the song with your hungry kisses on Aura's mouth, until you stop the dance with your crushing kisses on her shoulders and breasts.

You're holding the empty robe in your hands. Aura, squatting on the bed, places an object against her closed thighs, caressing it, summoning you with her hand. She caresses that thin wafer, breaks it against her thighs, oblivious of the crumbs that roll down her hips: she offers you half of the wafer and you take it, place it in your mouth at the same time she does, and swallow it with difficulty. Then you fall on Aura's naked body, you fall on her naked arms, which are stretched out from one side of the bed to the other like the arms of the crucifix hanging on the wall, the black Christ with that scarlet silk wrapped around his thighs, his spread knees, his wounded side, his crown of thorns set on a tangled black wig with silver spangles. Aura opens up like an altar.

You murmur her name in her ear. You feel the woman's full arms against your back. You hear her warm voice in your ear: 'Will you love me for ever?'

'For ever, Aura. I'll love you for ever.'

'For ever? Do you swear it?'

'I swear it.'

'Even though I grow old? Even though I lose my beauty? Even though my hair turns white?'

'For ever, my love, for ever.'

'Even if I die, Felipe? Will you love me for ever, even if I die?'

'For ever, for ever. I swear it. Nothing can separate us.'

'Come, Felipe, come ...'

When you wake up, you reach out to touch Aura's shoulder, but you only touch the still-warm pillow and the white sheet that covers you.

You murmur her name.

You open your eyes and see her standing at the foot of the bed, smiling but not looking at you. She walks slowly towards the corner of the room, sits down on the floor, places her arms on the knees that emerge from the darkness you can't peer into, and strokes the wrinkled hand that comes forward from the lessening darkness: she's sitting at the feet of the old lady, of Señora Consuelo, who is seated in an armchair you hadn't noticed earlier: Señora Consuelo smiles at you, nodding her head, smiling at you along with Aura, who moves her head in rhythm with the old lady's; they both smile at you, thanking you. You lie back, without any will, thinking that the old lady has been in the room all the time;

> *you remember her movements, her voice, her dance,*
> *though you keep telling yourself she wasn't there.*

The two of them get up at the same moment, Consuelo from the chair, Aura from the floor. Turning their backs on you, they walk slowly towards the door that leads to the widow's bedroom, enter that room where the lights are for ever trembling in front of the images, close the door behind them, and leave you to sleep in Aura's bed.

V

Your sleep is heavy and unsatisfying. In your dreams you had already felt the same vague melancholy, the weight on your diaphragm, the sadness that won't stop oppressing your imagination. Although you're sleeping in Aura's room, you're sleeping all alone, far from the body you believe you've possessed.

When you wake up, you look for another presence in the room, and realize it's not Aura who disturbs you but rather the double presence of something that was engendered during the night. You put your hands on your forehead, trying to calm your disordered senses : that dull melancholy is hinting to you in a low voice, the voice of memory and premonition, that you're seeking your other half, that the sterile conception last night engendered your own double.

And you stop thinking, because there are things even stronger than the imagination : the habits that force you to get up, look for a bathroom off this room without finding one, go out into the hallway rubbing your eyelids, climb the stairs tasting the thick bitterness of your tongue, enter your own room feeling the rough bristles on your chin, turn on the bathroom faucets and then slide into the warm water, letting yourself relax into forgetfulness.

But while you're drying yourself, you remember the old lady and the girl as they smiled at you before leaving the room arm in arm; you recall that whenever they're together they always do the same things : they embrace, smile, eat, speak, enter, leave, at the same time, as if one were imitating the other, as if the will of one depended on the existence of the other ... You cut yourself lightly on one cheek as you think of these things while you shave; you make an effort to get control of yourself. When you finish shaving you count the objects in your travelling-case, the bottles and tubes which the servant you've never seen brought over from your boarding-house : you murmur the names of these objects, touch them, read the contents and instructions, pronounce the names of the manufacturers, keeping to those objects in order to forget that other one, the one without a name, without a label, without any rational consistency. What is Aura expecting of you? you ask yourself, closing the travelling-case. What does she want, what does she want?

In answer you hear the dull rhythm of her bell in the corridor telling you breakfast is ready. You walk to the door without your shirt on. When you open it you find Aura there : it must be Aura because you see the green taffeta she always wears, though her face is covered with a green veil. You take her by the wrist, that slender wrist which trembles at your touch ...

'Breakfast is ready,' she says, in the faintest voice you've ever heard.

'Aura. Let's stop pretending.'

'Pretending?'

'Tell me if Señora Consuelo keeps you from leaving, from living your own life. Why did she have to be there when you and I . . . Please tell me you'll go with me when . . .'

'Go away? Where?'

'Out of this house. Out into the world, to live together. You shouldn't feel bound to your aunt for ever . . . Why all this devotion? Do you love her that much?'

'Love her?'

'Yes. Why do you have to sacrifice yourself this way?'

'Love her? She loves me. She sacrifices herself for me.'

'But she's an old woman, almost a corpse. You can't . . .'

'She has more life than I do. Yes, she's old and repulsive . . . Felipe, I don't want to become . . . to be like her . . . another . . .'

'She's trying to bury you alive. You've got to be reborn, Aura.'

'You have to die before you can be reborn . . . No, you don't understand. Forget about it, Felipe. Just have faith in me.'

'If you'd only explain.'

'Just have faith in me. She's going to be out today for the whole day . . .'

'She?'

'Yes, the other.'

'She's going out? But she never . . .'

'Yes, sometimes she does. She makes a great effort and goes out. She's going out today. For all day . . . You and I could . . .'

'Go away?'

'If you want to.'

'Well . . . perhaps not yet. I'm under contract. But as soon as I can finish the work, then . . .'

'Ah, yes. But she's going to be out all day. We could do something . . .'

'What?'

'I'll wait for you this evening in my aunt's bedroom. I'll wait for you as always.'

She turns away, ringing her bell like the lepers who use a bell to announce their approach, telling the unwary: 'Out of the way, out of the way.' You put on your shirt and coat and follow the sound of the bell calling you to the dining-room. In the parlour the widow Llorente comes towards you, bent over, leaning on a knobby cane; she's dressed in an old white gown with a stained and tattered gauze veil. She goes by without looking at you, blowing her nose into a handkerchief, blowing her nose and spitting. She murmurs, 'I won't be at home today, Señor Montero. I have complete confidence in your work. Please keep at it. My husband's memoirs must be published.'

She goes away, stepping across the carpets with her tiny feet, which are like those of an antique doll, and supporting herself with her cane, and spitting and sneezing as if she wanted to clear something from her congested lungs. It's only by an effort of the will that you keep yourself from following her with your eyes, despite the curiosity you feel at seeing the yellowed bridal gown she's taken from the bottom of that old trunk in her bedroom . . .

You scarcely touch the cold coffee that's waiting for you in the dining-room. You sit for an hour in the tall arch-back chair, smoking, waiting for the sounds you never hear, until finally you're sure the old lady has left the house and can't catch you at what you're going to do. For the last hour you've had the key to the trunk clutched in your hand, and now you get up and silently walk through the parlour into the hallway, where you wait for another fifteen minutes – your watch tells you how long – with your ear against Señora Consuelo's door. Then you slowly push it open until you can make out, beyond the spider's web of candles, the empty bed on which her rabbit is gnawing at a carrot: the bed that's always littered with scraps of bread, and that you touch gingerly as if you thought the old lady might be hidden among the rumples of the sheets. You walk over to the corner where the trunk is, stepping on the tail of one of those rats; it squeals, escapes from your feet, and scampers off to warn the others. You fit the copper key into the rusted padlock, remove the padlock, and then raise the lid, hearing the creak of the old, stiff hinges. You take out the third portion of the memoirs – it's tied with a red ribbon – and under it you discover those photographs, those old, brittle, dog-eared photographs. You pick them up without looking at them, clutch the whole treasure to your breast, and hurry out of the room without closing the trunk, forgetting the hunger of the rats. You close the door, lean against the wall in the hallway until you catch your breath, then climb the stairs to your room.

Up there you read the new pages, the continuation, the events of an agonized century. In his florid language General Llorente describes the personality of Eugenia de Montijo, pays his respects to Napoleon the Small, summons up his most martial rhetoric to declare the Franco-Prussian War, fills whole pages with his sorrow at the defeat, harangues all men of honour about the Republican monster, sees a ray of hope in General Boulanger, sighs for Mexico, believes that in the Dreyfus affair the honour – always that word 'honour' ! – of the army has asserted itself again . . .

The brittle pages crumble at your touch : you don't respect them now, you're only looking for a reappearance of the woman with green eyes. 'I know why you weep at times, Consuelo. I have not been able to give you children, although you are so radiant with life . . .' And later : 'Consuelo, you should not tempt God. We must reconcile ourselves. Is not my affection enough? I know that you love me; I feel it. I am not asking you for resignation, because that would offend you. I am only asking you to see, in the great love which you say you have for me, something sufficient, something that can fill both of us, without the need of turning to sick imaginings . . .'

On another page : 'I told Consuelo that those medicines were utterly useless. She insists on growing her own herbs in the garden. She says she is not deceiving herself. The herbs are not to strengthen the body, but rather the soul . . .' Later : 'I found her in a delirium, embracing the pillow. She cried, "Yes, yes, yes, I've done it, I've recreated her ! I can invoke her, I can give her life with my own life !" It was necessary to call the doctor. He told me he could not quiet her, because the truth was that she was under the effects of narcotics, not of stimulants . . .' And finally : 'Early this morning I found her walking barefooted through the hallways. I wanted to stop her. She went by without looking at me, but her words were directed to me. "Don't stop me," she said. "I'm going towards my youth, and my youth is coming towards me. It's coming in, it's in the garden, it's come back . . ." Consuelo, my poor Consuelo, even the devil was an angel at one time . . .'

There isn't any more. The memoirs of General Llorente end with that sentence: '*Consuelo, le démon aussi était un ange, avant . . .*'

And after the last page, the portraits. The portrait of an elderly gentleman in a military uniform, an old photograph with these words in one corner: '*Moulin, Photographe, 35 Boulevard Haussmann*' and the date '1894'. Then the photograph of Aura, of Aura with her green eyes, her black hair gathered in ringlets, leaning against a Doric column with a painted landscape in the background: the landscape of a Lorelei in the Rhine. Her dress is buttoned up to the collar, there's a handkerchief in her hand, she's wearing a bustle: Aura, and the date '1876' in white ink, and on the back of the daguerrotype, in spidery handwriting: '*Fait pour notre dixième anniversaire de mariage,*' and a signature in the same hand, 'Consuelo Llorente'. In the third photograph you see both Aura and the old gentleman, but this time they're dressed in outing-clothes, sitting on a bench in a garden. The photograph has become a little blurred: Aura doesn't look as young as she did in the other picture, but it's she, it's he, it's . . . it's you. You stare and stare at the photographs, then hold them up to the skylight. You cover General Llorente's beard with your finger, and imagine him with black hair, and you only discover yourself: blurred, lost, forgotten, but you, you, you.

Your head is spinning, overcome by the rhythm of that distant waltz, by the odour of damp, fragrant plants; you fall exhausted on the bed, touching your cheeks, your eyes, your nose, as if you were afraid that some invisible hand had ripped off the mask you've been wearing for twenty-seven years, the cardboard features that hid your true face, your real appearance, the appearance you once had but then forgot. You bury your face in the pillow, trying to keep the wind of the past from tearing away your own features, because you don't want to lose them. You lie there with your face in the pillow, waiting for what has to come, for what you can't prevent. You don't look at your watch again, that useless object tediously measuring time in accordance with human vanity, those little hands marking out the long hours that were invented to disguise the real passage of time, which races with a mortal and insolent swiftness no clock could ever measure. A life, a century, fifty years: you can't imagine these lying measurements any longer, you can't hold that bodiless dust within your hands.

When you look up from the pillow, you find you're in darkness. Night has fallen.

Night has fallen. Beyond the skylight the swift black clouds are hiding the moon, which tries to free itself, to reveal its pale, round, smiling face. It escapes for only a moment, then the clouds hide it again. You haven't got any hope left. You don't even look at your watch. You hurry down the stairs, out of that prison cell with its old papers and faded daguerrotypes, and stop at the door of Señora Consuelo's room, and listen to your own voice, muted and transformed after all those hours of silence: 'Aura ...'

Again: 'Aura ...'

You enter the room. The votive-lights have gone out. You remember that the old lady has been away all day, without her faithful attention the candles have all burned up. You grope forward in the darkness to the bed.

And again: 'Aura.'

You hear a faint rustle of taffeta, and the breathing that keeps time with your own. You reach out your hand to touch Aura's green robe.

'No ... Don't touch me ... Lie down at my side.'

You find the edge of the bed, swing up your legs, and remain there stretched out and motionless. You can't help feeling a shiver of fear: 'She might come back any minute.'

'She won't come back.'

'Never?'

'I'm exhausted. She's already exhausted. I've never been able to keep her with me for more than three days.'

'Aura ...'

You want to put your hand on Aura's breasts. She turns her back: you can tell by the difference in her voice.

'No ... Don't touch me ...'

'Aura ... I love you.'

'Yes. You love me. You told me yesterday that you'd always love me.'

'I'll always love you, always. I need your kisses, your body . . .'

'Kiss my face. Only my face.'

You bring your lips close to the head that's lying next to yours. You stroke Aura's long black hair. You grasp that fragile woman by the shoulders, ignoring her sharp complaint. You tear off her taffeta robe, embrace her, feel her small and lost and naked in your arms, despite her moaning resistance, her feeble protests, kissing her face without thinking, without distinguishing, and you're touching her withered breasts when a ray of moonlight shines in and surprises you, shines in through a chink in the wall that the rats have chewed open, an eye that lets in a beam of silvery moonlight. It falls on Aura's eroded face, as brittle and yellowed as the memoirs, as creased with wrinkles as the photographs. You stop kissing those fleshless lips, those toothless gums : the ray of moonlight shows you the naked body of the old lady, of Señora Consuelo, limp, spent, tiny, ancient, trembling because you touch her, you love her, you too have come back . . .

You plunge your face, your open eyes, into Consuelo's silver-white hair, and you'll embrace her again when the clouds cover the moon, when you're both hidden again, when the memory of youth, of youth re-embodied, rules the darkness.

'She'll come back, Felipe. We'll bring her back together. Let me recover my strength and I'll bring her back . . .'

Translated by Lysander Kemp

Nicanor Parra

PORTRAIT OF THE AUTHOR

Consider, boys,
This tongue gnawed by cancer:
I'm a professor in an obscure day school,
I've lost my voice teaching classes.
(However it's worked out
I put in my forty hours a week.)
What do you make of my pounded face?
Really, it upsets you to look at me.
And what do you say to this nose rotted
By the lime of the degrading chalk.

Come to the eyes, at three yards
I can't make out my own mother.
What's happened to me? – Nothing!
I've ruined them teaching classes:
The bad light, the sun,
The wretched, venomous moon.
And all for what!
To earn an unforgivable loaf
Hard as a bourgeois face
And smelling and tasting of blood.
Why were we born men
If we're to be led on to die like beasts!

Sometimes, out of overwork,
I see strange shapes in the air,
I hear the clatter of demented footsteps,
Laughter, criminal conversations.
Look at these hands
And these cheeks white as a corpse's,

These few hairs I have left,
These hellish black wrinkles !
Just the same I was like you,
Young, full of high ideals,
I dreamed of melting copper
And polishing the facets of diamonds :
And now they've set me here
Behind this uncomfortable table
Brutalized by the singsong
Of five hundred hours a week.

PIANO SOLO

Since man's life is nothing but an action at a distance,
A bit of froth shining on the inside of a glass,
Since the trees are nothing but fluttering furniture,
Nothing but chairs and tables in perpetual motion,
Since we ourselves are nothing but beings
(As god himself is nothing but god)
Since we don't talk to be heard
But to make others talk
And the echo precedes the voices that raise it,
Since we haven't even the consolation of chaos
In a garden that yawns and fills with air,
A puzzle we have to solve before we die
So that we can be tranquilly restored to existence
After we have overdone it with women,
Since there is also a heaven in hell
Allow me also to do a few things :

I want to make a noise with my feet,
I want my soul to discover its body.

THE PILGRIM

Your attention, ladies and gentlemen, your attention for one
　　moment:
Turn your heads for a second to this part of the republic,
Forget for one night your personal matters,

Pleasure and pain can wait at the door:
There's a voice from this part of the republic.
Your attention, ladies and gentlemen! Your attention for one
　　moment!
A soul which has been bottled up for years
In a sort of sexual and intellectual abyss,
Nourishing itself most inadequately through the nose,
Desires to be heard by you.

I'd like to find out about certain things,
I need a little light, the garden's covered with flies,
My mental state's a disaster,
I work things out in my peculiar way,
As I say these things I see a bicycle leaning against a wall,
I see a bridge
And a car disappearing between the buildings.

You comb your hair, that's true, you walk in the gardens,
Under your skins you have other skins,
You have a seventh sense
Which lets you in and out automatically.
But I'm a child calling to its mother from behind rocks,
I'm a pilgrim who makes stones jump as high as his nose,
A tree crying out to be covered with leaves.

Translated by W. S. Merwin

Alberto Girri

EPISTLE TO HIERONYMUS BOSCH

How well you knew
all that we children of wrath
did not understand,
the source of that evil
which deforms our substance,
an incorporeal evil which you examined
like one who piles corpses
and with cold scalpel
extracts the madness from their heads,
and from their anatomies
the confusion of the three kingdoms.
Trees with faces
stones that are also plants,
animate and poisonous metals,
an insect astride a bird
and the bird sharpening its knife;
for of this you spoke and shouted,
and in visual form
established that properly joined
we form a single body,
deprived of the great benefit,
withdrawn from love of the seed
that fell on the ground and died,
not its own loss but ours.
But always man,
I, someone else, or you,
man and his nakedness
stupidly rambling through
gardens of fair delights
and the plateaux of hell,

and behind and above
the haywain of the world,
on which everyone snatches anything he can;
his nakedness, not sex,
homesick for the sum of nakedness,
the primal hermaphrodite unity,
the complete being Adam-and-Eve.

Vagabond of the strange,
hand that aspired to consciousness,
may the prayers of your mass
have mounted straight
like a perfume.

Translated by J. M. Cohen

Mario Benedetti

THE IRIARTES

Five families used to phone the Boss. I was always in charge of the telephone on the morning shift and I knew the five voices by heart. We had all cottoned on to the fact that each family was a nice little bit of homework and we sometimes compared notes.

For example, I thought of the Calvo family as being a little, fat aggressive woman with lipstick plastered over the edges of her lips; the Ruiz family a commonplace chick with hair over one eye; the Durán family a thin intellectual – the bored, broadminded type; the Salgado family a thick-lipped female, the type that gets by on pure sex appeal. But the only one with the voice of an ideal woman was the Iriarte family. Neither fat nor thin, just enough in the way of curves for the natural gift of touch to appreciate, neither too unyielding nor too easy – a real woman, that is, a woman of character. So I imagined her. I knew her open contagious laugh and from this I imagined her manner. I knew her silences and from these I created her eyes – black and melancholy. I knew her friendly, welcoming voice and from this I imagined her tenderness.

About the other families, there was disagreement. Elizalde, for example, thought that Salgado was an ordinary little bint; Rossi believed Calvo to be a kinky-haired brunette. Correa thought that Ruiz was simply another old pro. But about the Iriarte family, we were all agreed that she was adorable. What is more, we had all imagined almost the same image from her voice. We were all certain that if, one day, she should open the office door and smile without saying a word, we should all recognize her at once because we had all imagined the same unmistakable smile.

The Boss was a pretty indiscreet type when it came to confidential matters concerning the office; he was silent as a tomb about the five families. On this point, our conversations with him were dishearteningly brief. We simply answered the call, pressed the button to sound the buzzer in his office and said to him, for example, 'The Salgados'. He just said, 'Put them through' or 'Tell them I'm not in' or 'Tell them to call back in an hour.' Never a comment, nor even a joke. And yet he knew he could trust us.

I couldn't understand why, of the five, the Iriartes were the ones who called least often, sometimes once a fortnight. True, on these occasions, the red light which marked 'Engaged' didn't go out for a quarter of an hour. How much it would have meant for me to have listened for a whole fifteen minutes to that tender, sweet, assured little voice.

Once I plucked up courage to say something, I don't remember what and she answered something, I don't know what. What a day! From then on I cherished the hope of speaking to her for a little while or better still of her recognizing my voice the way I recognized hers. One morning I had the idea of saying: 'Would you mind waiting for a minute until I can get through?' and she replied: 'Sure, as long as you help me while away the time.' I know that I sounded half-witted that day because I could only talk about the weather and work and about a change of schedule they were planning. But on another occasion, I plucked up courage and we talked about general things but with special significance. From then on, she recognized my voice and greeted me with 'Hi, Secretary', which completely melted me.

A few months after this development, I went on holiday, to Este. For years, my holidays in Este had been my strongest hope from the love angle. I always thought that one of these leaves, I should meet the girl who incarnated my private dreams, and on whom my latent tenderness could be lavished. Because I'm definitely the sentimental kind. Sometimes, I reproach myself for it, and tell myself that these days it's better to be selfish and calculating, but it's no use. I go to the movies. I swallow one of those Mexican vulgarities about illegitimate children and poor old men, and I know without a shadow of doubt that it's idiotic, and yet I can't keep the lump from my throat.

Now about this question of meeting a woman in Este, I have gone into this very thoroughly, and I've discovered other motives which are not so sentimental. The truth is that in a holiday resort, you only see clean, fresh, relaxed women who are ready to laugh and enjoy everything. It's obvious that there are clean women in Montevideo, but the poor things are always tired. Tight shoes, stairs, buses make them jaded and sweaty. In the town you practically don't know what a happy female is like. And though it might not seem so, it is important. Personally I consider myself able to put up with any sort of feminine depression. I'd even go so far as to say that I feel able to withstand any kind of tears, shouting or hysteria. But I realize that I am much more exacting when it comes to happiness. There is some female laughter which frankly I could never stand. On the beach, where everybody laughs from the minute they go in for their first bathe till they reel out of the Casino, you know one from the other and which laugh is disgusting and which wonderful.

It was precisely in the resort that I heard her voice again. I was dancing among the tables of a terrace café by the light of the moon that nobody was bothering about. My right hand had tightened on a shoulder that was half peeling and that still had not lost the heat of the afternoon. The owner of the shoulder was laughing, and it was a good laugh, there was no getting away from it. Every time I was able to, I looked at some almost transparent little blonde hairs which she had around her ears and really I felt quite moved. My partner spoke little but she always said something silly enough to make me appreciate her silences.

It was just in the agreeable course of one of these silences that I heard the phrase as clearly as if she had framed it specially for me: 'And what do you want to drink?' It isn't important for now or later, but I remember it word for word. One of those slow, trailing knots that you get in the tango had formed. The sentence had been spoken very near but at that moment I couldn't associate it with any of the thighs that had rubbed against me.

Two nights later in the Casino, I lost about ninety pesos and I got the wild idea of putting fifty on the last ball. If I lost, so much the worse; I'd have to go straight back to Montevideo. But 32 came up and I felt greatly relieved and optimistic as I reviewed the eight orange chips which I had put on it. Then someone said in my ear almost as if into a telephone, 'That's the way to gamble. You have to take a risk.'

I turned round calmly, certain of what I was going to find, and the Iriarte family standing beside me was as delightful as the one that I and the others had reconstructed from her voice. Afterwards, it was quite easy to take up the thread of her own conversation, invent a gambling system and persuade her to gamble with me, to talk at first, dance later and to meet me on the beach next day.

From then on we went steady. She told me she was called Doris, Doris Freire. This was strictly true (I don't know for what reason she showed me her identity card) and besides quite explicable. I had always thought that the 'families' were only telephone names. From the first day, I made this plan of action; it was obvious that she was having an affair with the Boss and it was equally obvious that this hurt my pride; but (and notice what a good but), she was the most delightful woman I have ever met, and I risked losing her for ever (now that chance had placed her within earshot) if I took too much notice of my scruples.

Besides, there was another possibility. Just as I had recognized her voice, why shouldn't Doris recognize mine? True, she had always been someone beautiful and unattainable to me whilst I was only now entering her sphere. Nevertheless, when I ran to meet her one morning with a happy 'Hi, secretary', the fact that she had been worried as if some suspicion had suddenly dawned on her did not escape me, although she took the blow without flinching, laughed, gave me her arm and teased me about a dark woman who went in front of us in a jeep. Afterwards, however, she seemed to accept fatalistically the possibility that I was the one who answered her calls to the Boss. And this certainty which was now reflected in her conversations, in her unforgettable looks of complicity and promise finally gave me new hope. It was clear that she appreciated the fact that I did not speak to her about the Boss and (though this was not so obvious) it was probable that she would reward my tact by breaking it off with him soon. I have always known how to read another person's looks and those of Doris were particularly sincere.

I went back to work. Every other day, I once again did the morning shift by the telephone. The Iriartes did not call any more.

Almost every day, I met Doris when she came out of work. She worked in the Law Courts, earned a good salary, was the chief clerk in her office and everyone appreciated her.

Doris did not hide anything from me. Her present life was extraordinarily honest and transparent. But what about the past? At bottom, it was enough that she was not deceiving me. Her affair – or whatever it had been – with the Boss was certainly not going to poison my portion of happiness. The Iriartes had not called any more. What more could I want? I was the Boss's favourite and soon this would be relegated to the unpleasant memory in Doris's life which all girls inevitably have.

I had warned Doris not to telephone me at the office. I don't know what excuse I found. Frankly, I didn't want to take the risk of Elizalde or Rossi or Correa answering the call, recognizing her voice, and inventing in consequence one of those dubious interpretations to which they were so prone. Certainly, friendly and ungrudging as she always was, she made no objection. I liked the fact that she was so understanding in everything to do with this forbidden topic, and I was really grateful that she had never made me enter into unpleasant explanations, and used those words of ill repute which sully everything and destroy all good intentions.

She took me home and I met her mother. She was a good, tired woman. She had lost her husband two years before and still had not got over it. She watched Doris and myself with mild complacency, but at times her eyes filled with tears, perhaps remembering some faraway incident during her engagement to Mr Freire. Three times a week, I stayed till eleven but at ten she discreetly said good-night and went out of the room so that Doris and I were left with an hour in which to kiss to our heart's content, talk of the future, add up the price of sheets and the number of rooms we should need, exactly like a hundred thousand other couples scattered over the whole of the Republic who at this very same moment were interchanging similar plans and caresses. Her mother had never mentioned the Boss nor anyone else who had been sentimentally involved with Doris. She always treated me with the consideration which any respectable home reserves for the little girl's first boyfriend. And I let her do it.

Sometimes I couldn't help feeling a sordid smugness knowing that I had secured (for my use and my delight) one of those unattainable women kept only for Ministers, public figures and important Civil Servants. I . . . an assistant secretary.

Doris, it is only fair to admit, was more delightful every night. She never held back her tenderness with me; she had a way of caressing my neck, of kissing my throat, of whispering little things whilst she was kissing me that frankly made me come out dizzy with happiness and – why not admit it – with desire. Afterwards, alone and wakeful in my bachelor flat, I felt rather bitter thinking that this refined skill proved that someone had carefully assisted her initiation. After all was this an advantage or a disadvantage? I couldn't help thinking of the Boss so stiff and respectable, so encrusted in his respectability, and I couldn't manage to envisage him in the role of this enviable instructor. Had there been others then? But how many? Most of all, which of them had taught her to kiss like that? I always ended by reminding myself that we were not living in the Middle Ages, that now I was the one who mattered to her, and I went to sleep embracing the pillow as if in vast anticipation and as a weak substitute for other embraces that figured in my plan.

Up to the twenty-third of November, I had the feeling that I was slipping helplessly and graciously into matrimony. It was a fact. We only needed to find a flat of the type that I liked with light, air and plenty of big windows. We had been out several Sundays in search of the ideal, but when we found something that was near to it, the price was too high or there wasn't good transport, or it was in some suburb that Doris found dull and remote.

On the morning of the twenty-third of November, I was doing my shift. The Boss had not appeared in the office for four days; so that I was alone and peaceful reading a magazine and smoking a fag. Suddenly I heard a door open behind me. Lazily I turned round and caught a glimpse of Doris's adorable little head peeping round in a questioning manner. She came in with a certain slightly guilty air because – as she said – she thought I was going to be annoyed.

The reason for her presence in the office was that she had finally found a flat of the type we were looking for and at the right rent. She had made a neat little plan and she showed it with satisfaction. She was lovely in her light dress and that wide belt that showed off her waist better than any other. As we were alone, she sat on my desk, crossed her legs, and began to ask me where Rossi and Correa and Elizalde sat. She didn't know any of them personally but she was acquainted with their mannerisms and their anecdotes through my caricatured versions. She had begun to smoke one of my fags and I had her hand in mine when the phone rang. I lifted the receiver and said: 'Hullo.' Then the phone said: 'Hi, secretary' and apparently everything was the same as before. But in the few seconds during which the call lasted, while I, only half-recovered from the shock, asked mechanically: 'Where on earth have you been all this time?' and the phone replied: 'I went on a trip to Chile,' really nothing was the same. Like the last few minutes of a drowning man's life, there went through my brain a multitude of ideas without order or sense. The first was: 'So the Boss had nothing to do with her' and represented the triumph of dignity. The second was more or less: 'But Doris . . .' and the third, literally: 'How on earth could I have mistaken this voice?'

I explained to the telephone that the Boss was not in, said good-bye, put the receiver back in place. Her hand was still in mine. Then I looked up and I knew what I would find. Sitting on my desk, just like any other chick, Doris waited, smiling, still thinking about her ridiculous little plan. It was, of course, an empty superficial smile, just like anybody else's. I ran the risk of being bored from here to eternity with her. Later on, I would try to find the real reasons; but, meanwhile, in the deepest layer of my consciousness, I put an end once and for all to the misunderstanding. Because I am really in love with the Iriartes.

Translated by Jean Franco

Vinicius de Moraes

CHRISTMAS POEM

For that we were created:
To recall and to be recalled
To weep and to cause to weep
To bury our honoured dead –
Therefore our long arms for farewells
Hands to catch what was given
Fingers to dig the earth.

So this is always our life:
An afternoon to forget
A star ending in darkness
A roadway between two tombs –
Therefore we need to hide
To speak low, to tread soft, to see
Night sleeping in silence.

There is not much to say:
A song about a cradle
A verse, perhaps of love
A prayer by whoever departs –
But do not forget this hour
And by it may our hearts
Be left, sober and guiltless.

Then for that we were created:
For hope in the miracle
For disclosure of poetry
For seeing the face of death –
Suddenly no more shall we wait . . .
Tonight is young; from death
We are scarcely born, immensely.

SONNET ON SEPARATION

Suddenly from laughter grew tears
Gravely silent and white like mist
And mouths united became foam
And hands outstretched grew astonished.

Suddenly from calm issued wind
That extinguished all flame from eyes
And passion became foreboding
And the still moment became drama.

Suddenly, no more than suddenly
One who was sad made himself loving
And from loneliness made himself pleased

The close friend moved in the distance
Life turned to a vagrant adventure
Suddenly, no more than suddenly.

Translated by Ashley Brown

José Donoso

ANA MARÍA

I

'Funny that they should leave a girl as small as that in this huge garden,' thought the old man, wiping the sweat from his face with a handkerchief, which he then put back in the pocket of his torn jacket.

The child was in fact very small. She could scarcely have been three, and was like a particle that floated for a moment and then disappeared, among the trunks of the chestnuts and walnuts, right at the end of the blue perspective thrown by their shade. The old man's eyes searched for the child: the unkempt vegetation seemed to have devoured her. There was a silence peopled only by the hum of insects and the flowing of a drain that wandered through the matted bracken and thickets. Unable to discover her, the man was for a moment disturbed. Soon, however, his eyes found the little figure crouching in a pool of flowers, which assumed a false yellow in a shaft of sunlight that pierced the deepest shadow. Then the old man sighed with relief, muttering: 'Poor little thing!'

He sat down under a willow which shadowed the footway from a corner of the property. With dry twigs he was kindling a tiny fire, on which he put his tea to boil in a small billy-can. He took out a piece of bread, some tomatoes, and an onion, and ate, thinking how funny it was that he hadn't seen the little girl before. He had always thought that this property inside the barbed wire fence was deserted, though sometimes he had thought he saw among the trees at the back, a house, small and unworthy of the site, that looked as if it were a temporary structure. He had inspected the garden on more than one occasion, surprised never to see anyone. Then he had ceased to be surprised.

Every day he came to eat his lunch under the willow and doze for a bit beside this island of greenery, the only vegetation in that quarter. And at two in the afternoon he would return to the building on which he was working, two blocks further along a road on which almost all the sites were parched and still unbuilt on.

The man lay down on his stomach beside the fence. Protected from the harsh midday heat, he listened to the flowing of the drain, and, listening attentively for the lightest rustle of the leaves, watched the garden. In the far distance – perhaps she had sprung up spontaneously as part of the vegetation – he saw the little girl; tiny and almost naked, she was standing beside a huge trunk covered with red roses; the roses seemed to climb over it with a sort of animal vigour. He lay watching her for a while; saw her slip away as she played between two bushes; saw her suddenly disappear; saw an especially heavy shadow blur the whiteness of her little body. Later the man washed his billy-can and after stamping out what remained of the fire, went back to work.

When the day's job was over, the old man did not leave with the group of workmen who went off laughing and swinging the bags that held their working clothes. He hung back with the idea of stopping in front of the garden, to see if he could see the little girl. He did not see her.

At nightfall he sat down to smoke beside the door of the shack in which he lived, on the opposite edge of the city. His wife, squatting in the doorway, was blowing on the brazier on which she was going to put the stewpan as soon as the coals were red. The old man did not know whether to tell her or not. In thirty or more years of marriage, he had never managed to understand what it was possible to say to his wife without annoying her . . . though really for a long time he had been indifferent to his wife's bursts of annoyance. Finally he told her that he had seen a tiny little girl alone in a huge garden.

'Alone?' For a moment the woman's face was softened by a few wrinkles.

'And she was so fair. . . .' added the man softly.

When she caught the tone of his voice, the woman's face resumed its hard, closed look. She blew so hard at the brazier that a trail of sparks flew out into the wretched night. Then she went in to fetch the stewpan, more certain than ever that her husband despised her. This was the long expected moment, no doubt, at which, sick of secretly loathing her failure as a woman, the man would call her 'Mule'. It was what the local wives called her in their pride. Exhausted by the labour of feeding their innumerable children, they always avoided dealings with her, saying that she was bitter and silent. In the course of years she had concealed herself in a cloud of ill-temper and despair, awaiting the moment to retire and give her place to some other woman who would deserve it better. At the beginning, when perhaps they still kept some of their youth, the man was a little sorry for her. But afterwards it was too difficult to get through to her. And as they grew old, such a distance sprang up between them that an almost silent bitterness remained their only tangible and positive link.

That night the woman brusquely served her husband his plate of soup. He spooned it up without thinking this time that it was the same soup as always which in all their years of marriage he had never managed to like. Then they went to bed. The woman habitually stirred and talked so much in her sleep that it was often difficult for the man to doze off. But sometimes she lay tensely wakeful for hours on end, and then she did not move. The night on which the man told her he had seen a tiny girl alone in a huge garden, the woman lay still and silent as if waiting for something.

Every day, at the lunch hour, the man lay down on the footway in the shade of the willow, beside the fence and watching the garden. Sometimes he caught sight of the little girl in the distance, always alone, almost naked, and floating in that island of green light. But at other times he missed her because he fell asleep, for he was weak and old, and the heat and the day's work tired him. As he had no one else to discuss it with, he several times said something about the little girl to his wife, whose spirits gradually recovered until there was not even any bitterness between them.

One day the man woke up with a start beneath the willow. He carefully observed the overgrown garden; there was no one. But suddenly, behind the fence, where the shade of a bush fell heaviest, he saw two large eyes, deep and bright, looking fixedly at him out of the darkness. Fear shook him briskly awake.

It was the little girl's eyes. Her body had half disappeared in the green reflections of the leaves. Ashamed as if he had done something wrong in sleeping under someone else's willow, the man began to get on his feet to walk away. But before he could do so, the child had come up to the fence and exclaimed: 'My love!'

All the amazement that lay unexpended in the old man burst out in a smile.

'Bootiful!'

The little girl's eyes were so clear and bright that they seemed to glow in the little face surrounded with a mop of fair hair. Both stayed still, looking at one another. Then the man asked: 'What's your name, little miss?'

She did not understand immediately and the man had to repeat his question. This time the girl answered with a smile: 'Ana María.'

Unable to resist, the old man put one hand through the wire to caress Ana María's hair. She became serious and seemed to reflect. Then, with a laugh, she looked straight into his eyes which swam with amazement and showed him a shoebag that she carried dangling from her arm.

'A han'bag ... a 'ittle han'bag!' the child exclaimed.

'It's a pretty bag you've got, little missy!'

'Bootiful! And you're bootiful too, my love!'

And leaving the fence, almost vanishing in the shadows of the leaves, she waved her hand to bid the old man good-bye.

'Poor little thing!' said the man to himself.

That night he told his wife that the little girl's name was Ana María. He did not tell her any more. But the woman's body bent savagely humiliated over the fire on which she was boiling the clothes. Later she told her husband that there was nothing to eat that night. But this was something the old man was used to, and he went to bed early, because one does not feel hungry when asleep. The woman went to bed in silence and lay down quietly beside him.

II

In the house at the end of the garden Ana María's father and mother lay side by side on the narrow rumpled bed. The fictional underwater light that seeped through the closed green shutters fell on their bodies which shone with sweat, and flooded the small bedroom. A persistent buzz of flies and horse-flies kept the air athrob, an air moist with the smell of exhausted bodies, cigarettes and foul sheets.

The man hardly moved. He passed a hand over his chest and belly to dry the sweat, and as he wiped his palm on the dirty pillow, screwed up his face in disgust without opening his eyes. Then he slowly opened them a little as if the sweat were too heavy on his lids, and turned on his side to observe his wife's body. It was beautiful; white and beautiful. Too large and fleshy perhaps, but beautiful, and where it touched the sheet its contours were emphasized by a fold of heavy, generous flesh. The man knew that she was only half asleep. On her white flesh where her neck joined her breast, he saw one of his own black, strong, curly hairs embedded. He removed it slowly, leaving a slight reddish furrow in her skin, which gradually paled. Then with sensual relish he killed several very frail green insects that had come in from the overgrown garden where everything bred, and settled on his wife's skin. There was one almost invisible in her armpit, that he had noticed because she was sleeping with her arms crossed under her head; he squashed it with a deliberate pressure. The woman smiled. He stroked the hair in her armpit, the underside of her arm, which was even whiter than the rest of her body. The woman turned towards the man and they lay embraced.

Then they dozed for a while, until opening his eyes wide the man exclaimed: 'It's two in the afternoon. I'm hungry!'

The woman stretched, murmuring in the midst of a yawn: 'I don't think there's anything to eat. . . .'

The pair yawned together.

'I saw some eggs.'

'I gave the kid eggs this morning.'

'Bah! What's it matter?' said the man turning in the bed and going to sleep with one leg resting on his wife's thigh.

She threw off the weight, sitting up a little as she did so and leaving a sweat stain on the sheet. She propped herself on her husband's hard back and her fingers played with the muscles of his shoulders. But no. Suddenly remembering, she pulled herself together. She took a comb which she found on the floor beside the bed, next to a shell full of half smoked cigarettes, and with a deft movement gathered up her damp hair at the nape of her neck. Then she stuck her feet in her dirty, white high-heeled shoes and walked naked into the kitchen.

In fact there were only eggs in the refrigerator. On seeing the dirty plates from the morning's breakfast and last night's supper, she shrugged her shoulders and got out clean ones so as not to have to wash the others. While she was cooking, she put on the radio, a programme of noisy dance tunes. She beat time to the music with the high heel of her shoe. She swayed her naked body as she scrambled the eggs.

'Now you've woken me up with your music,' shouted the man from the bedroom.

'Bah! You've slept long enough!'

The man got up, and began to do exercises in front of the long mirror. Between one movement and the next he asked: 'Say, what can have become of the kid?'

'She's somewhere around,' replied the woman. 'She knows she mustn't be a nuisance because it's Sunday.'

'She's too small to know it's Sunday.'

'But she knows she mustn't be a nuisance when you're at home.'

The woman served a plate for her husband and one for her daughter. She put her own portion in a cup because she could not find another clean plate or make up her mind to wash the others. She put on a dressing-gown, and her husband put on pants. Then when she'd shouted to Ana María through the house door, the three of them sat down at the little table in the living-room where they generally ate.

When Ana María saw the eggs, she said: 'Don't want.'

But they didn't listen because they were laughing at the jokes in a picture paper. Afterwards the woman noticed that Ana María had not eaten and that she was looking at them with her enormous bright translucent eyes. She felt uncomfortable, and said to her sharply : 'Eat up !'

Ana María looked at the eggs and said once more : 'Don't want.'

'Take some bread then and go away.'

Ana María went.

'Did she eat this morning ?' asked the man.

'Yes I think so. I was half dopey, so I didn't really notice.'

'Dopey ? And why ?'

'You're not going to ask me why after all last night, are you ? Don't be so stupid.' They laughed.

'Give the dishes a rinse.'

'Not much ! Do you think I married you to be the servant for you and the kid ?' Leaving everything in the same mess as before they went back to the bedroom. After a few moments' ambiguous play and dozing, the man suggested : 'Say, shall we go to the pictures tonight ?'

'All right. But we'll have to put the kid to sleep first and lock up.'

'All right . . . just as usual.'

'Yes. But she's so queer I don't know what might happen. Haven't you noticed ? Sometimes I find her . . . I dunno . . . she seems to . . . frighten me. The other night you know, when we came back from the pictures she was awake. She was only pretending to be asleep, and it must have been something like one o'clock in the morning.'

'Well, what's odd about that ?'

'I dunno, she's so little.'

'Don't be silly. What's it matter ? She's got the whole day to sleep if she wants to.'

'She's always been rather strange. I think she's a bit backward in her talking. The only thing she likes to play with, you know, is the bag I keep her shoes in. I don't know what she finds so wonderful about it. Her han'bag she calls it.'

'Mm, she's strange.'

'And a bit tiresome too sometimes when she stares at me with those eyes of hers. Like an animal's eyes they are. Only the other day, when I was asleep in the deckchair in the garden, you know how sleepy the heat makes me . . .'

'Only sleepy?'

Laughing, the woman stroked the damp hair on her husband's chest.

'Well, I'd just gone off to sleep when I woke up suddenly. The first thing I saw, a little way away, in the shadow of that lilac bush, was the kid. Or rather the kid's eyes looking at me in a daft sort of way from the shadows. When she noticed that I was awake, she ran away.'

'Bah ! Don't be so silly. What's important about that?'

'I don't know, but it's odd. And yesterday. She'd been hanging around me all the morning wanting me to pick her up or something, though she didn't say anything or come up close. But I didn't want to do anything at all, I was sort of tired, I dunno.'

'Aren't you always tired, lazy?'

'So in the end I picked her up. Then she began to cuddle me and laugh and make a fuss of me in such a sickly way that . . . I dunno . . . it made me feel sort of frightened or disgusted. Though sometimes she's such a pet. But she went on calling me "My love" and "Bootiful", you know, the first words she learnt to say, goodness knows where because you never call me that.'

'Never? What?'

'No. Never.'

'But I call you better names.'

'Yes, but not those. Well, she was making such a fuss of me when she suddenly gave me a fright. D'you know what she did?'

'No.'

'She bit my ear.'

The man burst out laughing.

'Bit your ear? And how did the little devil know you like it?'

'Don't be silly, not like that. Stop laughing. She didn't bite my ear gently. She gave it a fierce bite as if she wanted to bite it off with those sharp little teeth of hers. It hurt so much that I shouted and dropped her. And she went running off as fast as she could go, as if she knew she'd done something naughty. That was in the morning. She didn't come back for lunch, nor for the rest of the day. And as you know it depresses me to go down the garden, among all those trees, I didn't go and look for her. But when she came back at night, with a scared look on her face, I punished her.'

'What did you do to her?'

'I don't know. How should I remember?'

The man burst out laughing again, this time at a joke in the illustrated paper that he was leafing through during their conversation. He felt the whole rather moist shape of his wife's body beside his own. They smoked, and one of them went to turn on the wireless for some music. The green light of the shutters and the garden began to fade.

III

The old man went on going there every day to eat his lunch under the willow. Now he did not have to search the garden because the little girl was always waiting for him beside the fence. Somehow she seemed to guess the time, and if the man came late, she would look at him rather sternly. But soon she would smile at him and murmur: 'My love. Bootiful.'

The old man plucked up courage and lifted Ana María over the fence to sit down beside him. He let her light the fire to warm the tea. Then he ate his bread, occasionally a slice of meat, and onions and tomatoes, sharing his food with her, for she always seemed hungry.

A workman from the building site once surprised the old man talking to Ana María, and from that time his mates never gave him a moment's peace.

'How's your girlfriend, buffer, eh? The old boy's in love.'

He bore their laughter patiently. As he pushed his barrow-load of clay his legs were so tottery with age that they scarcely supported him. He almost fell on his way down the plank. His eyes were clouded with soil and sweat, and he could hardly see the young workers who threw scurrilities at him from the scaffolding: 'Listen here, you old devil, you take good care or they'll shove you in jail!'

And thinking of what Ana María had said to him at lunchtime, he flushed beneath the grime.

The girl had sat down beside him in the shade, and suddenly opened her eternal bag to show him a pair of shoes.

'Shoe-shoes! Pretty tootsies?'

She also had in the bag a creased shiny ribbon. With clumsy hands the old man tied it round the little girl's fair hair, and she proudly felt the bow of blue ribbon. The child showed him other things too, a dice, a box of medicines, a matchbox, the broken head of a doll. She took this out of the bag last as if she did not want her friend to see it, as if not wishing to see it herself. It had fair hair, chubby cheeks, and a sensual self-satisfied expression.

'And this? What's this, little missy?'

Ana María's eyes suddenly brimmed with tears, which did not fall but stayed there, magnifying them hugely.

'Bad,' muttered the child.

'Why?'

Then she shook the broken doll roughly, exclaiming: 'Bad, bad, bad!' And she threw it into the tangled garden. At that moment the tears overflowed her eyes, and she stood motionless, looking at the old man with streaming cheeks and moist lashes.

The old man took Ana María in his arms, cradling her head on his shoulder till her silent tears subsided. He washed them away with his own handkerchief. Then stroking his wrinkled and unshaven face with her tiny hand, the child said: 'Bootiful . . . my bootiful love.' Later the man walked away happy.

In the evenings, smoking in the doorway of his shack, he watched the darkness fall on the makeshift roofs of the shantytown. Then he thought of that tiny little girl alone in the huge garden. He made no plans, he remembered no happenings, but opened himself entirely, allowing Ana María's presence to engulf him. And his wife watched him, almost without looking at him, certain that her moment was now coming to go away and yield her place to another.

Time passed and the building on which the old man worked was finished. The workmen were dismissed and soon found new jobs, but nobody was willing to employ anyone so frail as the old man.

He realized the situation without anxiety. But it worried him to think of Ana María waiting for him behind the wire fence on the opposite side of the city, waiting to chat with him and for him to give her bread and onions. The old woman was a laundress and on her work they kept themselves alive. Though her silence began to acquire an almost solid consistency, the old man was sure that she would never throw his idleness in his face. But the woman said nothing because she had no right to anything. She merely watched him sitting in the doorway of the shack thinking, morning, noon and evening. His hands resting slackly one on each knee and faintly smiling, he seemed to be counting the seconds in every hour. The old man's lips moved imperceptibly :

'Poor little thing !' the woman read on them, and in those words said for another she found her own condemnation.

Nevertheless the man went to see the little girl two or three times. He stole a hunk of bread from his wife and set out very early in the morning, muttering between his teeth that he was going off to look for work. The woman knew that this was not true.

The old man walked slowly, resting every now and then beside a tree in the park, and picking up the page of a newspaper to read while he rested. When he felt refreshed, he slowly resumed his way till he had crossed the whole city and reached the garden where Ana María was waiting for him, at the time when he had once eaten his lunch under the willow.

The first thing that the old man saw was those deep eyes, shining stealthily among the branches. When she saw him come, the little girl came forward excitedly for her friend to lift her over the fence. Then as they ate and talked under the willow, it was as if nothing in the world could disturb them.

The woman could bear the situation no longer. The little that remained to her of a world that had never been generous and that the years had gradually whittled away, finally collapsed. She spent the days working fiercely and hard, to kill in herself anything that she might dare to feel. But before completely surrendering to the inevitable, some hidden coals of energy drove her to a decision.

One sunny day she bought a bag of sweets and, taking a bus,

made her way to the garden beside the building site, where the little girl lived. She sat herself down under the willow. The garden was certainly huge and green, cool, deep and rich with foliage. Beside her in the shade were the black traces of the bonfires on which her husband had boiled his tea. She sat down to wait.

Suddenly she spied in the distance the little girl splashing in the drain, her white body smudged with the reflections of the water. Terror, and hatred dumbly gripped her heart at the sight. She got up and went to the barbed wire fence so that Ana María should see her from over there and come to her.

But Ana María did not look at her. She came out of the water, nevertheless, and little by little skirting the brambles and thickets, though the woman could not follow her, approached the willow. But she kept herself concealed a little way off.

Then the woman caught sight of those deep blue eyes, looking harshly at her from the shadows, catching her in their hostile light. With a final effort the woman from somewhere in herself squeezed a smile. But the little girl stayed quietly behind the thicket, looking at her.

The woman began to weaken. It had all come to nothing. Everything always did come to nothing. As a last resort, she showed her the sweets and said: 'Would you like a sweet, little miss?'

The little girl shook her head. The woman went on trying: 'They're very good.'

'Don't want,' answered Ana María.

Finally the woman's face fell into lines of failure and despair. It was like a mask. She turned to go, and at this moment the little girl came some paces nearer.

'Bad, bad, bad!' she called, staring at her. And the woman rushed away defeated.

When she got home she told her husband that a family for whom she washed had asked her to come and work for them indoors. She could be sure of food and a roof. What was more, a neighbour wanted to take over the shack they lived in. She was going off next morning. Silence fell. Then the old man thought he heard his wife ask from the corner of the room: 'And you? What are you going to do?'

'I don't know,' he answered aloud. And the woman looked at him in surprise.

It was a month since the man had seen the little girl. He was so old, and wearier every hour, that it was almost impossible for him to walk to the opposite side of the city.

But next day, when his wife had ceased to exist, he went to say good-bye to the little girl. What came afterwards did not matter. Perhaps the best thing would be to go to some deserted spot, to a hill perhaps, and wait for night, to die. He was certain that he had only to curl up on the ground and want it, and death would come.

Next morning he took the last hunk of bread and went more slowly than ever to the garden. And, as on the first occasion, he was struck with astonishment at the sight of such a tiny girl in such a huge garden.

'Poor little thing !' he said to himself.

'My love !' murmured the child on seeing him.

He lifted her over the wire, and Ana María kissed him, throwing her arms around him and laughing.

'My pretty little miss !' exclaimed the old man again and again, stroking her with his dark hands.

'And your little handbag,' he muttered a few minutes later.

Ana María's face suddenly darkened. She shrugged her shoulders and said : 'No. Not got it.'

They stayed a long time together in the shade of the willow, till the old man thought it was time to go. He lifted her over the fence and, stroking her fair head between the wire, murmured : 'Good-bye, little miss.'

She looked at him in surprise, as if she understood everything.

'No, no, my love, no !' she said, her eyes growing large with tears.

'Good-bye,' he repeated.

Ana María took a firm hold of the man's hand. But suddenly, as if an idea had struck her, she smiled. Her tears dried and she said: 'Wait, wait . . . Little bag.'

The man saw his small friend disappear among the vegetation, as if this was the last time he would see so small a child running alone among the trunks and thickets of such an enormous garden.

Ana María opened the house door and went into the living-room, muttering: 'Bag . . . bag,' and looking for it in the kitchen, in the living-room itself and in the cupboard. But she did not find it.

Before going into her parents' room she hesitated for a moment. She pushed the door. In the green light, humming with insects, the pair brusquely broke their embrace. Ashamed and furious, they half covered themselves with the sheet on seeing the child. The woman's eyes stopped her daughter at the door.

'You stupid kid !' she screamed, half getting up.

Her hair was in disorder. She covered herself with the corner of the sheet.

'Didn't we tell you not to bother us?' shouted the man.

'Bag,' murmured Ana María, searching for it with her eyes all over the room which was heavy with the smell of her parents being alone together.

'I've told you I don't want you to play with that bag. You'll only lose it. Now off with you !'

'Oh, give her the bag and then we'll be rid of her,' muttered the man, stretching the sheet to cover his body.

'There it is, on the chair . . . Now, off with you !'

The child seized the bag and ran out without looking at her parents, who sank back into bed, relieved but uncomfortable.

Ana María ran across the garden. She jumped or rather flew across the drain, passing beneath the circles of floating light that pierced the trees and made everything indistinct. The old man was waiting for her beside the wire. The child cried : 'Upsy ! upsy !' The old man picked her up and put her down beside him. He was trembling a little because he was very old and knew what was going to happen though he did not know much. Ana María sat down on the ground beside him and took the shoes out of the bag.

'Shoe-shoes. Put them on tootsies,' she asked the old man.

He knelt down to put on her shoes with his clumsy hands. Then they stood up under the willow, the bent and dark old man beside the little girl with the bag over her arm. He looked at her as if expecting something. Then Ana María smiled at him as in their happy times, from the depths of her sparkling blue eyes :

'My love,' she said.

And taking the old man's hand she led him out of the shade of the willow into the harsh midday heat of summer. She guided him, taking him with her, and saying: 'Let's go . . . Let's go.'

The old man followed her.

Translated by J. M. Cohen

João Cabral de Melo Neto

From 'THE DEATH AND LIFE OF A SEVERINO'

A Pernambuco Christmas Play, 1954-5

I

THE 'RETIRANTE' EXPLAINS TO THE READER WHO HE
IS AND WHAT HE DOES

– My name is Severino,
I have no Christian name.
There are lots of Severinos
(a saint of pilgrimages)
so they began to call me
Maria's Severino.
There are lots of Severinos
with mothers called Maria,
so I became Maria's
of Zacarias, deceased.
But still this doesn't tell much:
there are many in the parish
because of a certain colonel[1]
whose name was Zacarias
who was the very earliest
senhor of this region.
Then how explain who's speaking
to Your Excellencies?
Let's see: the Severino
of Maria of Zacarias,
from the Mountain of the Rib,
at the end of Paraiba.
But still this doesn't mean much.

1. 'Colonel' means any big land-owner.

There were at least five more
with the name of Severino,
sons of so many Marias,
wives of so many other
Zacariases, deceased,
living on the same thin,
bony mountain where I lived.
There are lots of Severinos;
we are exactly alike:
exactly the same big head
that's hard to balance properly,
the same swollen belly
on the same skinny legs,
alike because the blood
we use has little colour.
And if we Severinos
are all the same in life,
we die the same death,
the same Severino death.
The death of those who die
of old age before thirty,
of an ambuscade before twenty,
of hunger a little daily.
(The Severino death
from sickness and from hunger
attacks at any age,
even the unborn child.)
We are many Severinos
and our destiny's the same:
to soften up these stones
by sweating over them,
to try to bring to life
a dead and deader land,
to try to wrest a farm
out of burnt-over land.
But, so that Your Excellencies
can recognize me better

and be able to follow better
the story of my life,
I'll be the Severino
you'll now see emigrate.

II

HE MEETS TWO MEN CARRYING A CORPSE IN A
HAMMOCK AND CRYING 'BROTHERS OF SOULS!
BROTHERS OF SOULS! I DIDN'T KILL HIM, NOT I!'[1]

– Whom are you carrying,
    brothers of souls,
  wrapped in that hammock?
    kindly inform me.
– A defunct nobody,
    brother of souls,
  travelling long hours to
    his resting place.
– Do you know who he was,
    brothers of souls?
  Do you know what his name is,
    or what it was?
– Severino Farmer,
    brother of souls,
  Severino Farmer,
    farming no more.
– From where do you bring him,
    brothers of souls?
  Where did you start out
    on your long journey?
– From the driest of lands,
    brother of souls,
  from the land where not even
    wild plants will grow.

1. The 'brother of souls' refrain refers to a religious sect in the north of
Brazil – one of whose duties is the burial of pauper dead.

– Did he die of this death,
    brothers of souls,
  was it this death he died of,
    or was he killed?
– It wasn't that death,
    brother of souls,
  it was death by killing,
    in ambuscade.
– And who hid in ambush,
    brothers of souls?
  And with what did they kill him,
    a knife or a bullet?
– This was a bullet death,
    brother of souls.
  A bullet's more certain
    (it goes in deeper).
– And who was it ambushed him,
    brothers of souls,
  who let this bullet bird
    out, to harm him?
– That's hard to answer,
    brother of souls,
  there's always a bullet
    idle and flying.
– But what had he done,
    brothers of souls,
  what had he done,
    to harm such a bird?
– He owned a few acres,
    brother of souls,
  of stone and leeched sand
    he cultivated.
– But did he have fields,
    brothers of souls,
  how could he plant
    on the barren rock?

– In the thin lips of sand,
  brother of souls,
 in the stones' intervals,
  he planted straw.
– And was his farm big,
  brothers of souls,
 was his farm so big
  that they coveted it?
– He had only two acres,
  brother of souls,
 on the mountain's shoulder,
  and neither one level.
– Then why did they kill him,
  brothers of souls,
 why did they kill him
  with a shotgun?
– It wanted to spread itself,
  brother of souls,
 this bullet bird wanted
  to fly more freely.
– And now what will happen,
  brothers of souls,
 will measures be taken
  against that gun?
– It has more space to fly in,
  brother of souls,
 more space and more bullets
  to teach to fly.
– And where will you bury him,
  brothers of souls,
 with the seed still in him,
  the seed of lead?
– In the graveyard of Torres,
  brother of souls,
 (now Toritama)
  at break of day.
– And can I help you,

brothers of souls,
since I pass Toritama,
it's on my way.
– Yes, you can help us,
brother of souls,
it's a brother of souls
who hears our call.
And then go back,
brother of souls,
you can go back
from there to your home.
– I'll go back; it's far,
brothers of souls,
it's a long day's march
and the mountain is high.
The defunct is luckier,
brothers of souls,
since he won't be going
the long way back.
– Toritama is near,
brother of souls,
we'll reach holy ground
by break of day.
– Let's go while it's night,
brothers of souls,
for the dead's best shroud
is a starless night.

XIV

(A *child has just been born*)

NEIGHBOURS, FRIENDS, TWO GIPSIES, ET AL. ARRIVE
AND STAND TALKING IN THE DOORWAY OF THE MAN'S
HOUSE

– All the heaven and earth
are singing in his praise.

It was for him the tide
didn't go out tonight.
– It was for him the tide
made its motor stop.
The mud stayed covered up
and the stench didn't rise.
– And Sargasso lavender,
acid and disinfectant,
came to sweep our streets,
sent from the distant sea.
– And the sponge-dry tongue
of wind from the interior
came to suck the moisture
out of the stagnant puddle.
– All the heaven and earth
are singing in his praise.
And every house becomes
an inviting refuge.
– Every hut becomes
the kind of ideal refuge
highly thought of by
the sociologists.
– The orchestra of mosquitoes
that broadcasts every night,
because of him, I think,
is off the air tonight.
– And this river, always blind,
opaque from eating dirt,
that never reflects the sky,
has adorned itself with stars.

Translated by Elizabeth Bishop

Juan Rulfo

THEY GAVE US THE LAND

After walking for so long without seeing the shadow of a tree nor the seed of a tree, nor the root of anything, we hear dogs barking.

Half-way along this featureless road, we thought at times that we would find nothing beyond, nothing at the end of this flat plain split by cracks and dry rivulets. But there is something after all. There is a village. We hear dogs barking and sniff the smell of smoke in the air and savour this scent of people as if it offered hope.

But the village is still far ahead. It is the wind that brings it nearer.

We have been walking since dawn. Now it is about four in the afternoon. Someone peers up at the sky and opens his eyes wide towards where the sun hangs motionless and he says:

'It's around four o'clock.'

This someone is Melitón. With him are Faustino, Esteban and myself. There are four of us. I count: two in front, two more behind. I look behind and see nobody. Then I say to myself: 'There are four of us.' Some time ago, around eleven, there were twenty odd; but they dropped away a few at a time until only our little group remains.

Faustino says:

'Maybe it'll rain.'

We all raise our heads and look at a heavy, black cloud passing over us. And we think: 'Maybe it will.'

We don't say what we are thinking. Some time ago, we lost the urge to talk. We lost it with the heat. You'd willingly talk anywhere else, but here it's hard work. Here, when you talk, the words warm up with the heat from outside and they dry on your tongue and end up as a gasp. Here things are like that. That's why no one feels like talking.

A big, fat drop of water falls making a hole in the ground, leaving a paste like that of spittle. It's the only one that falls. We hope that more will follow and our eyes search for them. But there are no more. It is not raining. Now if we look at the sky, we see the rain cloud racing off far away at full speed. The wind from the village meets it and pushes it against the blue shadows of the hills. And the drop which fell by mistake is eaten up by the land and disappears in its thirst.

Who the hell made such a great plain? What's it all for, eh?

We have started walking again; we had stopped to watch it raining. It didn't rain. Now we start walking again. And it occurs to me that we have walked further than the distance we have covered. This occurs to me. If it had rained, perhaps other things would have occurred to me. Even so, I know that since I was a kid, I have never seen it raining on the plain, not what you'd really call raining.

No, the plain is not a useful thing. There are no rabbits or birds. There isn't anything. Except for a few miserable thorn trees, and an occasional little patch of coarse grass with dried-up blades; apart from this, there isn't anything.

And here we are. The four of us on foot. Previously, we went on horseback and we had rifles slung over our shoulders. Now we aren't even carrying rifles.

I have always thought that they did right when they took away our rifles. In these parts, it is dangerous to go around armed. They kill you without warning when they see you with your 30-bore always tied to the straps. But horses are a different matter. If we'd been on horseback, we would already have tasted the green water of the river and we would have paraded our full stomachs through the village streets in order to get our dinner down. We would already have done this, if we had had all those horses that we used to have. But they took our horses as well, along with our rifles.

I turn round and look at the plain. Such a great stretch of land for nothing. Your eyes slip when they meet nothing to stop them. Only a few lizards put their heads out of the tops of their holes and as soon as they feel the baking sun run to hide themselves in the thin shade of a stone. But what about us when we have to work here? How are we going to cool ourselves from the heat of the sun? Why did they give us this dead scab on which to sow our seed?

They told us:

'From here to the village belongs to you.'

We ask:

'The plain?'

'Yes, the plain. The whole of the Great Plain.'

We have it on the tips of our tongues to say that the plain was not what we wanted. What we wanted was near the river. On the other side of the river, along the meadows where there are those trees called casuarinas and grass and good land. Not this hard cowhide which is called the Plain.

But they didn't let us have our say. The delegate hadn't come to chat with us. He put the papers in our hands and said:

'Don't get a shock at having such a lot of land all to yourselves.'

'But the plain, sir . . .'

'There are thousands and thousands of acres.'

'But there's no water. There isn't even enough water to fill your mouth.'

'What about rainstorms? Nobody said you were going to be given irrigated lands. As soon as it rains there, the corn will come up as if it had been stretched.'

'But, sir, the land is hard and eroded. We don't think that the plough will sink into that rock of a land you get on the plain. You would have to make holes with a hoe to sow the seed and even then it's not certain that anything will grow; neither corn nor anything else will grow.'

'Put that in writing. And now go away. It's the big estates you should be attacking, not the Government that has given you the land.'

'Wait, sir. We haven't said anything against the Government. It's all against the plain. You can't fight against what you can't do anything about. That is what we said. . . . Wait while we explain. Look, let's begin again at the beginning. . . .'

But he didn't want to listen to us.

So they gave us this land. And on this hot earthenware dish, they want us to sow seeds of something to see if something germinates and grows. But nothing will grow here. Not even vultures. You see them up there, now and then, flying very high up at top speed, trying to get away as quickly as possible from this white, hardened rocky earth where nothing moves and where you walk as if you were slipping backwards.

Melitón says:

'This is the land they gave us.'

Faustino says:

'What?'

I don't say anything. I think: 'Melitón isn't thinking straight. It must be the heat that makes him talk like this. The heat has gone through his hat and warmed his head. Otherwise, why does he say what he says? What land have they given us, Melitón? There isn't enough here for the wind to play at raising eddies with.'

Melitón is talking again:

'It'll do for something. It might even do for exercising mares.'

'What mares?' Esteban asks him.

I hadn't noticed Esteban very closely. Now that he is speaking, I notice him. He is wearing a jacket that reaches his belly and below the jacket there appears the head of something that looks like a hen.

'Listen, 'Teban, where did you swipe that hen?'

'She's mine!' he says.

'You weren't carrying her before. Where did you buy her, eh?'

'I didn't buy her. She's the hen from my own yard.'

'Then you brought her for food, didn't you?'

'No, I brought her to look after her. I left my house empty and there was no one to feed her. I always carry her with me when I have to go far.'

'She's going to suffocate under there. You'd better take her out into the air.'

He tucks her under his arm and blows warm air into her mouth. Then he says:

'We're nearly at the ravine.'

I no longer hear what Esteban is saying. We have formed into a single file in order to descend the ravine and he is right in front.

You can see that he is holding the hen by its feet and he swings it from side to side all the time so as not to hit its head against the stones.

The lower we go down, the better the land is. Dust rises from us as if we were a string of mules going down there, but we like covering ourselves in dust. We like it. After eleven hours' journey, treading the hardness of the plain, we feel completely in our element wrapped in that stuff that leaps on to us and tastes of land.

Above the river, over the green tops of the casuarinas, fly flocks of green chachalachas.[1] That too is what we like.

Now we hear the barking of dogs right here, near us, and it's because the wind from the village bounces against the ravine and fills it with all its sounds.

Esteban again holds his hen in his arms as we approach the first houses. He unties its legs to get the numbness out of them and then he and his hen disappear behind some mezquite trees.

'Here's where I pull in !' Esteban says to us.

We go further on towards the middle of the village.

The land they gave us is back there.

Translated by Jean Franco

1. A type of wild fowl native to Mexico.

Jaime Sabines

LIKE CRABS

Like those wounded crabs
that leave their claws on the beach,
so I get rid of my desires,
bite and cut my arms,
prune my days,
dissolve my hope,
destroy myself.
I am on the point of tears.

Where did I lose myself, at what moment
did I come to inhabit my house,
so like myself that even my children take me for their father
and my wife says the usual things to me?

I gather myself piece by piece,
at intervals from the dust-heap of memory,
and try to reconstruct myself,
to make myself like my image.
Nothing, alas, remains !
The dishes slip broken from my hands,
the chairlegs, the soiled pants,
the bones I dug up
and the portraits that show me loves and phantoms.

Take pity on me !
I want to ask someone for pity.
I am going to ask the first person I meet for forgiveness.
I am a stone rolling
because night is on the slope and no one can see the end.

My stomach and my soul ache
and my whole body is waiting in fear
for a kind hand to throw a sheet over me.

I HAVE SEEN THEM IN THE PICTURES

I have seen them in the pictures,
outside theatres,
in trams and parks,
their fingers and eyes glued together.
In the dark cinemas the girls
offer their breasts to hands,
and open their mouths to the moist kiss
and open their thighs to invisible satyrs.
I have seen them living by anticipation, guessing
the enjoyment concealed by clothes, the illusion
of a tender word of desire,
each strange to the other.
It is the flower that blooms
through the longest day,
the art that hopes,
that trembles like a blind man at an omen.
That girl I saw today was just fourteen,
beside her her parents watched her laughter
as if she had stolen it from them.
I have seen them often
– them, the lovers
in doorways at night,
on pavements, on the grass, under a tree
meeting in the flesh,
sealing one another with their lips.
And I have seen the black sky
in which there are not even birds,
and steel structures
and poor houses and yards,

forgotten places.
And faithful, trembling,
they entrust themselves to one another,
and love smiles to itself, moves them, teaches them,
like an old grandfather who has lost his illusions.

Translated by J. M. Cohen

Gabriel García Márquez

THE DAY AFTER SATURDAY

The trouble began in July when Señora Rebeca, an embittered widow who lived in an enormous house with two corridors and nine bedrooms discovered that her wire screens were broken as if they had been stoned from the street. She first discovered this in her bedroom and thought that she ought to mention it to her maid, Argenida, who had acted as her confidante since her husband's death. Later on, when she was sorting out odds and ends (for some time Señora Rebeca had done nothing except sort out odds and ends), she noticed that not only the screens of her bedroom but those of the whole house were damaged. The widow had a rigid respect for authority, inherited from her paternal great-grandfather, a creole who had fought on the royalist side during the War of Independence and who had afterwards made an arduous journey to Spain with the sole purpose of visiting the palace built by Charles II in Saint Ildefonso. So that when she discovered the state of the other wire screens, she no longer thought of mentioning it to Argenida but put on her straw hat with velvet flowers and made for the Town Hall to inform the Mayor of the offence. When she arrived there however, she saw that the Mayor himself, hairy, with no shirt on and with what she considered to be brutal strength, was engaged in repairing the municipal wire screens which were damaged like her own.

Señora Rebeca burst into the dingy, untidy office and the first thing that she saw was a heap of dead birds on the writing-desk. But she was dazed partly by the heat and partly by her indignation at the destruction of the screens. So that she had no time to be shocked at the unusual spectacle of dead birds on the desk. She was not even scandalized by the sight of the degraded authority on top of the ladder, repairing the metal mesh of the window with a roll of wire and a screw-driver. She was not at that moment thinking of anyone else's dignity but her own, which had been exposed to ridicule because of the wire screens; and her dazed condition even prevented her from connecting the windows of her house with those of the Town Hall. She installed herself with discreet solemnity two paces from the door on the inside of the office and, leaning on the long, ornate handle of her parasol, said:

'I have to register a complaint.'

From the top of the ladder, the Mayor turned a face which was bloated by the heat. He showed no surprise at the unaccustomed presence of the widow in his office. With surly nonchalance, he went on unfastening the damaged mesh and asked from above:

'What is it?'

'That the neighbourhood boys have broken my wire screens.'

Then the Mayor looked at her. He examined her carefully from the pretty velvet flowers to her shoes which were the colour of old silver and it was as if he were seeing her for the first time in his life. He came carefully down, without ceasing to look at her and when he reached solid earth, he put a hand on his waist and motioning his screw-driver towards the desk, said:

'It isn't the boys, Señora. It's the birds.'

And it was then that she connected the dead birds on the desk with the man on top of the ladder and with the damaged screens in her bedrooms. She trembled imagining that all the bedrooms of her house were full of dead birds.

'The birds,' she exclaimed.

'The birds,' the Mayor confirmed. 'It's odd that you shouldn't have noticed that for three days we have had this trouble with birds breaking windows and dying inside the houses.'

When she left the Town Hall, Señora Rebeca felt embarrassed; and rather resentful against Argenida who dragged all the village rumours into her house and had never mentioned the birds. Dazzled by the brilliance of an impending August, she put up her parasol and as she walked along the burning, deserted street, she had the impression that all the rooms of her house gave out a strong, penetrating stink of dead birds.

This was during the last days of July and never in the existence of the village had it been so hot. But the inhabitants, alarmed by the deaths among the birds, were not conscious of this. Although the strange phenomenon had not seriously interfered with village activities, by the beginning of August the majority of people were preoccupied by it; a majority among whom was not numbered Reverend Antonio Isabel of the Most Holy Sacrament of the Altar, the mild parish priest who at the age of ninety-four declared that he had seen the devil on three occasions and who, nevertheless, had only seen two dead birds without attributing the slightest importance to them. He found the first one on a Tuesday in the sacristy after mass and he thought that it had been dragged to the spot by some neighbourhood cat. The other he found on Wednesday in the corridor of the presbytery and he pushed it with the tip of his boot into the street, thinking: 'Cats oughtn't to exist.'

But on Friday, when he arrived at the station, he found a third bird dead on the bench on which he had chosen to sit. It was like a sudden inner flash when he picked up the corpse by its little feet, raised it to the level of his eyes, turned it over, examined it and thought in sudden terror: 'Gracious, that's the third one that I've found this week.'

From that moment, he began to be aware of what was happening, though in an indistinct manner, because Father Antonio Isabel, partly because of his age, and partly because he had declared that he had seen the devil on three separate occasions (a thing which the village found a little crazy), was regarded by his congregation as a good, peaceful and obliging man who was, however, always in the clouds. So he became aware that something was happening to the birds, but even then he did not believe it to be worth a sermon. He was the first to notice the smell. He noticed it one Friday night when he awoke in alarm, his light sleep disturbed by a nauseating stink; but he did not know whether to attribute it to a nightmare or to a new and original Satanic method of disturbing his sleep. He sniffed about and turned in his bed, thinking that this experience might come in useful for a sermon. It could be a dramatic sermon, he thought, on Satan's skill at penetrating the human heart through any one of the five senses.

He heard the dead birds mentioned for the first time as he was passing through the church porch on the following day before mass. He was thinking about his sermon, about Satan and about the sins which can be committed through the sense of smell, when he heard someone saying that the bad smell at night came from the dead birds collected during the week; and a confused jumble of evangelical prophecies, bad smells and dead birds formed in his mind. So that on Sunday, he had to improvise a sermon on charity which he himself did not understand very clearly and he forgot for ever the connexion between the devil and the five senses.

However, those experiences must have remained lurking in some remote corner of his mind. This was always happening to him, not only once seventy years ago in the seminary but also more particularly since he had reached the age of ninety. In the seminary, on a clear afternoon on which a heavy shower of thunderless rain had fallen he had been reading a piece of Sophocles in the original tongue. When it stopped raining, he looked out of the window on to a tired countryside and the fresh, cleansed afternoon and entirely forgot about the Greek theatre and the classics, which he did not differentiate, calling them all, in general 'the ancients of long ago'. One rainless afternoon, perhaps thirty, perhaps forty years later, he was crossing the cobbled square of the town in which he had been visiting and, unintentionally, he recited the verse of Sophocles that he had been reading in the seminary. That same week, he conversed for a long time about the 'ancients of long ago' with the apostolic vicar, a talkative and impressionable old man who loved certain complicated puzzles for learned people which he claimed to have invented and which later became very popular under the name of crossword puzzles.

That meeting allowed him to recover at once all his old, deep affection for the Greek classics. At Christmas that year, he received a letter. And if it had not been that at this period he had acquired a strong reputation for being too imaginative, too bold in his interpretations and a little mad in his sermons, he would then have been made a bishop.

Since long before the war of '85, however, he had been buried in the village, and in the period when the birds came to die in the bedrooms, they had been asking for years for his replacement by a younger priest, particularly after he said that he had seen the devil.

From then on, they started to ignore him, a thing which he himself did not perceive very clearly despite the fact that he could still decipher the tiny letters of his breviary without the need for glasses.

He had always been a man of regular habits. He was small and insignificant with strong prominent bones, a relaxed manner and a voice that was soft in conversation but too soft for the pulpit. He would stay in his bedroom till lunchtime, twiddling his thumbs, lounging carelessly in a canvas chair wearing no clothes except for a pair of long, twill trousers with the legs tied at the ankles.

He did nothing except say mass. Twice a week he sat in the confession box but for years nobody had confessed. He simply believed that the congregation were losing their faith because of the modern way of life. Hence he had thought it a very timely occurrence to have seen the devil on three occasions, although he knew that people gave little credit to his words despite the fact that he was not very insistent when he talked of those experiences. He for his part would not have been surprised to discover that he had been dead not only for the past five years, but also during those extraordinary moments when he had found the first two birds. When he found the third, however, he came back to life a little so that lately he had been thinking with some frequency about the dead bird on the station seat.

He lived a few paces from the church in a small house without wire screens, with a corridor to the street, and two rooms which served as office and bedroom. He considered, perhaps in his less lucid moments, that it is possible to attain happiness on earth when it is not very hot, and this idea disconcerted him a little. He loved to wander along metaphysical by-paths. This is what he was doing when he sat in the corridor every morning with the door ajar, his eyes closed and his muscles relaxed. However he himself was not aware that his thoughts had become so thin, that for three years in his periods of meditation he had no longer been thinking of anything.

At the stroke of twelve, a boy crossed the corridor with a food tray in four sections which contained the same thing every day; soup made from a bone with a piece of yucca in it, white rice, meat cooked without onion, fried banana or maize cake and a few lentils which Father Antonio Isabel of the Most Holy Sacrament of the Altar had never tasted.

The boy would put the food tray near the chair on which the priest was lying but Father Antonio Isabel would not open his eyes until he heard the footsteps in the corridor again. Because of this the village believed that the priest had his siesta before lunch (which was another thing that seemed crazy to them), when the truth was that he did not sleep properly even at night.

About this time, his habits had been simplified to the point of being primitive. He lunched without moving from his canvas chair, without taking the food out of the tray, without using plates or fork or knife, but simply using the same spoon with which he had eaten his soup. Afterwards, he would get up, throw a little water over his head, put on the white cassock which was mended with big, square patches and make for the station at exactly the hour when the rest of the village was lying down to take its siesta. For several months whilst making this journey, he had murmured a prayer which he himself had composed on the last occasion on which the devil had appeared to him.

One Saturday, nine days after the dead birds had begun to fall, Father Antonio Isabel of the Most Holy Sacrament of the Altar was making for the station when a dying bird fell at his feet exactly in front of Señora Rebeca's house. A sudden flash of lucidity burst in his mind and he realized that this bird, unlike the others, could be saved. He picked it up and knocked at Señora Rebeca's door at the precise moment when she was undoing her bodice before going to sleep her siesta.

The widow heard the knocking from her bedroom and instinctively her eyes flew to the wire screen. No bird had entered this bedroom for two days. But the mesh was still torn. She had thought it an unnecessary expense to have it repaired before the invasion of birds (which kept her nerves in a constant state of irritation) was over. She heard the knocking at the door over the hum of the electric ventilator and remembered impatiently that Argenida was having her siesta in the bedroom at the far end of the corridor. It did not even occur to her to wonder who could be bothering her at such an hour. She buttoned her bodice again, pushed aside the mesh door, walked straight down the corridor, and across the drawing-room which was crammed with furniture and ornaments, and before opening the door, she saw through the grille that there stood Father Antonio Isabel, his eyes dimmed, a grim expression on his face and holding a dead bird in his hand. Even before she had opened the door, he was saying: 'If we throw some water over it and then put it under a bowl, I'm sure that it will get better.' And when she opened the door, Señora Rebeca felt as if she was going to faint with terror.

He did not stay there for more than five minutes. Señora Rebeca thought that it was she who had cut short the incident, but in reality it had been the priest. If the widow had reflected for a moment, she would have realized that, in all the thirty years he had lived in the village, the priest had never stayed in her house for more than five minutes. It seemed to him that, despite the owner's remote though recognized family connexions with the Bishop, her greed was plainly apparent in the lavish furnishing of the drawing-room. Besides there was a legend (or a true story) about Señora Rebeca's family which, the priest thought, could certainly not have reached the episcopal palace despite the fact that the widow's first cousin, Colonel Aureliano Buendía (whom she considered to have no natural feelings) once declared that the Bishop had not visited the village in the new century in order to avoid calling on his relative. In any case, whether true story or legend, the truth was that Father Antonio Isabel of the Most Holy Sacrament of the Altar did not feel at ease in a house whose only occupant had never shown signs of piety and confessed only once a year and who replied evasively when he attempted to find out something definite about the mysterious death of her husband.

Whilst he waited for the widow to return, the priest sat down in a sumptuous rocking-chair of carved wood; he again felt the strange dampness of that house which had never recovered its tranquillity since the day, twenty years ago, when there had been the sound of a pistol shot and José Arcadio Buendía, the colonel's and his own wife's cousin, had fallen, with a noise of buckles and spurs, full-length on the warm leggings he had just taken off.

When Señora Rebeca again burst into the drawing-room, she saw Father Antonio Isabel sitting on the rocking-chair with that vague look which made her feel such horror.

'The life of an animal,' the priest said, 'is as precious to our Lord as that of a man.'

When he said it, he was not thinking of José Arcadio Buendía. Nor was the widow thinking of him. Besides she was used to giving no weight to the priest's words ever since he had spoken in the pulpit of the three occasions on which the devil had appeared to him. Without paying any attention to him, she took hold of the bird, plunged it in the glass and then shook it. The priest noted that there was a lack of piety, a carelessness about her movements and an absolute lack of consideration for the creature's life.

'You don't like birds,' he said, in a gentle though positive manner.

The widow raised her eyes in a gesture of impatience and hostility. 'Even if I had once liked them,' she said, 'I'd detest them now that they have taken to dying in the houses.'

'Many have died,' he said, implacably. It might have been thought that there was a great deal of guile in the monotony of his voice.

'All of them,' the widow said. And she added as she squeezed the bird with distaste and then placed it under a bowl : 'And I wouldn't care if they hadn't broken my wire screens.'

And he felt that he had never known such hardness of heart. A moment later, as he held it in his own hand, the priest realized that this tiny, defenceless body had stopped breathing. Then he forgot everything : forgot the dampness of the house, the widow's greed, the unbearable smell of gunpowder on José Arcadio Buendía's body and he became aware of the great truth which had encompassed him from the beginning of the week. Then and there, whilst the widow watched him leaving the house with the dead bird in his hands and a menacing expression on his face, he experienced the marvellous revelation that a rain of dead birds was falling on the village and that he, the minister of God, the predestined one who had known happiness when it was not hot, had entirely forgotten the Apocalypse.

That day he went to the station as usual, but he was not fully conscious of his actions. He realized in a confused manner that something was happening in the world, but he felt dull and stupid, unworthy of the occasion. As he sat on the station seat, he tried to remember if there had been a rain of dead birds in the Apocalypse, but he had completely forgotten it. He thought suddenly that the delay in Señora Rebeca's house had made him miss the train, and he stretched his head to look out over the dusty, broken window-panes and saw by the Town Hall clock that it was only twelve minutes to one. When he returned to his seat, he felt that he was going to suffocate. Then he remembered it was Saturday. For a moment, he moved his fan of plaited palm, absorbed in his dark, nebulous inner thoughts. And then he was irritated by the buttons of his cassock and the buttons of his boots and by his long, tight twill trousers and he realized in alarm that he had never felt such heat in all his life.

Without leaving his seat, he unbuttoned the neck of his cassock, took out a handkerchief from his sleeve and wiped his bloated face, thinking in a moment of self-pity that he was perhaps witnessing the formation of an earthquake. He had read about it somewhere. However, the sky was clear; a transparent blue sky from which all the birds had mysteriously disappeared. He was aware of the blueness and transparency but had momentarily forgotten the dead birds. He was thinking of something else now, of the possibility of a storm breaking. But the sky was as diaphanous and calm as if it were the sky of another village remote and different where they had never felt heat: and as if they were not his eyes but those of another person contemplating it. Then he looked northwards over the roofs of palm thatch and corrugated iron and saw the slow, silent, symmetrical patch of vultures upon the manure heap.

For some mysterious reason, he felt that in that moment he was living again the emotion he had felt one Sunday in the seminary before receiving his first orders. The Rector had given him permission to use his personal library and he would remain for hours and hours (especially on Sundays) immersed in reading some aged, yellow books which smelt of old wood and had Latin notes in the margin written in the Rector's diminutive, spiky scribble. One Sunday, after he had been reading for a whole day, the Rector had come into the room and with a start of surprise had hastened to pick up a card which had evidently fallen out of the pages of the book he was reading. He observed the embarrassment of his superior with discreet indifference but he managed to read the card. There was only one sentence written in purple ink in a clear, straight hand. '*Madame Ivette est morte cette nuit.*' More than half a century later, seeing a patch of vultures over a forgotten village, he remembered the Rector's melancholy expression as he sat in front of him in the orange twilight, his breathing imperceptibly altered.

Amazed at this association of ideas, he did not feel the heat at that moment but precisely the contrary – a touch of ice in his groin and on the soles of his feet. He felt fear without knowing the exact reason for this fear which was inseparable from a tangle of confused ideas among which it was impossible to distinguish between a feeling of nausea and the hoof of Satan caught in the mud and a flock of dead birds falling on the world whilst he, Antonio Isabel of the Most Holy Sacrament of the Altar, remained indifferent to that event. Then he sat up straight, lifted a startled hand as if to initiate a greeting which was lost in the void, and exclaimed in fear : 'The Wandering Jew.'

At that moment the train hooted. For the first time in many years he did not hear it. He saw it entering the station wrapped in dense smoke and heard the hail of soot upon the corrugated iron. But that was like a remote and enigmatic dream from which he did not awaken completely until that afternoon, a little after four o'clock, when he put the finishing touches to the great sermon he would preach on Sunday. Eight hours later, they went to fetch him to administer extreme unction to a dying woman.

So that the priest did not know who arrived on the train that afternoon. For many years he had gone to watch the four broken-down, discoloured wagons go past and during the last few years at least, he did not remember anyone getting down to stay in the village. Before then it had been different for he could spend a whole afternoon watching a loaded banana train go past; a hundred and forty wagons laden with fruit which passed without stopping until, late in the night, the last wagon went by with a man holding a green lamp. Then he would see the village at the other side of the line with the lights already lit and it would seem to him that the train had carried him on to another village merely because he had watched it go by. Perhaps his habit of going to the station started at this period, a habit which continued even after the workers had been fired and the banana plantations were finished and with them the trains of a hundred and forty wagons; and there only remained the yellow, dusty train which neither brought anyone nor took anyone away.

But that Saturday somebody arrived. As Father Antonio Isabel of the Most Holy Sacrament of the Altar was going away from the station, a peaceful-looking boy with nothing extraordinary about him except his hunger saw him from the carriage window at the precise moment when he remembered that he had eaten nothing since the day before. He thought: If there is a priest, there must be a hotel. And he got out of the carriage, crossed the street which was baked by the metallic August sun and entered the cool shade of a house which was situated in front of the station and in which a worn gramophone record was playing. His sense of smell, sharpened by two days' hunger, told him that this was a hotel. And he went in without noticing the sign, Hotel Macondo, a sign which he was not to read at any time at all.

The landlady was more than five months pregnant. She was the colour of mustard and had the appearance of looking exactly like her mother when her mother had been pregnant with her. He asked for 'a lunch as quickly as possible' and without making any attempt to hurry, she served him a plateful of soup with a meat-less bone and a hash of green bananas. At that moment the train hooted. Enveloped in the warm, healthy smell of soup, he measured the distance that separated him from the station and was imme-diately afterwards assailed by that bewildered feeling of panic which comes when one misses a train.

He tried to run. He reached the door in panic but had not even stepped out of the threshold when he realized that he would not have time to reach the train. When he returned to the table, he had forgotten his hunger: near the gramophone, he saw a girl watching him mercilessly with a horrible expression like a dog wagging its tail. For the first time that day he took off the hat which his mother had given him two months before and clasped it between his knees whilst he finished eating. When he got up from the table he no longer seemed bothered about missing the train or by the prospect of spending a weekend in a village whose name he did not trouble to find out. He sat down in a corner of the room with the bones of his back resting against a hard, straight chair and remained there for a long time without listening to the records till the girl who was choosing them said:

'It's cooler in the corridor.'

And he felt bad. It was difficult for him to start talking to people he did not know. He hated looking people in the face and when there was nothing for it but to speak, the words came out differently from what he had been thinking. 'Yes,' he replied. And he felt a slight tremor. He tried to rock himself, forgetting that he was not in a rocking-chair.

'People who come here push a chair into the corridor where it's cooler,' the girl said. And he listened to her with the agonized realization that she wanted to talk. He stole a glance whilst she was winding up the gramophone. She seemed to have been sitting there for months, for years perhaps and showed not the slightest intention of moving from that place. She was winding up the gramophone but her whole being was concentrated upon him. She was smiling.

'Thanks,' he said, attempting to get up and to move easily and spontaneously. The girl went on looking at him. She said, 'They also leave their hats on the hat-stand.'

This time he felt his ears burning. He shuddered as he thought of that way of insinuating things that she had. He felt uneasy and intimidated and was once again panic-stricken at having missed the train. But at that moment the landlady came into the room.

'What's the matter?' she asked.

'He's taking his chair into the corridor just as they all do,' the girl said.

He thought he detected a note of derision in her words.

'Don't bother,' the landlady said, 'I'll get you a stool.'

The girl laughed and he felt disconcerted. It was hot. There was a dry, monotonous heat and he was sweating. The landlady pushed a wooden stool with a leather seat into the corridor and he was going to follow her when the girl spoke again.

'The trouble is that the birds will scare you.'

He intercepted the hard glance which the landlady gave the girl. It was a rapid, intense glance. 'You ought to keep your mouth shut,' she said and turned towards him smiling. He felt less lonely then and more like talking.

'What is she talking about?' he asked.

'About the dead birds that fall into the corridor at this time of day,' the girl said.

'It's one of her ideas,' the landlady said. She bent down to arrange a bunch of artificial flowers on the little occasional table. There was a nervous tremor in her fingers.

'It's not just one of my ideas,' the girl said. 'You swept up two of them yourself, the day before yesterday.'

The landlady looked at her in exasperation. There was a pitying expression on her face and she obviously wanted to explain everything until there remained not the slightest shadow of doubt.

'What happened, sir, is that the day before yesterday some boys left two dead birds in the corridor to tease her then they told her that dead birds were falling out of the sky. She swallows everything they tell her.'

He smiled. This explanation seemed very amusing to him. He rubbed his hands together and looked at the girl again; she was staring at him in desperation. The gramophone had stopped playing. The landlady went out of the room and as he made for the corridor, the girl insisted in an undertone.

'I've seen them falling. Believe me. Everyone has seen them.'

And he thought that he then understood her attachment to the gramophone and the landlady's irritation. 'Yes,' he said pityingly. And then as he moved towards the corridor: 'I've seen them too.'

It was not so hot outside in the shade of the almond trees. He leaned on the stool against the door-frame, put his head back and thought of his mother; he thought of his mother lying in the

rocking-chair and scaring away the hens with a long broom-handle
and he was conscious that for the first time he was not at home.

A week ago he had been able to think of his life as a straight,
smooth thread stretching from the rainy dawn of the last civil war
when he had come into the world within the four clay and bamboo
walls of a rural school to that morning in June when he had
reached the age of twenty-two and his mother had come to his
hammock to present him with a hat and a card: 'To my dear son
on his birthday.' Occasionally he would shake off the rust of idleness and would feel nostalgic for the school, the blackboard and
the map of the country with its heavy concentrations of fly excrement, and for the long row of beakers hanging on the wall under
each child's name. It wasn't hot there. It was a placid, green village
with hens with big ashen feet which wandered through the school-
rooms to lay their eggs underneath the shelves for the water-jars.
His mother was a sad, withdrawn woman in those days. She would
sit down in the evening to enjoy the breeze which wafted through
the coffee plantations and she would say: 'Manaure is the most
beautiful village in the world'; and then as she turned towards
him and saw him growing quietly in his hammock, she would say:
'You'll realize that when you get older.' But he hadn't realized
anything. He hadn't realized it when he was fifteen and too big
for his age and overflowing with careless, insolent health induced
by idleness. Until he was twenty years old his life amounted to
nothing much more than a few changes of position in his hammock. But about this time, his mother's rheumatism obliged her
to leave the school which she had looked after for eighteen years,
so that they went to live in a two-roomed house with an enormous
yard where they raised hens with ashen feet like those which
wandered through the class-rooms.

Looking after the hens was his first contact with reality. And
it had been his only one until the month of July when his mother
remembered her retirement pension and decided that her son was
now sufficiently shrewd to apply for it. He was useful in helping
her fill up the papers and even had tact enough to persuade the
priest to alter the birth certificate by six years since his mother
was not yet old enough for a pension. On Thursday, he received

his last instructions which were carefully detailed, thanks to his mother's pedagogical training, and he began his journey to the city with twelve pesos, a change of clothing, a bundle of papers and a completely rudimentary idea of the meaning of the word 'retirement pension' which he thought of as a lump sum which the government was to hand over to him so that he could start a pig farm.

Dozing in the hotel corridor, dazed by the heat, he had not paused to consider the seriousness of his situation. He supposed that the return of the train next day would resolve the difficulty so that his only preoccupation now was to wait till Sunday and resume his journey and never again think about this village where it was so unbearably hot. Just before four he fell into an uncomfortable, sticky sleep thinking, during the times when he was not sleeping, that it was a pity that he had not brought his hammock. It was then that he realized the full significance of his situation and that he had left his bundle of clothes and the pension papers on the train. He woke up abruptly, assailed by fear and thinking of his mother; and once again he felt panic-stricken.

When he pushed his seat back into the room, the lights of the village were lit. He had not seen electric light before so that he was greatly impressed when he saw the feeble, stained light-bulbs of the hotel. Then he remembered that his mother had talked about it and he went on pushing his chair into the room trying to avoid the blue-bottles which banged against the mirrors like projectiles. He ate without appetite, shocked by the unmistakable realization of his situation and by the bitterness of the loneliness which he was experiencing for the first time in his life. After nine o'clock, he was taken to the far end of the house to a wooden room papered with newspapers and magazines. By midnight, he had plunged into a feverish, difficult sleep whilst five blocks away, Father Antonio Isabel of the Most Holy Sacrament of the Altar lay on his back thinking of that night's experiences and improving the sermon which he had prepared for seven in the morning. Amidst a thick buzz of mosquitoes, the priest was lying down in his long, tight twill trousers. Just before twelve, he had passed through the village in order to administer extreme unction to a woman and he was feeling nervous and excited so that he had put the sacra-mental objects by the side of his bed and had lain down to rehearse his sermon. He remained lying on his back in the bed in this manner for some time until he heard the distant dawn call of a bittern. Then he tried to get up; he had some difficulty in sitting up and trod on the mass bell and went headlong on to the hard, solid floor of his room.

He was hardly conscious when he felt the ominous sensation which crept up his side. In that moment he was aware of his entire weight; the weight of his body, of his sins and his age all in one. Against his cheek, he felt the solidity of the stone floor which so often, when he prepared his sermons, had served to give him an idea of the road that leads to hell. 'Heavens,' he murmured fear-fully, thinking: 'I'll certainly never be able to get to my feet again.'

He did not know how long he lay on the ground, without think-ing of anything, not even remembering to ask for a good death. It was as if he had really been dead for a time. But when he recovered consciousness, he no longer felt pain or fear. He saw the livid streak of light beneath the door and heard the sad, distant clamour of the cocks and knew that he was alive and remembered the words of his sermon perfectly.

When he drew back the bolt of the door, it was dawn. He no longer felt any pain and it even seemed to him that the blow had taken away his age. All the goodness, the misdoings and the sufferings of the village entered his heart as he swallowed the first breath of that blue moist air which was filled with the sound of cocks. Then he looked round as if to reconcile himself to his lone-liness and saw in the tranquil dawn twilight one, two, three dead birds in the corridor.

For nine minutes, he contemplated the three bodies thinking (just as he had said in the sermon he had prepared) that the dead birds needed an expiation. Then he walked to the other end of the corridor, picked up the three dead birds and went back to the water tank which he uncovered, throwing the birds into the green, still water without exactly knowing the reason for his action. Three and three made half-a-dozen in a week, he thought, and a great burst of lucidity revealed to him that he had begun to suffer the great day of his life.

At seven o'clock it had already begun to be hot. The one guest in the hotel was waiting for his breakfast. The gramophone girl had not yet got up. The landlady approached and the seven strokes of the clock seemed to be sounding at that moment in her bulky stomach.

'And so you missed the train,' she said – with belated sympathy. Then she brought breakfast : white coffee, a fried egg and some slices of green banana.

He tried to eat but did not feel hungry. He felt alarmed because it was hot already. He was sweating in bucketfuls. He was suffocating. He had slept badly and in his clothes and now he felt a bit feverish. Again he remembered his mother and was stricken with panic just at the moment when the landlady came to take away the plates, radiant in a new dress with big, green flowers. The landlady's dress reminded him that it was Sunday.

'Is there a mass?' he asked.

'Yes,' the woman said. 'But there might as well not be one because hardly anyone goes. You see they won't send us a new priest.'

'And what's the matter with the one you've got?'

'He's a hundred years old and half crazy,' the woman said and she stood there motionless and thoughtful with all the plates in her hands. Then she said : 'The other day in the pulpit he swore that he had seen the devil and since then no one has been to mass.'

So that he went to church, partly from desperation and partly out of curiosity to see a hundred-year-old man. He noted that the village was a dead place with interminable, dusty streets and dark, wooden houses with corrugated iron roofs which seemed to be uninhabited. This was the village on a Sunday ; windowless streets, houses with wire screens and a deep marvellous sky above the suffocating heat. He thought that there was no means which would enable him to distinguish Sunday from any other day of the week and as he walked along the deserted street, he recalled his mother saying : 'All the streets in a town lead inevitably to the church or the cemetery.' At that moment he came out into a little paved square with a limestone building with a tower and a wooden cock on the top and a clock that had stopped at ten past four.

He crossed the square without haste and mounted the three steps of the front porch and immediately he smelt an odour of stale human sweat mixed with the scent of incense and entered the warm shade of the almost empty church.

Father Antonio Isabel of the Most Holy Sacrament of the Altar had just entered the pulpit. He was about to begin his sermon when he saw a boy come in with his hat on. He saw him examine the almost empty church with his big, serene, clear eyes. He saw him sit down in the farthest seat, his head on one side and his hands on his knees. He knew that the boy was a stranger. He had been in the village for more than twenty years and he could have recognized any one of its inhabitants just by his smell. That is how he knew that the boy who had just come in was a stranger. In one brief, intense glance, he observed that the boy was taciturn, rather sad and that his clothes were dirty and wrinkled. It's as if he had been sleeping in them for some time, he thought with a feeling of mingled repugnance and pity. And then, seeing him on the seat, he felt his soul overflow with gratitude and he prepared to preach the greatest sermon of his life. Lord, he thought meanwhile, let him remember his hat so that I shall not have to send him out of church. And then he began his sermon.

At the beginning he spoke without realizing what he was saying. He was not even listening to himself. He just heard the clear, fluent melody that issued from a source which had lain dormant in his soul since the beginning of the world. He had the confused certainty that his words were coming out opportunely, with precision and exactly in the order and on the occasion which he had foreseen. He felt a warm vapour pressing against his entrails. But he knew also that his soul was cleansed of vanity and that the feeling of pleasure which his senses experienced was not pride or rebellion or vanity but pure spiritual joy in Our Lord.

In her bedroom, Señora Rebeca felt herself growing weak, and she realized that the heat would soon be intolerable. Had she not felt tied to the village by a deep fear of change, she would have put her things into mothballs in a trunk and gone to see the world as they had told her that her great-grandfather had done. But inside herself, she knew that she was destined to die in the village amongst those endless corridors and the nine bedrooms whose wire screens she was thinking of having replaced by wired glass as soon as the hot weather was over. So she would stay there, she decided (and she made this same decision every time that she did out the clothes in her wardrobe), and she also decided to write to 'my most illustrious cousin' to ask him to send a young priest so that she would be able to go to church again in her hat with the tiny velvet flowers and hear once again a well-conducted mass and sensible, edifying sermons. It's Monday tomorrow, she thought and immediately began to think of the heading of her letter to the Bishop (a heading which Colonel Buendía had described as frivolous and disrespectful), when Argenida abruptly opened the mesh door and exclaimed:

'Madam, they say the priest has gone mad in the pulpit.'

The widow turned her autumnal, bitter, entirely individual face to the door. 'He's been mad for at least five years,' she said. And still absorbed in the rearrangement of her wardrobe, she said:

'He must have seen the devil again.'

'It wasn't the devil this time,' Argenida said.

'Then who was it?' Señora Rebeca asked stiffly and indifferently.

'Now he says that he has seen the Wandering Jew.'

The widow felt her skin contract. On hearing those words 'Wandering Jew' which she had not remembered since the evenings of her far-off childhood, there passed through her brain a mass of confused ideas amongst which she could not distinguish between broken wire screens, heat, dead birds and the plague. And then she began to move, cold and livid, in the direction of Argenida who was staring at her with open mouth.

'It's true,' she said in a voice that issued from her entrails. 'Now it's clear to me why the birds are dying.'

Under the impulse of fear, she put a black, embroidered mantilla on her head and sped like the wind down the long corridor and the drawing-room that was full of ornaments, out through the street door and along the two blocks which separated her from the church in which Father Antonio Isabel of the Most Holy Sacrament of the Altar was saying:

'. . . I swear that I saw him. I swear that he crossed my path this morning at dawn as I was returning from administering the holy oils to the wife of Jonas the carpenter. I swear that his face had been blackened by the curse of Our Lord and that he left behind a trail of burning ashes.'

His words broke off and remained floating in the air. He realized that he could not stop the tremor in his hands and that his whole body was trembling and that a thread of icy sweat was slowly descending his vertebrae. He was ill, feeling the tremor and feeling thirst and a fierce twisting of his bowels and a noise which sounded like a deep organ note in his entrails. Then he realized the truth.

He saw that there were people in church and that Señora Rebeca was coming up the central aisle looking spectacular and pathetic with her arms wide open and her cold, bitter face turned towards Heaven. He dimly understood what was happening and even had sufficient lucidity to understand that it would have been vanity to believe that he was sponsoring a miracle. He rested his trembling hands humbly on the wooden ledge and resumed his speech.

'Then he came towards me,' he said. And this time he heard his own voice, passionate and convincing – 'He came towards me and he had the green eyes, the rough skin and the smell of a male goat. And I raised my hand to rebuke him in the name of Our Lord and said: "Stop. Sunday has never been a good day on which to sacrifice a lamb."'

When he had finished, the heat had started. The intense, solid, burning heat of an unforgettable August. But Father Antonio Isabel was no longer aware of the heat. He knew that once again, behind him, the village knelt down, carried away by his sermon but he did not even rejoice at this. He did not even rejoice at the immediate prospect of the wine soothing his rasped throat. He felt uneasy and out of place. He felt dazed and could not concentrate on the supreme moment of sacrifice. For some time the same thing had been happening to him but this time the distraction was of a different kind because his mind was filled with a definite feeling of uneasiness. It was then that he knew pride for the first time in his life. And just as he had imagined and described it in his sermons, he felt that pride was a pressure like thirst. He closed the tabernacle energetically, saying:

'Pitágoras.'

The acolyte was a child with a lustrous shaven head who was Father Antonio Isabel's godson and had been christened by him. He went up to the altar.

'Take the collection,' the priest said.

The child blinked, turned right round and said in an almost imperceptible voice: 'I don't know where the plate is.'

It was true. No collection had been taken for months.

'Find a big bag in the sacristy then and collect as much as you can,' the priest said.

'And what shall I say?' the boy said.

The priest pensively contemplated the blue, shaven skull with the pronounced bumps. Now he was the one who blinked.

'Say that it is for exiling the Wandering Jew,' he said and as he said it he felt as though he were bearing a great weight on his heart. For a moment he heard nothing except the hissing of the candles in the silent church and his own excited, difficult breathing. Then, putting his hand on the shoulder of the acolyte who was looking at him with frightened round eyes, he said:

'Then take the money and give it to the boy who was the only one at the beginning, and tell him that the priest has sent it so that he can buy a new hat.'

Translated by Jean Franco

G. Cabrera Infante

AT THE GREAT 'ECBO'

It was raining. The rain came crashing down between the old, dilapidated pillars. They were both sitting down and the man was staring at the white table-cloth.

The waiter came up to take the order in an unusually courteous fashion. At least he's civil, the man thought: it must be because of her. He asked her what she wanted.

She looked up from the menu. The dark stiff paper cover bore the inscription: 'La Maravilla – Menu'. Her eyes seemed lighter now with the snow-white light coming in from the park and the rain. 'The timeless light of da Vinci,' he thought. He heard her talking to the waiter.

'And you sir?' The waiter was addressing him now. Well then! He really means to be polite. The fellow's not at all bad-mannered.

'Something simple. Have you any meat?'

'No, not today. It's Friday.'

These Catholics. Obsessed with their rules and regulations. He thought it over for a moment.

'No dispensation?' he asked.

'What did you say?' asked the waiter.

'Bring me lamb chops. Grilled. And mashed potatoes. Oh yes, and a black beer.'

'Would you like something to drink?'

I could bet on it. She said she would have a beer. Just like a woman.

While they were fetching the lunch he looked at her. She seemed to have become a different woman. She looked up from the table-cloth at him: You never give up, he thought. Why don't you look beaten today? You ought to.

'What are you thinking about?' she asked and her voice sounded strangely soft and calm.

If only you knew. He said:

'Nothing.'

'Were you examining me?' she asked.

'No. I was looking at your eyes.'

' "Eyes of a Christian in a Jewish face",' she quoted.

He smiled. He was slightly bored.

'When do you think it'll stop raining?' she asked.

'I don't know,' he said. 'In a year's time maybe. Perhaps in a minute or two. You never know in Cuba.'

He always spoke like that: as if he'd just got back from a long trip abroad or had been brought up there, as if he were a tourist and just passing through. In fact he'd never been out of Cuba.

'Do you think we shall be able to go to Guanabacoa?'

'Yes, I do. Though I don't know if there'll be anything going on. It's raining pretty hard.'

'Yes, it is.'

They stopped talking. He was looking out at the park beyond the mutilated pillars, along the roadway there still with its cobbles and the old, creeper-choked church: at the park with its sprinkling of puny trees.

He realized she was looking at him.

'What are you thinking about? Remember we swore we would always tell each other the truth.'

'I'd have told it you anyway.'

She checked herself. First she bit her lips and then opened her mouth extremely wide as if to utter words larger than her mouth. She did this habitually. He had advised her not to, as it didn't suit an actress.

'I was thinking,' he heard her and wondered if she had started to speak then or earlier, 'I don't know why I love you. You're exactly the opposite of the sort of man I dreamed about, but all the same I can look at you and feel in love with you. And you're nice.'

'Thank you,' he said.

'Oh dear!' she said, upset. She looked again at the table-cloth, at her hands and unpainted nails. She was tall and slim and she looked beautiful in the dress she had on, with its broad, square décolletage. Her breasts were in fact small, but the prominent bone structure of her chest made her appear to have a large bust. She wore a long, ornate pearl necklace and had her hair done up in a high bun. Her lips were full and even and very pink. And she used no make-up, except perhaps for some mascara which made her eyes bigger and lighter. She was put out and didn't speak again before the end of the meal.

'It's not stopping.'

'It isn't,' he said.

'Anything else?' said the waiter.

He looked at her.

'No thank you,' she said.

'I want some coffee and a cigar.'

'Very good,' said the waiter.

'Oh yes, and the bill please.'

'Yes sir.'

'Are you going to smoke?'

'Yes,' he said. She loathed cigars.

'You do it on purpose.'

'You know I don't. I do it because I like it.'

'It's not good to do everything one likes.'

'Sometimes it is.'

'And sometimes it isn't.'

He looked at her and smiled. She didn't smile.

'Now I wish it hadn't happened.'

'Why?'

'What do you mean why? Because I do. Do you think everything is so easy?'

'No,' he said. 'On the contrary, everything is hard. I'm serious. Life is complicated and hard. Everything is hard.'

'It's hard to go on living,' she said. He could follow her train of thought. She was back on the old subject. At the beginning she had spoken only of death, all day, all the time. Then he had made her forget the idea of death. But yesterday, yesterday evening to be exact, she began talking about death again. Not that he found the topic unpleasant, but he was more interested in its literary aspects and although he thought a lot about death, he didn't like to talk about it. Especially with her.

'Dying presents no problems,' she said finally. Now it had come out, he thought and looked out at the street. It was still raining. Just like *Rashomon*, he thought. All we need is an old Japanese to come on and say: I don't understand, I don't understand . . .

'I don't understand,' he ended up saying out loud.

'What exactly?' she asked. 'That I'm not afraid of death? I always told you I wasn't.'

He smiled.

'You look like the Mona Lisa,' she said. 'Always smiling.'

He looked at her eyes, her mouth, her décolletage – and remembered. He liked remembering. Nothing was better than remembering. Sometimes he believed that he found things interesting only in so far as he could go over them again later. Like this now: this moment exactly: her eyes, her long eyelashes, the yellow-olive colour of her eyes, the light reflected from the table-cloth on to her face, her eyes, her lips: the words they pronounced, the tone and the quiet, caressing sound of her voice, her teeth, her tongue which at times reached the edge of her mouth and was quickly withdrawn: the murmuring rain, the tinkling glass and the rattling plates and cutlery, a remote, inscrutable music coming from nowhere: the cigar smoke: the damp, fresh air from the park: he was deeply moved by the idea of knowing what his exact recollection of this moment would be like.

'Let's go,' he said.

'But it's still raining,' she said.

'It's going to go on all afternoon and evening. It's three o'clock already. Besides, the car is just outside.'

They ran to the car and got in. He felt that the atmosphere inside the small car was going to asphyxiate him. He settled himself carefully and started the engine.

They passed and left behind the narrow, winding streets of old Havana, the old beautiful houses, some of them mercilessly demolished and turned into blank, asphalt car parks, the intricately-worked iron balconies, the huge, solid and beautiful customs building, the Muelle de Luz and the Alameda de Paula, a faultless pastiche, and the church of Paula looking like a half-built Roman temple and the stretches of city wall and the tree growing on top

and Tallapiedra and its stench of sulphur and putrefaction and the
Elevado and Atarés castle looming up through the rain and the
Paso Superior, dull and grey, and the criss-cross of railway lines
down below and of electric cables and telephone wires up above
and at last the open highway.

'I should like to see the photographs again,' she said in the end.

'Now?'

'Yes.'

He brought out his wallet and passed it to her. She looked at
the photographs silently in the dim light inside the car. She didn't
say anything when she gave him the wallet back. Then, when they
left the highway and turned into a side road, she said:

'Why did you show them to me?'

'Because you asked to see them of course,' he answered.

'I don't mean now,' she said.

'I don't know. I suppose it was the sadist in me.'

'No, it wasn't that. It was vanity. Vanity and something else.
You did it to get hold of me completely, to assure yourself that I
was yours above everything: above the act, desire and remorse.
Especially remorse.'

'And now?'

'Now we're living in sin.'

'Is that all?'

'Yes. Don't you find it enough?'

'And remorse?'

'Where you'll always find it.'

'And pain?'

'Where you'll always find it.'

'And pleasure?'

It was an old game. Now she was supposed to say where pleasure was to be found exactly, but she didn't say anything. He
repeated:

'And pleasure?'

'There's none to be had,' she said. 'We're living in sin.'

He pushed the waterproof flap back a little and threw his cigar
away. Then he told her:

'Open the compartment in the dashboard.'

She did so.

'There's a book in it : take it out.'

She did so.

'Open it at the book-mark.'

She did so.

'Read what it says.'

She saw that it said in capital letters : 'Neurosis and Guilt Feelings'. And she closed the book and put it back in the compartment and closed it.

'I've no need to read anything to know how I feel.'

'But,' he said, 'it's not supposed to tell you how you feel but why you feel the way you do.'

'I know quite well why I feel like this and so do you.'

He laughed.

'Of course I do.'

The small car bounced and then turned off to the right.

'Look,' he said.

Ahead of them, to the left, a small graveyard shone all white, damp and wild through the rain. Its sterilized symmetry belied thoughts of worms and foul corruption.

'Isn't it beautiful !' she said.

He slowed down.

'Why don't we get out and walk round it for a few minutes?'

He gave her a brief, half-taunting look.

'Do you know what time it is? It's four already. We're going to get there when the party's over.'

'You're insufferable,' she grumbled.

That was the other half of her personality : the little girl. She was a monster, half woman and half child. Borges should include her in his fantastic fauna, he thought. The infanti-female. Along with the catoblepas and the amphisbaena.

He saw the village and stopped the car at a fork in the road.

'Could you tell me where the baseball ground is please?' he asked a group of people and two or three of them described the way in such detail that he knew he would get lost. At the next crossing he asked a policeman who showed him the road.

'Aren't people obliging here,' she said.

'They are. Man on foot and man on a horse. Serfs will always oblige a feudal lord. Nowadays a car is a horse.'

'Why are you so arrogant?'

'Me?'

'Yes, you.'

'I don't think I am quite. It's just that I know what people think and have the courage to say it.'

'It's the only sort of courage you have . . .'

'Perhaps.'

'Not even perhaps. You know yourself . . .'

'All right, I do. I warned you from the beginning, though.'

She turned round and looked at him closely.

'I don't know how I can love such a coward,' she said.

They had arrived.

They ran through the rain to the building. At first he thought there wasn't going to be anything on because he couldn't hear anything for the rain and – amongst some corporation buses and a few cars – saw nothing but a few boys dressed in baseball kit. When he went in he felt as if he had penetrated a magic world:

there were a hundred or two hundred Negroes dressed in white from head to toe: white shirts and white trousers and white socks and their heads covered with white caps which made them look like a conference of coloured cooks and the women were also dressed in white and there were a few white-skinned women among them and they were dancing in a ring to the rhythm of the drums and in the middle a huge Negro who was already old but still powerful and wore dark glasses so that only his white teeth could be seen as another part of the ritual dress and who thumped on the floor with a long wooden stick that had a carved Negro's head with human hair as a handle and this Negro with the dark glasses sang and the others answered he shouted olofi and paused while the holy word resounded against the walls and the rain and he shouted olofi again and then sang tendundu kipungulé and waited and the chorus repeated olofi olofi and in that atmosphere so strange and turbulent yet cool and damply lit the Negro sang again naní masongo silanbasa and the chorus repeated naní masongo silanbasa and again his slightly guttural and now hoarse voice sang out

sese maddié silanbaka *and the chorus repeated* sese maddié silanbaka *and again*

She came up close to him and whispered in his ear :

'It's divine !'

Damned theatre slang, he thought, but he smiled because he felt
her breath on the back of his neck and her chin resting on his
shoulder.

the Negro sang olofi *and the chorus answered* olofi *and he said*
tendundu kipungulé *and the chorus repeated* tendundu kipungulé
*and all the time keeping the rhythm with their feet and going end-
lessly round in a circle in a close group knowing they were singing
to the dead and praying that the dead might rest in eternal peace
and that those still alive might be comforted and waiting for their
leader to say* olofi *again so that they could say* olofi *and begin again
with the invocation* sese maddié

'Olofi is God in their language,' he explained to her.

'What does the rest of it mean?'

For me to have to explain what Olofi means is bad enough, he
thought.

'They're hymns to the dead. They sing to the dead so that they
may rest in peace.'

Her eyes shone with curiosity and excitement. She clutched his
arm. The dance went on, round and round, tirelessly. Young and
old alike. One man wore a white shirt completely covered with
white buttons in front.

'Look,' she said into his ear. 'He's got hundreds of buttons on his
shirt.'

'Sh !' he said, because the man had looked up.

silanbaka bica dioko bica ndiambe *and he thumped his stick
rhythmically against the floor and great drops of sweat ran down
his arms and face and made faintly dark patches on the immaculate
whiteness of his shirt and the chorus said after him again* bica
dioko bica ndiambe *and close to the man in the middle other lead-
ers were dancing and repeating the chorus's response and when
the Negro in dark glasses murmured take it!* one of them chanted
olofi sese maddié sese maddié *and the chorus repeated* sese maddié
ses maddié *while the Negro in dark glasses thumped his stick*

*against the floor and wiped away the sweat with a handkerchief
that was also white*

'Why do they dress in white?' she asked.

'They are worshipping Obbatalá, the god of the pure and un-
blemished.'

'Then I can't worship Obbatalá,' she said as a joke.

But he looked at her criticizingly and said:

'Don't talk nonsense.'

'It's true. It's not nonsense.'

She looked at him and then turned her attention to the
Negroes and said, ridding what she had said before of all insinua-
tion:

'Besides, it wouldn't suit me. I'm much too pale for white
dresses.'

*and at his side another Negro swayed in time to the music and
something indeterminate which went against the rhythm and interrupted it with his fingers on his eyes and he opened his eyes
extremely wide and pointed to them again and emphasized the
sensual and somewhat disjointed and mechanical movements of his
body which nevertheless seemed possessed by a superior power and
now the chanting reverberated against the walls and olofi olofi sese
maddié sese maddié invaded the whole building and reached two
Negro boys in baseball kit who listened and looked on as if un-
willing to embrace something that was theirs and reached the
other spectators and drowned the noise of the beer bottles and the
glasses in the bar at the back and flowed down the steps of the
stands and danced among the puddles in the baseball pitch and
went on over the sodden fields and through the rain reached the
aloof and distant palm trees and went on further into wild country
and seemed to want to surmount the far off hills and scale them
and crown their summits and go on higher still olofi olofi bica
dioko bica dioko ndiambe bica ndiambe ndiambe y olofi y olofi y
olofi but again sese maddié but again sese maddié but again sese
but again sese*

'That man's being sent,' he said, pointing to the mulatto who
had his fingers in his huge ears.

'Is he really?' she asked.

'Of course. It's only the hypnotic effect of the music, but they don't realize it.'

'Would I be affected by it, do you think?'

And before telling her that she would, that she could be intoxicated by that rhythm, he became afraid that she would rush off and dance with them and so he said:

'I don't think so. It's only for the benighted, not for people like you who have read Ibsen and Chekhov and know Tennessee Williams off by heart.'

She felt slightly flattered but said:

'They don't seem benighted to me. Primitive I agree, but not benighted. They believe. They believe in something neither you nor I can believe in and they are guided by their belief and live according to its rules and die for it and afterwards they sing ritual songs to their dead. I think it's wonderful.'

'Mere superstition,' he said pedantically. 'It's something barbaric and remote and alien, as alien as Africa, where it comes from. I prefer Roman Catholicism with all its hypocrisy.'

'That's remote and alien too,' she said.

'Yes, but there's the Bible and Saint Augustine and Saint Thomas and Saint Teresa and Saint John of the Cross and Bach's music . . .'

'Bach was a Protestant,' she said.

'It doesn't matter. A Protestant is a Catholic who can't sleep at nights.'

He felt easier now because he felt he was witty and capable of talking above the drums and the chanting and the dancing, and because he had overcome the fear he had felt when he came in.

and sese *but again* sese *and* olofi sese olofi maddié olofi maddié maddié olofi bica dioko bica ndiambe olofi olofi silanbaka bica dioko olofi olofi sese maddié maddié olofi sese sese *and* olofi *and* olofi *and* olofi olofi

The music and the singing and the dancing suddenly stopped, and they witnessed how two or three Negroes grabbed the mulatto with the frenzied eyes by the arms and prevented him from knocking his head against one of the pillars.

'He's gone,' he said.

'You mean he's been sent?'

'Yes.'

They all gathered round him and carried him to the end of the hall. He lit two cigarettes and offered one to her. When he had finished his cigarette he went over to the wall and threw the stub out on to the damp field, and then he saw the negress coming up to them.

'If you'll allow me, sir,' she said.

'Of course,' the man said, without knowing what it was he had to allow.

The old Negress said nothing. She could have been sixty or seventy. But you never know with Negroes, he thought. Her face was small and fine-boned; her skin was intricately wrinkled and glistened about the eyes and mouth, but was taut over her prominent cheek-bones and pointed chin. Her eyes were keen and gay and wise.

'If you'll excuse me sir,' she said.

'What is it?' he said and thought: I'm sure she wants some money off me.

'I should like to speak to the young lady,' she said. And so she thinks she can touch her more easily. She's doing the right thing because I hate charity.

'But of course!' he said, standing back a little and wondering uneasily what the old woman really wanted.

He saw the girl listening carefully at first and then lowering her earnest gaze from the old Negress's face to the ground. When they had finished talking he came up again.

'Thank you very much sir,' the old woman said.

He didn't know whether to proffer his hand or bow slightly or smile. He chose to say:

'Not at all. I must thank you.'

He looked at her and noticed that something had changed.

'Let's go,' she said.

'Why? It's not over yet. It goes on till six. They go on singing till sunset.'

'Let's go,' she said again.

'What's going on?'

'*Please*, let's go.'

'All right, let's go. But first tell me what's going on. What's happened? What was that old nigger woman on to you about?'

She looked at him unkindly.

'That *nigger woman*, as you put it, is a great person. She has lived a lot and knows a lot and if you really want to know she has just taught me something.'

'Really?'

'Really.'

'And may one know what the schoolmistress had to say?'

'Nothing!'

She moved away towards the door, finding her way with her graceful courtesy through the groups of Faithful who had come to worship Obbatalá. He caught her up at the door.

'Wait a minute,' he said, 'I did bring you here.'

She said nothing and let him take her arm. As he was unlocking the car a boy came up to him and said:

'Hey mister, can you settle an argument? What sort of car's that? German?'

'No, it's English.'

'It's not a Renault, is it?'

'No, it's an MG.'

'Just like I said,' the boy said with a satisfied smile, and rejoined his friends.

Always the same thing, he thought. Never say thank you. And they're the ones who breed most.

It had stopped raining and the air was fresh and he drove carefully until he found the road out to the highway. She hadn't broken her silence and when he looked into the driving-mirror, he saw that she was crying.

'I'm going to stop and put the hood down,' he said.

He pulled over to the side of the road and saw that he was stopping close to the little graveyard. As he lowered the hood and fastened it down behind her he wanted to kiss the nape of her neck, but he felt as if he was being repulsed as strongly as he had been attracted on other occasions.

'Were you crying?' he asked her.

She lifted up her face and showed him her eyes without looking at him. They were dry, but very bright and slightly red at the rim.

'I never cry darling. Except at the theatre.'

He was hurt and said nothing.

'Where are we going?' he said.

'Home,' she said.

'You're quite sure?'

'Surer than you might think,' she said. Then she opened the compartment, took the book out and turned towards him.

'Here you are,' she said shortly.

When he looked he saw she was handing him the two portraits – the one of the smiling, solemn-eyed woman and the one of the little boy, taken in a studio, with huge, solemn eyes and no smile on his lips – and realized that he was taking them automatically.

'I'd rather you kept them.'

Translated by J. G. Brotherston

Marco Antonio Montes de Oca

THE FOOL'S FAREWELL

My clothes are soiled by coloured dust,
I have returned my motley to the bottom of the sea;
I have stayed blind beside the pool,
beside the river stunned by a blow from the tail of its own foam.

In vain I sought my reflection
looking at myself in the dark mirror of the sunflowers;
I lost the immortal brightness, dissolving it in great gulps
and also my flannel for cleaning the moon
and the port where evening falls on its knees.

I lost my dearest possessions,
my penniless man's luxuries,
the ancient glance that grew
at the speed with which the trunk pursues its foliage.

Where could they be, my palaces of dreaming water,
where the enormous white leaves
that winter stripped from the stem?

The eagles of the earth's centre,
the sweet sawdust inventions,
all my goods hardly measurable in the heartbeats and happiness,
in what fold of chaos did they find burial?

Ladies and gentlemen, stones and birds,
it is the beauty of life that leaves us so poor,
the beauty of life
that slowly sends us mad.

O men, women, children, flowers,
my heart appears for the last time before you :
my clothes are soiled by coloured dust,
I have returned my motley to the bottom of the sea.

THE LIP CRACKS .

For my good friend Arturo González Cosío

The lip cracks the word is born
An autumn arises of green and everlasting leaves
Here is there now the North does not exist
Let us all go travelling
The island throws her millennial anchor in the teeth of the wind,

Words are pronounced singly
Pale rubies that spring up from the perfect weather
Ploughs of light on the waters
Words in union that are like
A wood that has become one tree
One selfsame tree growing
Like a solitary and fabulous perch for birds.

They must be piled up like fiery coins
And used as payment for the miracle they confer
Or thrown flying like a pack of cantharides
Under the skin of certain blind men.

The lip cracks the word is born
We travel through a window bristling with smiles
The badger plunges his tiny tooth in pillars of ashes,
Words make their way along the tortuous road
That goes from the throat to the infinite
Words march in perfect order
Into the twittering ambush of their own making.

They reveal us or kill us
Intrepid words
Skeleton keys of the breast
That also open the porous strongbox of stones
They reveal us or kill us
And at night they climb the roofs
On which automata dry their tinplate shirts.

The lip cracks the word is born
The sky shakes its resounding necklace its bell bracelets
Let us ride mounted on the deer we pursue
Here is there
Let us cross the blazing furnace
That stirs marble curls on the cornice
We have come
Through a cleft in the mystery
We have come to the heart of the word.

Translated by J. M. Cohen

C. Vasconcelos Maia

SUN

The train stopped and the fat man lifted down his case.

'What a wilderness,' he heard somebody say.

He squinted through his dark glasses to where the voice came from: a shrunken old woman, her mummy's face wrapped in a dusty shawl, was looking out of the window.

'Like a cemetery,' she grunted depressingly.

Huge rocks, bare and white as marble and uniform as tombstones, stuck sharply up from the scorched plain. The sun, falling fully on to them, set off dazzling reflections. The fat man took off his dusty coat and moved through the packed compartment on to the train steps. The violent sunlight made him stagger and close his eyes. Then, as he opened his lids slowly his eyes became accustomed to the glare and he got down on to the platform. Before him was a station almost in ruins, a faded name-plate with letters missing, bundles of wood stacked beside the rails. And a crowd of beggars rushed to the train displaying their sores and twisted limbs. Huddled in a patch of shade, sheltering from the sun, a group of Negroes propped against barrels eyed him indifferently.

'Revolting!' he muttered.

A taste of bile rose sourly from his empty stomach. Hunger ate him. And the heat crushed him like a sharp fever. The engine groaned and the beggars became more frantic. Out came the station master in wooden shoes, with a cap pulled over his eyes, to ring the bell. The air was filled with the squeaking of brakes, the grating of iron wheels and the sighs of the engine: the train, puffing furiously, began to drag itself across the burning scrubland. A cloud of dust made the fat man move. Coughing angrily, he picked up his bag and walked past the Negroes. They eyed him lazily, unmoved. He put his head into the little window of the signal-box.

'Which way to the town centre?' he asked.

A pale young man with a thin moustache and vaseline-plastered hair lifted his yellow eyes from his signal mechanism and stuck his lower lip out towards the beginning of a road.

'If you go along there you won't go far wrong.'

'Isn't there anyone to carry my bag?' asked the fat man.

The signalman made a sour face. Suddenly he opened his mouth to shout but his throat swelled up and all that came out was a feeble squeak.

'Ze!'

One of the Negroes stared across at them. Moving lethargically he rubbed his eyes, straightened his frayed trousers and dragged himself towards them.

'Yes, boss?'

'Would you like to earn a little money?'

'If you want.'

'Carry this bag to the centre.'

The Negro said neither yes nor no but just waited until the stranger had begun to walk away. Then he went after him, limping like a distempered dog. They got to the road. The fat man loosened the knot of his tie, took off his coat and folded it over his arm, wiping his face, neck, and bald head. The sweat soaked his starched collar. The sun beat down on him. He had never felt so awful in his life. Around him all was bare and threatening, hard ground, an unrelenting landscape, unrelieved by shade or tree tops. Even the occasional bushes of prickly pear were drab and thin, like dry excrement. Along the road the granite rocks he had seen from the train rose with a menacing strength. The ground seemed to boil and the steam made the air hot and unbreathable. A pitiful, undisturbed silence fell, harsh as the sun. And at each step, the fat man felt he had lost a molecule of himself, that he was being consumed by the primitive brutality of the strange, scorched landscape.

From a rise in the ground he saw the centre of the town. It was a single, treeless street writhing like a snake along a thin, dark, stagnant stream. No movement was discernible – neither man nor beast nor smoke curling from a chimney. He moved further down the slope and saw barrels in doorways, an unharnessed ox-wagon, faded clothes in back yards and scattered agricultural tools, all abandoned (as if a war or a plague had descended on the small town and had killed all its inhabitants). The Negro at his side had, in the interval, put the bag down. His arms hung limply by his side, his tongue was out.

The boarding-house was given over to flies and silence. The fat man paid the Negro and clapped his hands. The door of a bedroom opened and an ugly old half-caste came out rubbing her eyes. Embarrassed at finding herself before a stranger, she began to straighten her dishevelled hair, apologizing. She didn't know there were visitors about. He stopped her short, booked a room for three nights, and asked for something to eat. He would faint if he didn't have lunch soon. The woman grumbled again. There was no lunch ready. They never had visitors. Or hardly ever.

'But don't you eat?' the fat man asked impatiently.

'Well, if you won't turn up your nose at a poor person's food.' She produced a piece of dried meat fried in lard, a plate of porridge, two eggs and an onion. The fat man devoured it all and finished off with a couple of bananas and a glass of water.

Even inside the house the heat was oppressive. It was as if the sun were pouring molten lead over the roof. The stranger took off his clothes and stretched himself out on the bed completely nude, trying to sleep, needing to sleep. An unhealthy and inexorable stupor weighed on his eyelids and enfeebled his brain. The heat got no better. The dust of the journey had buried itself deep in the pores of his skin, but even worse was the buzzing of the flies settling on his body and irritating his inflamed skin. He tossed about, his stomach distended with the effort of digesting his unpalatable meal; he was dizzy and felt sick. Lifting himself up on his elbows, eyes closed and head heavy with drowsiness, the fat man belched painfully. Finally he lay still, in a troubled and uncomfortable sleep. A bitter reality took hold of his brain as he slowly sank into the dark, stagnant stream, feeling the touch of the foul clammy water, warm with the heat of the sun. He made no effort to resist. He had lost the power to resist; the sun had entered his head destroying his will power and torturing his brain. He dived and the water licked his body like a slimy serpent. The water was boiling. The small snails that lived in the muddy bottom woke up, stretched themselves and expelled armies of excited microbes. In a shocked moment of terror and disgust the fat man found that his body was not made of flesh, but was of the same soft and repugnant matter as millions and millions of bacteria.

Soaking with sweat, he woke up and frightened away the mass of flies which had been torturing him. His mouth was bitter and his tongue dry. He got up, opened his suitcase, got out a bottle of fruit salts, and took a stiff dose. Then he looked at his watch. Putting on his pyjamas, he called the landlady and asked for a bath. There was no running water and no shower. He managed with difficulty to cool his body with a bucket of cold water. He went back to his room determined to finish his job in the town as soon as possible.

It was not yet three o'clock when the fat man went out. He wore a hat, dark glasses, a tie and a fine clean linen suit. The town was beginning to stir: a few windows were open and a woman stared at him in surprise. There were children playing in the shady corners of the street among the pigs and hens. The Negro who had carried his suitcase was in a bar drinking away the money he had earned. The street had no pavement. The fat man walked to the main square, past a line of small, squat, monotonous, tumbledown houses without fences or gardens, interspersed with wooden shacks. He found the church.

'The Town Hall is beside the Church,' the landlady had said. 'The Inspectorate is next to that.'

The Inspectorate was still closed. The fat man had to knock three times before anyone opened the door. A shrivelled man, with an emaciated face, sucking at a straw cigarette, answered with a frown. His attitude changed quickly. He flung open the door in welcome and bowed his whole body with exaggerated politeness. The other man accepted it all, unmoved. There were apologies for having taken so long to open the door, and for his shabby clothes.

'It's the sun ... the heat ...'

'Yes,' agreed the fat man, sitting down, 'I understand. The sun is enough to drive anybody mad.'

'Everybody is having their siesta now,' he said to justify himself. 'Nobody has the strength to go back to work straight after lunch.' The newcomer interrupted him.

'I am Evaristo Peixoto.'

'I know. I guessed it must be you immediately. I had been advised of your arrival.'

'Awful journey.'

'I was going to meet you at the station, but the train must have arrived on time. Everybody missed it probably. It must have arrived on time deliberately – just so that I shouldn't be there to meet you.'

'No matter. I'm not the kind of man to hold a small thing like that against you.'

'Well then. Make yourself at home while I go to change my clothes.'

Evaristo Peixoto unbuttoned his jacket, took off his glasses and cleaned the green lenses meticulously. The family woke up surprised at the arrival of a visitor. The fat man heard muffled noises from the bedrooms, and voices, women nagging, children crying. The wailing of children made him feel nervous. He hated children.

The tax collector was soon back.

'The sooner I finish my job here the better,' said Evaristo Peixoto quickly.

'There is not much to do,' the tax collector answered, 'you've probably seen for yourself that there are not many shops here. There are very few tax-payers. This used to be an important town with a considerable income, but what with this sun – the sun caused it all. Do you know,' he added as if to himself, 'I feel sometimes that my brain will melt if I go out in the sun for ten minutes – and then there is the stream !'

'Bacteria !'

'It's as well to be warned. Always drink boiled water. And wash in boiled water too.'

'I wouldn't like to live here. I would come to a bad end, mad, drunk or a murderer. This sun makes one want to kill.'

'There is not a healthy person in the place,' the tax collector agreed, 'you don't get normal people with this sun. I hope to God the Government move me somewhere else. There couldn't be a worse posting !'

'The sooner I finish my job here the better,' said Evaristo Peixoto also thinking of himself.

The tax collector had sat down and opened an enormous ledger.

'There is not much work here – only one place could properly be called a shop. The others are garbage. There are no difficulties. All you have to do is sign on the dotted line. In the old days there was business here all right but the sun has destroyed everything. The town only sells cachaça[1] nowadays – isn't it funny that in spite of all this misery the production of cachaça should have increased?'

There was a silence. Evaristo Peixoto's eyelids were as heavy as if he hadn't slept for nights and his head ached like a swollen globe. The child's whining had stopped, but the enervating music of the flies went on. He felt like leaving the work until the following day, but he knew that if he left it once he would leave it for ever.

'Let's make a start,' he said.

The two men went out. It was mid-afternoon. The sun's rays shone obliquely now, but the heat had not diminished. The shops, fruit stalls and offices were open. There was a click of cues and billiard balls from a bar. An ox-wagon carrying barrels of cachaça creaked by. The fat man was bathed in sweat again.

'Bloody sun,' he muttered entering the first shop.

He worked until sundown, and then went on by lamplight. Even at night time there was no cooling breeze, only a hot, fetid smell that the earth had stored up during the day. When Evaristo Peixoto had exhausted himself, the tax collector took him back to the boarding-house.

'Well, the work's getting on. Didn't I say there was nothing to it?'

'I'm dying to get away. I should have finished the audit by to-morrow. There's a train early the day after tomorrow, isn't there?'

'If it's not late.'

'It had better not be. I'm sick and tired of this town.'

'I felt the same at first.'

'It will be different with me,' the fat man assured him.

1. Cachaça, a brandy distilled from the sugar cane.

'I trust to God,' murmured the tax collector lowering his eyes, 'that the Government will give me a new post.'

The fat man said good night and went to lie down. He tried to relax his nerves and his muscles, but his body ached strangely. Sleep overcame him, but a sleep disturbed by nightmares. The sickening stream enlarged and swelled, boiling with an inner fire, threatening to drown him. The shop-people looked on without raising a finger to save him. Then came the audit books – Chief Cash Book, Cash Sales, Credit Sales. He got up various times during the night suffocated by the rows and rows of figures and the microbes. Sweating and panting he lit cigarette after cigarette until his fingers scorched. When he was awake and fully conscious he thought like a fugitive of the landscape seen from the train, of the huge white tombstones piercing the heavens and burning in the sun, and the bad omen of the old mummy's face:

'Like a cemetery.'

When his depression became unbearable he got dressed, went out and strolled about in the countryside until daybreak.

Barrels of cachaça on sharply creaking ox-wagons; beggars on the steps of small shops; pot-bellied urchins nibbling mud; pigs, goats and donkeys grazing unfettered in the streets. He saw ugly, deformed women so decayed and wretched as to seem sexless, repugnant to look at. The small businessmen stopped work and stared at him as if he were some loathsome animal. Beside him the tax collector gabbled on, asking him to put in a good word for him with the Government to get his transfer. And the fat man walked on, his nerves on edge, cursing the sun that even at this hour in the morning was an affliction. They stopped in front of a grocer's shop with four doors and a freshly painted façade, its prosperous appearance contrasting violently with the surrounding decay. The tax collector went in first.

' 'Morning, Senhor Miguelinho.'

' 'Morning.' The thin voice came from a hammock behind the counter. Evaristo Peixoto took off his glasses. The hammock creaked: slowly and lazily somebody climbed out. The tax collector introduced them but Senhor Miguel said no word of welcome. The fat man wished to shake hands conventionally, but noticing that the other had no intention of doing so, stopped himself in time. He examined him carefully. There wasn't much to see. Like a dried fruit, small, withered and shapeless; it seemed inconceivable that he could have had a normal boyhood – he must have jumped straight from sickly puberty to anaemic maturity. In his yellow, shrunken, chinless, thin-lipped, small-nosed face only the two big protruding eyes appeared to be alive. The stains around them seemed to indicate a ruined liver. He wore wooden shoes and blue cloth trousers. The rolled-up sleeves of his shirt revealed two tiny arms as thin as vine-stems. His swollen little stomach sticking out from his dry body seemed not to belong to it. He threw away the end of his straw cigarette without inviting the tax inspector in, merely ordering the shop assistant to give him a chair on the opposite side of the counter. The fat man saw that this was openly offensive.

'We've been everywhere else. Since your shop is the most important I left it until last.' The fat man measured his words, intending to be equally contemptuous.

Senhor Miguel pulled out a huge drawer and took out a pile of heavy books with great effort.

'The books are here,' he said dryly.

'I hope they're in order,' mocked the other.

The proprietor's face gave nothing away. The fat man went on trying to frighten him.

'I hope I shan't be forced to prosecute, Senhor Miguel – I have had to prosecute every other businessman in the square except two who begged to be let off. You know what it is – illegal cachaça. I have prosecuted every businessman in the square – I hope I shan't have to prosecute you.'

The shrivelled man had been quiet before and he was quiet now. But for an instant their eyes met. There was a moment of apprehension. The fat man shivered – a shiver of disgust. Something foul in the shrunken little man emanated from his greenish skin and swam in his bulging eyes. He was, felt the auditor, a hyena. Exactly. A hyena. Curiously he had never seen a hyena – but hyenas must be like that. And he experienced the first feeling of pleasure he had had since arriving, when the hyena looked down and stepped back. He turned to the other two men to make them witnesses of his power. He sat down and the proprietor returned to his hammock, shutting his eyes as if to escape from the presence of power. Time passed. The sun rose in the sky. It grew hotter. The auditor worked on, noting down figures, checking them and adding them up. The tax collector helped him. Bent over the books they looked surprisingly alike in spite of their physical differences, like a pair of twins, twin vultures.

The church clock struck twelve. The hammock creaked and Senhor Miguel slowly got up.

'Nandinho.'

The assistant got up from the gas meter where he had been sitting.

'Boss?'

His voice was thin and weak. The auditor blushed. Tapping the counter with his pen, he lifted his eyes from the books.

'Are you going to close the shop?'

'It's lunch time.'

'But I haven't finished yet.'

'Nobody works from twelve to three.'

The fat man's face went from pink to red.

'If you want to go, do. I'm not ill, and I'm going on working. Your assistant can stay with me.'

The shrivelled man was standing motionless, only the muscles of his mouth working.

'My assistant is coming to lunch with me.'

'I'll stay here alone then.'

The swollen eyes of the businessman met those of the auditor. For the second time there was a moment of struggle.

'I give orders here.'

The blood boiled in the fat man's veins. But he could do nothing but control himself.

'All right,' he said, in his coldest voice. 'I'll be back at three o'clock.' But he felt that the little man had got his revenge. As he reached the door, a group of onlookers he had not noticed before dispersed. He didn't go back to the boarding-house as the tax collector had invited him to lunch. He didn't enjoy his meal. The

company of the crushed little man, his ageing, ridiculously cere-
monious wife and their squabbling, sickly children, nauseated
him. After the coffee, wishing to be polite, they stayed entertaining
him in the drawing-room, making it impossible for him to take his
siesta. As soon as the clock struck three, he went to put on his
coat. The sun was beating down on the street; there were no
animals. But leaning against the walls of the houses, squeezed in
the windows and huddled on the doorsteps, the whole of the township waited, whispering.

'Isn't anybody having a siesta today?' asked the fat man feeling
a certain uneasiness.

The tax collector spoke in a low voice, almost to himself.

'The people are waiting.'

The fat man looked at him wonderingly, noticing the foul in-
flection of fear in his companion's voice. They arrived, but the
grocer's shop was still closed.

'Didn't we say three o'clock?'

The tax collector spoke again, careful not to annoy the other
man.

'You said so – Senhor Miguel said nothing.'

Evaristo Peixoto took out his cigarette case and lit a cigarette.
The tax collector noticed that his hands were not shaking.

'Senhor Evaristo, it is better that I should warn you.'

'Warn me of what?'

'Of Senhor Miguel.'

'He's a swine.'

'It's better to be warned. He's not really such a swine – a different kind of person altogether, a sick man. Haven't you seen
how everybody's sick here? Who could feel well with this sun?
But his sickness is different. It's better to be warned.'

'The man is nothing but a walking corpse,' shouted the fat man
in reply, 'without even the strength to open his own silly front
door.'

From the hard steel-blue sky, the relentless sun continued to
pour fire over the wretched township. Beyond the roofs, the stone
obelisks, straight as tombstones, shimmered against the desolate
gloom of the landscape.

'Senhor Miguelinho is no ordinary decent kind of person,' the tax collector went on nervously. 'He can't bear people interfering in his life. And he's got a mania – he hates auditors.'

The fat man turned, suddenly taking interest.

'I forgot to tell you – I can't think why I didn't tell you yesterday. I've told all the auditors who've been here. Apart from this Senhor Miguel knows all about accounting. Didn't you notice his books? They're all in order. You won't find a single mistake. It's better not to go on – put your signature and finish. The auditors who have been here have always done it, in spite of the fact that they knew, I know, everybody knows . . .' Without finishing his thought the tax collector stopped, looked uneasily from side to side and lowered his voice.

'Everybody knows,' he went on, 'that Senhor Miguelinho has barrel upon barrel of illegal cachaça in a store behind his shop.'

The fat man understood more than a simple piece of advice or the solicitude for a colleague's welfare in the tax collector's whisper. He smelled intrigue. He was sure that the other wanted to involve him in a struggle that he himself had never had the courage to face.

'Ah !'

'But it's not worth looking into. It wouldn't pay in the end. Senhor Miguelinho is a funny person. All the auditors who have been here have finished by agreeing with me. We're at the end of the world here. The police and the politicians are on his side – there's no point in picking a quarrel. It's this sun . . . this sun is the end of every living thing.'

The fat man took out his handkerchief and wiped his sweating face. He turned to look at the people waiting in the refuge of the rare shadows.

'Ah !'

He called a little boy, slipped him a coin and sent him with a message to Senhor Miguel's house. The boy ran off. The crowd stirred like wisps of straw in a wind. The answer came quickly.

'Senhor Miguelinho says that he is not going to open his shop today !' The fat man shouted loudly so that the crowd would hear him :

'I will not be played with.'

A new wave of excitement ran through the townspeople. New heads appeared at the windows; there was a sound of whispering; mothers called their children to them; steam rose from the hot ground.

'Tell him that if he doesn't come, I shall go and get him.'

Sweating nervously the tax collector rephrased the message. Senhor Evaristo had to go on the following day, so would Senhor Miguelinho kindly open his shop? Another wait beneath the fierce sun, under the staring eyes of the wretched township.

This time Senhor Miguel Noronha came. Accompanied by his assistant, he walked slowly, a bunch of keys in his hand, a sunshade open above his head, dragging his wooden shoes over the hard ground. He said good afternoon weakly and opened the door. Evaristo Peixoto noticed how calm he was: there was no trace of sweat on the shrivelled little man's skin – it was as if he were immune from sun and heat. Inside the shop the books lay on the counter as he had left them. He reopened them. He knew it was useless to continue his check because the fraud he had practised was not to be found in them. However, to give himself time to decide what to do, he pretended to work. An obstinate frown crossed his forehead, joining his eyebrows together. He hoped that Senhor Miguel would lie on his hammock, but this time the proprietor sat behind his desk – half-way between the counter and the door which led to the stockroom. The auditor breathed deeply to control his quickening pulse rate. He looked over his glasses at the wretched man. Seated and immobile, Senhor Miguel leaned to one side as if he were too weak to sit erect. His yellow bulging eyes expressed nothing. The fat man felt them fixed upon him and couldn't help beginning to feel uncomfortable. Tense already, he closed the last book, took off his glasses, put them in their case and their case in his pocket. Quietly, intently he turned to face the owner of the shop. Senhor Miguel stared back.

'Your books are in order,' said the auditor.

'I know,' answered the other.

'There is no point,' said the tax collector, trying to interfere. The others felt it physically.

'However, I must examine your stock.'

Senhor Miguel returned the auditor's stare unblinkingly.

'If my books are in order you will touch nothing else.'

'I must examine your stock,' the fat man repeated as if he hadn't heard. 'I know you have illegal stock at the back of your shop. Unregistered cachaça. I am going to prosecute you.'

The proprietor said nothing.

'There is no point,' said the tax collector trying to interfere. The fat man pushed him away.

'I am going to examine the cachaça,' he said again to Senhor Miguel. The shrivelled little man spoke at last.

'No auditor has gone or will go behind that counter.'

The fat man turned to the tax collector.

'Go and fetch the Mayor.'

The other went out. Neither the auditor nor the proprietor moved. The tax collector returned.

'The Mayor's not here. He went away at dawn.'

'Call the Chief of Police.'

'He's gone as well – this morning.'

Evaristo Peixoto breathed deeply.

'Get the Chief Inspector.'

'He went off to his farm at midday. Can't you see there's nothing to be done? This is the end of the world. And this sun . . .'

'Shut your mouth, you coward,' shouted the fat man. 'You will be dismissed from your duties. What kind of a tax officer are you to let a taxpayer cheat the state unpunished? Go and get two witnesses.'

'Nobody will come.'

Inside the shop the fat man sensed the hush of expectation from the wretched crowd outside, searching for little bits of shade to hide under, afraid to come near. And the sun was beating down on the roofs, falling furiously over this dried-up cluster of small houses. The faint noise of a drawer being opened put the fat man on his guard. He saw the assistant move to a corner and the tax collector sneak away from his side. He knew that he was completely alone. Senhor Miguel's hands were no longer resting on the desk. An unpleasant tremor ran down Evaristo Peixoto's spine.

'I must examine your stock,' he said as if it were the refrain of a song, a funeral dirge.

The proprietor did not answer. The fat man was sweating through all his pores. The sweat ran down his forehead and his bald neck, soaking his collar and sticking his shirt to his body. His tongue swelled with the taste of bile and his stomach tightened. His hand softly slid down to the pocket of his trousers. Between his fingers, delicate as a flower, was a small cocked Mauser.

'I must examine your stock.' In spite of everything his voice was firm. The shrivelled little man behind the desk leaning to one side, his hands hidden, didn't move. The fat man stepped forward. The throb of his pulse beat in his brain like an earthquake, his ears deafened by the pounding of his heart. His consciousness of the things around him, of what he was doing and what he had decided to do, became confused in his mind: he was only aware of two bulging eyes staring at him. He tried to jump over the counter, but his legs went stiff. He tried to press the trigger, but his fingers wouldn't move. His arm fell slowly. The drawer creaked again. It was being closed. He turned his back on the shrivelled little man and went slowly out into the street under the eyes of the wretched people of the little town, knowing now that he was one of them, pitifully one of them.

Translated by R. P. Joscelyne

Pablo Armando Fernández

ORIGIN OF EGGO

What the dead mouths say is that man
came in the change of light.
The boat was his body and his arms two powerful oars.
Alone, through a strait of turbulent waters
man was a light, the dead say;
before all vanished history, and long
before all time to come.
He was going towards the mountain, they say.
He was gazing ahead, he was gazing behind,
and at the profile his powerful hands
had always cut in the air. He went alone,
and the crystal, the gold pouring from his boat,
moulded the torso of each created thing,
until the time of his fulfilment.
Along the shore, in the blurred undergrowth,
ashes or smoking carrion, ruins.
And the tale the dead mouths tell is that
the mountain, man himself,
was born upon the waters.
But when he reached the centre of himself
he was no longer a man;
he was primordial tree, its branches countless oars,
its trunk so many boats identical in strength,
joined in a rounded flower of gold.
In front of him, on each side, and behind him
he saw the mountain multiply to an exact number
divided into equal parts,
each one of them whole, but always the same man
who came on the waters and in the change of light.

ABEL REFLECTS

They've painted the store in other colours
which time hungrily devours.
They've brought a new stock of things to sell
and there is no doubt this pleases death,
that this pleases his willing servants
who kept the figs and the apples
from the child's hands,
who kept the clockwork toys
from the child's hands.
The painted store is one more mask
of death.

DENUNCIATION

The informers talk about
the night the cock may crow;
the toad's eyes in the dew;
trucks that go by without stopping;
San Eleuterio or The Virgin of the Vanished;
dreams to guess the lucky number.
The room is the accomplice of the voices,
three boys die on their way.

Translated by John Gibson, Arthur Boyars, and Christopher Middleton

Breno Accioly

JOÃO URSO

The hills are torn bundles. From the distance come echoes of loud voices; but the city is an enormous silence of heavy sleep, of sleep broken by the sounds of the hills. And it seems that the night in the hills is different from the night which wraps the city.

In the hills are the red colours of the lightning, the loud cries of the breaking thunder, the trees quickly changing colour and quickly returning to the green of their leaves.

There are no stars shining above the hills. They are all burning dimly in the distance.

The winds, the raging clouds and the burning colours are far away. One could compare the city to a person at a play, sitting in the back row and having to use binoculars.

João Urso may never have seen binoculars. But he seems to be shielding his eyes, making of his two hands a screen against the fierce brightness.

Leaning from the window, João Urso sees the old hills fighting against the fury of the elements and even forgets the sadness which is always with him.

A machine has put out the lights. Only the white shapes of the cathedral tower stand out sharply, hanging cones, motionless, piercing the night.

The wall of the hospital and its wards are also visible but weaker blemishes; and if the prison had not been painted red, it would have been another blemish to take note of, a gross smear, with its old roofing, sleeping with its punished passions.

João Urso lifts the collar of his pyjamas and rubs his hands.

The fig-trees, the *caraiberas*, all the trees of the city and of the banks of the river are quiet. There is no wind to shake their branches, or turn the small weather-vane at the meteorological station.

Canoes wedged between punt-poles as if they are overloaded and unable to stir; like enormous abandoned wooden slippers; the streets without drunks, or prowlers, or howling dogs.

João Urso alone watches the spectacle in the hills. When the lightning, growing stronger, flashes through the window, his eyes ache; for a moment it lights up bits of the dining-room: chairs reflected in an oval mirror; a foot of wall covered with a picture of the Sacred Heart of Jesus, a God with a blue and red robe, holding in his left hand a globe of the world, his right hand lying on his chest as if to relieve some deep pain; numbers of portraits of João Urso's ancestors are coloured, bleeding in the flash of the lightning.

The old piano seems to be covered in blood.

When the lightning moves by the river, the glasses of the cupboard seem to be full of wine, left over from some strange party where nobody wished to drink.

João Urso sighs. He bows his head to the city, and lifts his eyes to see the towers and the stars shining. Yes! Those towers and those bells! He sighs again. So long ago. So many memories.

And he fixes his eyes as if he were actually seeing the bells inside the cones of the towers, the bells ringing, waking the city to proclaim: A Waterspout! Since he was small he had loved to think like this, terrifying things which would make shivers of fear run up his spine. How good it would be if a Waterspout fell and made a hole in the ground, so deep that a lantern was needed to explore it.

A Waterspout to tear up roofs, cut the statue of the Emperor in two, break the chains of the prison, the iron bars which cut the prisoners' faces as they look out on to the road; João Urso begins to laugh. To laugh as he had laughed throughout his childhood, a laugh which nobody understood, and which made many people call him mad.

Even he could not explain why. When he came to, his mother would be screaming in his ears, angry, worried, wanting to know the reason for these sporadic, inexplicable bouts of laughter. João Urso would begin to cry. For hours at a time, he would be in disgrace, perched on a high stool.

The hours would pass slowly, slowly. In disgrace João Urso's hands would hold a book of sonnets: how often had he memorized love poems, and stood before his mother to repeat his punishment!

Sometimes, before finishing a sonnet João Urso's voice would seem to run away: his mouth would open showing yellow teeth, his cheeks would become round and full, pressing against his eyes, transforming his face, while he laughed out that hidden and mysterious pleasure.

'Get back to the stool, you little fool. Three more, do you hear?' João Urso knew that three more meant three more sonnets to learn.

He would climb up once more and return to reality a long time after, his legs hanging from the high stool.

Suddenly the echoes of João Urso's laughter would cross the corridors, fill the room, disturb the monotony of the huge stone thick-walled house, with its enormous garden going down to the banks of the river. As he used to sleep in the next room, he would wake sometimes to hear a person cry. He recognized it as his mother.

He would press his ear against the wall, but the thick stone only allowed him to hear everything dimly.

But even without being sure, João Urso believed that his mother's sobbing at night was due to the bouts of laughter he loved so much. João Urso would be happy, would shiver with pleasure when he felt that coldness running up and down his spine before filling his body with repeated spasms.

On one occasion some people had called with their children. They had gone to play in the attic. Downstairs had been heard the happy cries of children at play; but suddenly a long bout of laughter had drowned all the noises, and shaken the children who had been jumping over boxes, playing at hiding behind wardrobes and mats, concealing themselves in doorways or in the dark, narrow steps of the staircase.

The children had begun to cry as if they were crying for help.

In the middle of the corridor was the figure of João Urso laughing nervously, possessed by uncontrollable laughter, filling the children with terror as they continued to cry, calling for their parents, begging somebody for help.

They were children crying as if they had heard voices from another world, the laughter of some terrible apparition.

He had thought he would be punished, and spend the whole afternoon perched on his stool, learning sonnets by heart, his mother slapping and shouting at him.

He had gone sadly downstairs, and had sadly looked out of the window on to the road, its paving of enormous stones burning, leading upwards as if it wished to reach the hills where the donkeys who came to steal water from the river were returning.

And João Urso had felt his heart burst, filling itself with hate and, at the same time, with cowardice.

And if, instead of being punished, he were to go to church, struggling for a lantern as it was carried slowly past the Stages of the Cross, and lighting them? It was impossible now. Even if he were to go to church, he would be unable to get hold of a lantern. The priest had forbidden him to do so. The pious old ladies had been full of loud condemnatory prayers before, and had crossed themselves repeating the word: Excommunicated!

When he had held the lantern, João Urso had laughed heartily, shaken in a convulsion of strange laughter: his hands had seemed to change the lantern into a glove, and had whirled the globe like a boy from a circus, a mighty-handed acrobat.

The procession had been interrupted. Everybody had stood back, the priest with his open book, his eyes heavy with surprise, his rosary abandoned on his right arm like a useless weapon.

The white dresses of the Daughters of Mary adorned bewildered virgins, terrified by the laughter of João Urso whirling the lantern, as the columns in the nave answered the screams with muffled echoes, echoes vanishing behind the altars, behind the pulpits, and creeping up towards the trap in the choir through the box of the staircase.

And amid João Urso's mysterious pleasure, they had sprinkled holy water, while the priest – from a distance, everybody at a distance – prayed in Latin. João Urso remembers that afternoon well; he remembers the holy water that dried out on the blue cuffs of his sailor suit, on the velveteen collar embroidered with anchors. Neither has he forgotten the priest, the pious ladies, the whole town.

Sant' Ana do Ipanema was a voice which told everything, unable to keep the deepest secret. The people in the neighbourhood had heard the story. And in the market, in the butcher's shop, in the town hall, in the brothels of Rua do Sebo, they had talked about João Urso's illness. They had imitated his bouts of laughter, and had cut the silence of the night with their mockery of his laughter. It was fashionable to laugh as João Urso laughed.

João Urso had thought of the punishment, and had soon abandoned all thought of the procession. He had been sure, absolutely sure, that his mother would punish him, bind him to the high stool, fill his hands with sonnets – romantic sonnets to be recited without a single mistake.

He had been expecting punishment. And, as if he were a condemned man with a few moments of life before him, had stayed at the window, his eyes following the street upwards, and then down the opposite way, losing themselves among the ox-wagons creaking along the roads. The flag-stones had shone, and the river of still, seemingly stagnant water had changed into a swamp where canoes rotted.

João Urso had sensed his mother's footsteps. To try and protect his ears, he had twined his arms, lowered his head – and waited. He had waited so long that he looked up.

And with surprise he had seen his mother crying, stretching out her arms to him, wrapping him in a long maternal embrace, crying still, moistening his hair with tears, searching out his mouth, his eyes to cover them with kiss after kiss.

In the corner of the room, the stool had become a friendly shadow like the other furniture. The agony of the stool, and of memorizing sonnets was over.

But instead of crying to accompany his mother's tears, he had filled the whole house with peals of laughter, laughing nervously as he had laughed in church, as he had laughed terrifying the children in the attic, as if he were saying good-bye to a punishment, fleeing from a hated prison.

And at school, whenever anyone was caught laughing without good reason, without an explanation, the teachers would say:

'Could this be João Urso's disease?'

There was no school which would teach him.

Everything over there seems to be on fire. Flashes of lightning tearing the hills, covering the trees with blood, bending their streaks over the city, streaks with huge reflections which are splashes of blood on the towers of the Cathedral, on the few large houses, on the walls of the cemetery. They are like lanterns, strange lanterns that torture the city with their red eyes, off, on, quickly off again.

And the stunted chest, the small hands, the strange head, the João Urso that the window sill cannot hide is a splash also.

The hills must have imprisoned the thunder. João Urso no longer hears mouths bursting as if they want to tear the sky and explode all the secrets of the hills.

He is only coloured by the lightning now, disturbed by the wind, nursed by the song of the rain that begins to fall. And he hears the rain surge in the gutter, the song of a rivulet flowing between the flag-stones, the strength of the wind sway hair and trees, uttering the wail of untidy and dishevelled hair.

João Urso sighs again.

He lowers the window. And stays watching the rain washing the glass, running its quick drops down until they disappear in the window frames.

He can hardly hear the song of the rain, now. He can see only the lightning through the window pane, and hear the distant murmur of tossed trees; enormous drops of rain hammer on the roofs, flowing rapidly by the flag-stones.

João Urso hears everything distantly, half hearing as if he has been wrapped by the silence of the house, his senses imprisoned in the big drawers in the dressing-tables, in the dark wood cupboards; he runs his fingers through his hair, framing the deformed head of his frail body. Such a long time ago!

A stronger lightning crosses the window pane, reddening the portrait of João Urso's mother. And the portrait seemed to revive João Urso's mother in the March afternoons, in those quiet, restful afternoons, when they had gone up the hills, João Urso breathing slowly. The doctor had ordered him to breathe very lightly, and João Urso had done so. His mother had lain in the shade, her hands useless, her fingers resting on crochet needles. And when she had seen João Urso putting down his penknife, tired of writing his name on the tree trunks, she had dried her face, moistened the sleeve of her blouse and shaken her head.

This was after the punishments, after João Urso had memorized endless sonnets, and stayed long hours perched on the stool. She had thought João Urso's laugh was insubordination or disobedience. And only after the scandal in the church, after the children had cried from fright in the attic, after everybody in the city had made fun of João Urso, and the schools refused to admit him – only after this had she thought to call a doctor.

And the prescription was to breathe the fresh air of the hills, breathing slowly 'as if he were asleep'. The doctor had said: 'as if he were asleep' and how often had João Urso seen his mother absent-mindedly talking to herself, muttering irreverently: 'as if he were asleep . . . as if he were asleep'.

How often had his mother in her morning prayers slipped in that phrase of the doctor's without noticing! And João Urso had breathed as if he were asleep, obedient, even to the extent of lying down on the leaves, pretending to be asleep. Since João Urso hadn't stopped his laughter, a horse ride at the end of a train journey had taken him away from the hills, from the gossip, and from his mother who had remained waving, full of tears, waving until the horses had disappeared.

The specialists had been alarmed and had held a joint consultation. They had never seen anything like it; no medical book had ever dealt with it. And João Urso had continued laughing, letting out enormous shouts, high-pitched screams which had run through the wards like the cries of a strange wounded bird.

They had forbidden João Urso to read his mother's letters. No emotion, nothing disturbing. The doctors had found him an unusual case.

They had written to Europe to consult with experts; cures had multiplied and a cupboard had been filled with bottles labelled:

THE TREATMENT – JOÃO URSO. And they had been down-
cast, and completely thrown off balance, when after each new
medical João Urso had laughed as if he had been with his mother,
climbing the hills to breath the purer air.

One, two, five years João Urso had stayed in the sanatorium,
five years of lost Christmases, separated from the eve of St João,
that he had anxiously awaited, counting the days. He had returned
laughing worse, much worse than when he had gone galloping
away, passing through the shrub country, travelling by the train
from Quebrangulo. 'Recife is over there.' His father's arm made a
curve, as if he had wanted to enclose the hillocks, the children of
dromedaries on the green hills.

The gesture had seemed to say: 'We are far away.' They had
whipped the horses, spurred on, and the horses had lengthened their
pace, whinnied, their flanks damp with sweat as if they had just
crossed a river. Afterwards the Recife train had passed through
miles of sugar-cane plantations, glimpsing factories with tall chim-
neys: João Urso had been delighted. The heat and dust hadn't
bothered him. His father had told him the names of the estates
and stories about the factories. João Urso had lifted his deformed
head and seen in his father's eyes the magic of adventure. When he
had met his father, he already knew how to talk, all his teeth had
already cut. And sometimes he had seen his mother leaning from
the window, absent-mindedly looking from the veranda up the
highroads, distantly searching for that shadow which she knew
so well. And one day, when he woke up, he had seen his mother
telling a tall broad-shouldered ruddy man:

'This is João Urso, your son!'

And he had felt that the hands of the stranger, the man who his
mother said was his father, were hard as rock, bumpy with corns.

Afterwards his father had taken him to his room and opened
leather cases and trunks stuffed with riches. And for the first time
João Urso had heard of diamonds, and precious stones which his
father said were worth a fortune.

He had gone away suddenly and without warning leaving in his
mother's eye that frequent sadness, a sadness that by its frequency
became normal.

Now João Urso had returned. He had seen his mother thirty years older and had heard that heart, which used to beat so strongly, almost silent.

He felt moved, an urgent wish to cry, to hold his mother and to sob. He had opened his arms, wrapped his mother's breast in a violent hug and had begun to laugh, to laugh as he had never laughed, a sick laugh, interspersed with deep cries and terrifying screams.

The doctor who had brought João Urso had felt ill, and for a moment petty and useless. But he had moved instantly forward and had tried to separate João Urso's arms, and release him from his mother's breast.

João Urso's arms had been like iron rods, immovable in their sudden strength. João Urso had torn his throat and forced open the cut of his mouth. And when João Urso had stopped laughing, the walls had returned his cries of laughter in distant echoes as if other João Ursos had been hidden and were answering him.

His mother had fainted. And in her unconsciousness, asleep under the effect of morphine, had shuddered, her legs shaking in convulsions, had waved her arms, and groaned distressingly.

And João Urso had never again seen those trunks full of riches, those leather trunks. Never again had he felt those calloused hands, never again had he heard talk of diamonds like his father's talks.

The town had remembered João Urso's father as it remembered the death of the powerful.

'He died sifting gold on the banks of the Rio Prata. He was the richest man there. He lit cigarettes with fifty-dollar notes. He had virtually an army of prospectors. And he was rich enough to be godfather to the Governor's son.' Other stories had been repeated from mouth to mouth. Stories like fairy-tales, unbelievable at that time.

His woman, for a whole year afterwards, would go with no one. She needed to rest and to restore her powers.

Another story had been told of a woman who went around the world, visiting all the night-clubs, and living in Paris like a princess because João Urso's father had liked her and wanted her to enjoy herself.

The window pane doesn't stop João Urso from being covered with a splash of blood. The hills are red flashes that have brought rain, furious rain, hammering the roof-tops, swelling the volume of the river. And the waters of the river become dark, each moment muddier.

João Urso's mind dwells on so many memories, so many broken recollections! So many fragments of his sad past João Urso lives again, so many, so many!

Not even the hands of the clock break the silence of the house. The clocks are like out-of-date maps showing the time of another age. Everything is far away.

And as if he is throwing a last glance over his life, João Urso sees himself orphaned of his mother, forgotten by his father from whom he has had no news for so long, dead perhaps, or dying amid the riches which the people spoke about.

He sees himself forsaken by the world, without even knowing whether his laughter was contagious (even at the sanatorium the doctors took precautions). He had lived like an animal that loves the dawn, the solitude of the sleeping streets. João Urso had felt happy when some passer-by in the night bid him good night or asked him for a match. He would watch the shadow move away with a look full of sadness. And João Urso too would go away, fearing to be recognized, terrified of seeing the passer-by take to his heels, fly away in fear at discovering that it was João Urso.

He had loved climbing up beside the cemetery to find the meteorological station and he had stood for hours watching the weather-vane turn, marking the direction of the wind, with those four letters which looked to the four corners of the earth. And once João Urso had seen the instrument house open.

He had marvelled at the thermometers, the tubes of mercury oscillating slowly and magically. He had touched the aluminium flasks with enchantment. His eyes had stared at everything, at that world enclosed by white boards, and striped by blinds. He had felt himself the lord of a world that only he visited at dawn. He had never tired of seeing the thermometers, the geography of the constellations, tracing the bright paths of the comets with shining tails, of distant stars.

João Urso had braved the rain, the cold, the heat of the stifling nights. And if on this night he didn't go out at dawn it was not for fear of the lightning or of the rain which failed to wash the blood from the hills. João Urso would have loved to be with his mercury tubes, walking beneath the rain. But he is a prisoner now.

They have turned the old house into a prison. Soldiers, shivering with cold, dig their hands into their coat pockets. They swear. They have received orders to let nobody in or out. Their guns are wet pieces of iron, as forgotten as the soldiers in the stormy night. The judge had spoken fiercely, in front of João Urso.

'You know what to do if this criminal tries to escape. Fire !'

And they had all thrown stones, breaking the glass of the veranda, shouting, with clenched fists raised with the anger of the crowd. The people had crowded together and had fought for a place in front of the house wanting to lynch João Urso. And from up there João Urso had heard his name slandered in the people's mouths. Fate? João Urso could not understand the reason for it all. Yes, it had been silly. He should have remembered that everybody was afraid of his laughter. He had always tried to hide himself. But the lights of the circus had seemed to call him : they pleaded with him. João Urso had hesitated.

The shadow of a woman balancing on a trapeze was a mark on the canvas, tracing complex movements.

From a distance João Urso had admired, following the shadow, balancing his eyes on those studied, dangerous movements. Another mark had outlined the shape of a sun-shade on the canvas. It was the end of the Balance of Death. There had been a long silence. They had all seemed dead, because nobody had breathed. The dancer had prepared to leap for another trapeze. The canvas had traced the silhouette of an Outstanding Act. A voice had called for more silence. Everybody had been in suspense, mouths open, waiting. The drummer had held up his arm to strike when the Jump of Death was over. But he had never been able to do so. João Urso had approached, arriving at the entrance to the circus. And at the moment of jumping, when the dancer's feet had flown like two sequin wings, with trousers of red satin, and a firm brassière, at this moment, João Urso had let out his sharp cry of strangled laughter, perhaps the greatest laugh of his life. And the dancer had been like a wounded bird, a falling flight.

Once more João Urso's eyes bleed in the lightning. The spectacle of the hills, the song of the rain hammering on the roof-tops, running by the flag-stones, tires him.

And he only feels the desire to sleep, as he waits to go on a long journey, a journey which not even he knows the end of.

He finds his bed, and closing his eyes, keeps inside them the uncommon geography of the constellations, the mathematics of the old thermometers, the beautiful uncertain flight of the dancer.

Translated by R. P. Joscelyne

Enrique Lihn

THE TREE-CLUMP IN THE GARDEN

What will become of us? Have we then retraced our steps or, confused actors
in this rapid domestic scene, were we false witnesses and, whilst
 they made us promise
that we would never repeat the adventure, did she who has taken
 everything from us,
linking us to her destiny, abandon us to the misery of our own?

Our parents prepared us a forgetful awakening. The well was sealed
and a wall was raised across the path to the wood; in a garden like
 other gardens, nothing to recall
the migration of the little savages.

And they count us perhaps among the absent
who have to be admitted to every party, a sort of ghosts
but the sort that nobody must evoke, because they are always there
 in their place
waiting for the moment to appear on the scene, only for a moment
 that nobody denies them,
that nobody would want to deny them.

THE INVASION

In the antiseptic council-chamber a plumed head was enthroned,
and as if nothing had happened in a thousand years a clamorous
 silence reigned once more,
which was soon to be broken by the fire with its single word
on the stone of sacrifices.

The eternal youths who never change struck their ritual postures
naked to the waist, with their feet on the table, chewing tobacco
their tattoo-marks spoke for them, those childhood treasures
were the selfsame number of a picture magazine
and at the end of history here they were reunited
waiting for the result of the election of their victim.

The sign of the cross of the sword was made.
The heraldic eagle was uncaged at the service-entrance and told to
    perform its carnage quietly
without losing a tell-tale feather. Other absurd precautions were
    taken.
The hand-basin was taken to the young Emperor's table for hands
    bloody with ink.
Their letters of assassination were acknowledged in hideously obse-
    quious tropical English.
Outside the evil step was marked by muted strings. There were
    more hours of waiting in the courtyard
in case anything had been forgotten upstairs.
And the mercenaries intoned the hymns
of the pack as they made for the island.

THE FRIENDS OF THE HOUSE

We were not born for song but the storing
of words in the gnashing of our teeth.
Music was all goodness. We were born only
for so-called muttering, silent
amidst the noise in which we muffle our voices
at fall of evening as in a bottomless well
– all blind goodness – in the courtyard
crowded with the peaceable old and sick.

Ours is the fever that declines and does not subside, impervious
to the sun of madness, the warming of the bones
in the blindness of the rainy courtyard.

They have shut up the madmen above our heads, which are
    warmed again and rotted
by the hidden face of the sun, and of their own volition the grilles
    have opened for us, the iron and rust transfused, since the time
      has come
in which not even the earth remains. Only the vapour
and moss-seed in the unworked gardens.

We were not born for love, we were born for the copulation that
    smears the blood
with the mortified seed, for the weak puff on the embers
as if the breath were ash and the flesh the waste-plot on which
    men warm themselves
by the heat of stones, a cruel dish.
The last supper of the tribe when all is sand
– even the night – in the length of the night
and the wind dries a scattered paradise :
the buckwheat and the wild spelt-wheat.
Impossible to distinguish between sweat and tears
that quarrel over two dry mouths.

And old inhabitants of the death-room, we shall go on bowing
to the whim of the lady of the house, persistent and docile
like the mark of dampness on the walls, like the passive infiltration
    of ghosts
on plinths stained by dirty water.
Trust will know how to dispense us
the friends of the house from the pains of panic.

JONAH

I could condemn all of it alike, but don't ask me in whose name.
In the name of Isaiah the prophet, but with the grotesque,
    inconclusive gesture of his colleague Jonah
who never managed to complete his little errand subject to the ups
    and downs

of good and evil, to the variations of historical circumstance
which plunged him into the uncertainty of a whale's belly.
Like Jonah, heaven's clown, always obstinately trying to complete
  his little errand, his incendiary brief-case under his sweaty arm-
    pit, his frayed umbrella as a lightning-conductor.
And Jehovah's uncertainty about him, wavering between pardon
  and wrath, taking him up and dropping him, that poor tool of
    doubtful utility
finally fallen into definite disuse.

I too shall end my days under a tree
but like those old drunken tramps who loathe everything alike,
  don't let them
ask me anything, I only know that we shall be destroyed.
I blindly see the hand of a lord whose name I don't remember,
the delicate fingers loosely clenched. Another thing, something else,
  that has nothing visible about it. I remember something like . . .
no, it was no more than this. An event, but no matter! Now I
  don't know where I shall go next time.
Help me, O Lord, who am cast out of thy sight.

Translated by J. M. Cohen

Onelio Jorge Cardoso

IT'S A LONG TIME AGO

Let me forget the ill-used
blood of days gone by.
MANUELA

One afternoon a man from my village came along to see us. We were all interested to know how things were back there and my father, who became a Civil Servant years ago and was then about to retire, put the first question:

'How's the Jiménez family? How are they managing with the farm?'

'Not very well, Don Braulio. The land doesn't seem to like the way they treat it.'

My stepmother, an old woman who kept very much to herself, looked up so as not to miss anything; then she went back to her medicine bottle and began puzzling out the writing on the label again. My father thought his question over and shook his head:

'Dad had no trouble getting good harvests.'

I was standing by the door, on my way out, when something came back to me and I stopped to ask the man from the village:

'Susana's still there isn't she?'

Before he had time to answer, my stepmother frowned and looked at me hurriedly as if she didn't want me to notice. But I had anticipated that would happen.

'Didn't you know? Susana died some time last year.'

'She's not dead!' The news made me straighten up as if there were still time to avoid the shock.

'I don't believe it,' I went on, but my father stopped me short.

'Did you want her to go on for ever, son?'

'Yes, I did,' I said simply; and I found excruciating pleasure in asking my stepmother her opinion of the matter: she had become too old to be able to dominate the household any longer.

'What do you think of that, Manuela?'

She expressed no opinion, said nothing and didn't even take her eyes off the medicine bottle label. I noticed a flicker of anxiety cross my father's face: he was afraid the situation might suddenly get out of hand. Since Manuela didn't answer I turned back to the man and saw that he had just put a parcel of lemons from my village down on the table.

'How did you get to know she was dead? Did you see her die?'

'What a daft question!' my father burst out. 'Do you think he's one of the family or something?' He broke off, flustered and smiling awkwardly, to make sure he hadn't given himself away. But I ignored his question and the man made no move. My step-mother kept staring at the medicine bottle as she turned it round in her withered hand.

'But the fact is I did, Don Braulio...'

'Did what?' my father asked, and the man answered:

'It's true I wasn't a relation or even a friend of Susana's and I didn't live near her at all, but strangely enough I did see her die.'

I looked at my stepmother instantly in the hope that she had caught what had just been said, but she didn't respond. She only leant forward, put the medicine bottle down on the table and said to my father:

'This medicine ought to do the trick.'

My father seemed about to say something, but I didn't want us to get off the subject so I enquired, coldly and deliberately, just so that she could hear the answer:

'Did Susana die of hunger by any chance?'

'There wasn't any chance about it. You could be sure of starving in Susana's house.'

'She didn't even have a handful of rice to feed herself with then?'

This time it worked; this time I hurt my stepmother just where I wanted to hurt her. She turned towards me before the man could answer and fastened her desperate eyes on me. She gazed at me wincing with all the pain a human being can feel when aged and ill and on the point of tears; I noticed that my father was fidgeting on his chair. He understood her perfectly although she hadn't said a word. In the end, since nothing came out of that look of hers, she withdrew into her shell while we waited to hear what the visitor had to say:

'The poor old woman was nothing but skin and bone. Bad food or none at all. She had lots of children and all of them were boys. They all went their own way as soon as they were old enough. Even the sixteen-year-old. It wasn't so much a question of rice: she was lucky if she got enough water to drink. Anyone would have been scared of dying in that house. But mind you, she never blamed her sons. She used to say they were too far away and had their own problems to bother about.'

At this my stepmother lowered her head. I was fairly certain there was a limit to her endurance, but I felt like making sure and insisted:

'A handful of rice would have made all the difference, don't you think?'

My stepmother stiffened and I hoped that she was deeply sorry for what she once did. There I was believing I could make her feel sorry when her voice, everything about her, regained its old strength. She succeeded in winning my father's complete attention and a tactful silence from the visitor before saying:

'Susana was a thief.'

'Why say that, Manuela? Both of us know that well enough. But don't you think that stealing things was her only chance of saving herself from starvation?'

We faced each other. My father looked at me, helpless and in despair. I felt his gaze on the side of my face, but I had gone for her, nobody else, and I braced myself for the fight. We had at last got round to arguing over the thing which lay beneath the endless series of rows we had every day.

'Nobody's forced to steal. Susana got what was coming to her and you'll get what's coming to you soon enough as a punishment for your insolence.'

'You're getting what's coming to you this very moment. Don't you think it would have been better to let Susana keep that handful of rice hidden in her blouse eleven years ago, Manuela?'

That was much more than I ought ever to have said, to my

father's mind, and much more than she could take as well, to judge by her eyes and ailing body. She got up, trembling all over.

'Damn you for saying that!' my father said and went over to her because she seemed unsteady on her feet. The expression on her face altered and she brought her hand up towards her chest.

'Be careful Manuela, hold on to me!'

She coughed, leant forward and doubled up in one of her spasms. With difficulty she made my father understand that he must take her to her room. He couldn't take his eyes off her. All at once he became so worried that he tried helping her along, bending to support her pitiful weight.

I looked at the visitor; despite his deferential attitude towards all that was going on I imagined I could read his thoughts, the thoughts he and everyone else who knew us in the village always had. 'You were always difficult people,' he seemed to say.

I felt strangely unsettled by what I had just done. I thought of Susana and, without expecting it, I saw her kind, dark face disapproving of my behaviour and saddened that I should have grown up just for that. Then I heard my father's footsteps hurrying back and I got ready for a flood of protests. He was sure to be angry with me once again. Up to the point when a father would like to kill his son and only succeeds in making his face go purple.

But nothing of the sort happened. I heard him fumbling anxiously for his stick in the umbrella stand and I turned to face him:

'What's the matter?'

'You stay here; I'm fetching the doctor,' he said; and he went off, tripping over himself with fright, without even mentioning my bad behaviour. Things had gone much too far; I realized this and looked nervously in the direction of her room, but the door was shut. I was sure my stepmother was going to die. Otherwise he would have spent longer with her, and longer with me afterwards, telling me off. He had seen her and he understood her even to the point of knowing when she must die. I had no idea what to do: it's one thing thinking you might get into a tight spot and quite another actually being in one. All things considered, I thought,

death was such a sublime punishment that she would die a martyr
and have the advantage over me.

I thought of Susana again. This time I saw her crying and the
rice falling from her blouse into a pile between her shoes and my
stepmother's expensive shoes. In the end I simply sat down beside
the door so as not to miss anything that happened. The minutes
went by quickly sometimes and then dragged. Eventually I heard
footsteps approaching; I looked round and saw the doctor with my
father. My father came up, opened the door, let the doctor in, went
in himself and shut the door. The minutes went by again, this
time more regularly. The man from the village walked past me
and then came back from the *patio* with his hat. Finally I noticed
that the doctor had left and that my father was standing in front
of me.

'Come along,' he said and walked off, with me following him.
We stopped in the kitchen. He looked me in the eye, searching
desperately for some way of understanding me; I didn't try to
help him.

'Don't you realize she's dying !' he said.

He checked himself, scared by his own thoughts. I didn't know
what to say. In the space of a moment I relived our life together,
the rows I had with her, the loathing I felt, and I saw that hand
again, shaking and pulling at the blouse, and the rice pouring
down on to the shoes below.

'Go and see her and let her see you're there !' he said harshly.

I did as he said without giving it a thought. I turned round and
walked off. On the way through to the bedroom I saw the man
from the village. He kept his eyes to himself, but his presence was
real as he stood there, like a statue, like someone from another
world; all at once I felt as if he was somehow meant to be there.
At last I turned the door-handle and went in. The room seemed to
broaden out visibly before me. The things in it first of all; the bed,
the pictures. The smell of medicine, the pungent smell of the dose
she had just taken still hanging in the air.

Gradually I began to want to look at her. I saw her lying under
the sheet, from her feet up to her chest. Her chest : there you could
see how she was struggling to stay alive. The sheet rose sharply as

she took in a breath. The mound stayed there as if her lungs wanted no more air, but then it collapsed as if her lungs were sinking for good and then it rose again, came up slowly and irregularly.

I wanted to go out again straight away, but she began to mumble something with great effort. I couldn't make out what she was saying but at last heard her ask, fairly distinctly :

'What would have happened if Susana had never existed?'

'I don't know,' I said.

'I do,' she said, and she seemed suddenly relieved; she began breathing deeply and reasoning clearly. 'It would have been different, a different life.'

She opened her eyes and looked up at the ceiling :

'Do you remember how it happened?'

'Yes, I do,' I snapped, because she and I could never have thought of that occasion in the same way.

'There was no need to have done it, was there?'

'Of course there wasn't ! You did it out of spite. You could never have considered what a forty-year-old woman crying with shame must feel like ! Do you remember the expression on her face?'

I couldn't help losing my temper as I spoke. I had leant forward with excitement, but she didn't seem to notice. I was unsure whether she wanted to stay alive a few moments longer or whether at that stage things didn't hurt her any more. Anyway she went on talking as if she hadn't heard me.

'I don't remember what she looked like. At that particular moment I was looking at you. I heard her crying but I had to see how you had reacted.'

'You can't have taken long to find out.'

'You were furious.'

'I was more than that.'

'I remember now.'

'But you must have known quite well that when I was a baby I shared Susana's milk with her youngest son. She was my mother, or at least she became my mother as far as I was concerned.'

Manuela didn't say anything to this. She just brought her head forward to look at me and spoke — I'm forced to admit it — she spoke kindly to me as she asked, quite simply :

'Will you listen?'

I nodded and she went on, still in that strange tone which I wish I had never heard.

'I came before your mother. Things were changed because of a single wish ... It was on your grandfather's farm, on the farm ... your father was the son of the house and I was the maid ... we were young and the fields opened out around us. It was springtime and the animals were mating ... we went behind the fence ... he couldn't hold himself back and I didn't know how to stop him. And so my mother had to pack her bags and your grandfather took us out on to the road ... my mother went first ... they didn't want anyone to catch up with her ... but I wasn't thinking about her ... I was thinking about the child I might have. Then your grandfather came one day to ask about the child ... things started again, as you'd expect. But all the time I've been like an empty pea-pod – sexy and vain, and childless ...'

She stopped talking and seemed to collapse. She was strangely altered and I believed that she would never speak again. I was turning round slowly to go out when I saw her hand coming up from the sheet; I stayed where I was.

'Are you looking? I'm not a bit like your mother was, look.'

I looked up at the portrait on the wall. She was right, they were not alike. My mother's neck was made for pearls, the sort of neck you associate with pearls. Manuela never had a neck. Besides, the portrait had an air about it, the same as my father had sometimes when Manuela wasn't there. She was different; even on her death bed her forehead was still marked with the lines left by a lifetime of doing the same chores day in and day out.

'Your mother had the same social background as your father ... they got married and you were born ... that same day she died. I was somewhere else and knew nothing about it ... Susana was already in the household ... she had a child a few months old and plenty of milk. Your father met me again later on and brought me back ... Well, what more could I have asked for? ... But make no mistake,' she said desperately, trying suddenly to get through to me with her restless eyes, 'I have always been what I am, Daniel: a dry, useless husk!'

This time she collapsed completely and her forearm rolled down from her side on to the sheet. I started counting automatically: one, two, ten, twenty seconds, until there was no point in going on.

There were chairs everywhere, even in the *patio*, and an over-powering smell of roses. The realization came almost as a shock. I was surrounded by an irritating buzz of people trying to keep their voices down. The man from the village had stayed the night with us. He looked as if he had been sent here, there and every-where, but he didn't seem downhearted or tired. He was simply there, smoking. He didn't care about his social superiors passing him by and dismissing him with a glance as they looked around for someone to talk to. I let my amusement at watching him keep more serious thoughts at bay, but I couldn't forget one particular question:

'Why did she look at me and not at Susana at that moment?'

I was trying to puzzle this out when I saw my father approach-ing. He had changed so much since six o'clock the previous evening that at times I felt as if I hardly knew him. He pulled up a chair and sat beside me; he began to talk in purposeless snatches:

'Manuela never wanted anyone to know . . . you know what women who never have children of their own are like.' Then he stopped and looked humbly for some time at the coffin, the candles and everything else before beginning again:

'From the very first she knew that Susana stole . . . I couldn't have sent her away and Manuela didn't want me to either. It was only later on, when she saw that you could never stand her. You always wanted to be with Susana. Just one of those things. A man thinks he needs a son badly but a woman needs one more badly still. It wasn't premeditated: the idea came to her all of a sudden: if only you could see Susana's bad side, she thought . . . Not having a child of her own drove her to it! Then things turned out the way they did; she spent the night crying over the mess she'd made of everything.'

My father stopped talking and I didn't know what to say and still less what to do. I turned my head first this way, then the next.

I should have liked to be able to slip away unseen, without having to face anybody. But whatever happens I realize now that even if I escape I shall never talk about Susana again. And wherever I am I shall be thinking of Manuela and wanting to know something more about her.

Translated by J. G. Brotherston

José Emilio Pacheco

THE ELEMENTS OF NIGHT

In the minimal empire that summer has corroded
days, faith, foresight, crumble.
In the final valley
destruction gorges itself
on each slow exile described by its flight.

Here sinks the brow of the vanquished.
All predictions
are weightless cities spoilt by ash,
quenched vortices in which the rain extinguishes
the indecipherable history revealed by the lightning.
And the moment
fulfils its deaths,
revives remains.

In the slow corpse of the hours
night deposits its transient poisons;
words, days shatter against the air.

Nothing is restored, nothing gives
greenness to the burnt valleys.
The banished water will not come back to the fountain,
nor the eagle's bones return for its wings.

For that time, fragile as a wall of frost,
allowed the sphinxes their unshakeable riddles.

Late, a broken sphere studded with light
it weighs anchor now from the ruins,
its successor, the tableland on fire.

Translated by J. M. Cohen

Biographical Notes on Authors

J. M. COHEN (b. 1903): Translator of the Penguin Classics *Don Quixote*, *Gargantua and Pantagruel*, etc. His interest in Spanish American literature began on a visit to Argentina in 1953 when he first met J. L. Borges. Since then he has kept in touch with writers and books in several countries, and has spent some time both in Mexico and Cuba. In Havana he was a member of the jury of the *Casa de las américas* poetry prize of 1965, with Nicanor Parra and Jaime Sabines. He has edited and introduced programmes of modern poetry from Spain, Mexico, Chile, Cuba, and Argentina for the BBC. He has in preparation a Penguin anthology of contemporary writing in Cuba, entitled *Cuba si*.

BRENO ACCIOLY (1921–1966): Born in the state of Alagoas. Published four volumes of short stories and two novels, *Dunas* and *Siracusa*. *João Urso*, his first volume, was awarded the Graça Aranha and Coelho Neto prizes of the Brazilian Academy of Letters. Was a doctor specializing in leprosy and lived in Rio de Janeiro where he wrote newspaper articles.

MARIO BENEDETTI (b. 1920): Uruguayan novelist, short story writer, critic and occasional poet. His stories are mostly set in Montevideo. He has a crisp, ironic appreciation of urban characters and situations.

JORGE LUIS BORGES (b. 1899): Argentinian writer, who gained his first reputation as a poet of startling imagery (*ultraism*) and interpreter of Buenos Aires. Two volumes of metaphysical tales, *Ficciones*, 1944 (English translation, Grove Press, Inc., and Weidenfeld and Nicolson Ltd; paperback by John Calder Ltd, 1963) and El *Aleph*, 1949, have become minor classics in many countries. 'The Handwriting of God' from the latter volume has not been translated before. Overtaken by almost complete blindness, Borges has latterly returned to poetry and very brief parables, which he completes in his mind and then dictates. The story here was invented in hospital, when he was recovering from an unsuccessful eye operation and was still blindfolded. Borges has a wide knowledge of English literature, particularly of Stevenson, Henry James, Chesterton and Wells, an enthusiasm for Anglo-Saxon and Scandinavian poetry, and for curious philosophies of many kinds. He is chief librarian of the Argentinian national library, a post from which he was dismissed under the Péron dictatorship, but to which he was restored on the fall of the dictator.

JOÃO CABRAL DE MELO NETO (b. 1920): The most impressive Brazilian poet of the last twenty years. In relation to the modernism of the previous generation, he is an 'anti-poet', who offers 'no emotion that is not thought out, no single word that does not introduce a concept, no cadence that does not come as an exact and naked sound' (Eduardo Portella). The English reader will see some resemblances to the wittily fantastic poetry of Marianne Moore.

GUILLERMO CABRERA INFANTE (b. 1929): Cuban novelist and short story writer. His collection *Así en la Paz como en la Guerra*, from which 'At the Great Ecbo' has been taken, has been translated into Italian and French. His panoramic novel of Cuba in the years before the revolution, *Vista del amanecer en el trópico*, won the Premio Joan-Petit-Biblioteca-Breve of 1964. He has been a newspaper editor and cultural attaché in Brussels.

ONELIO JORGE CARDOSO (b. 1914): Cuban short story writer of peasant life. His *Cuentos completos*, 1962, contains the whole of his small, very economimal output until that date. A later volume, *La otra muerte del gato*, appeared in 1964.

ALEJO CARPENTIER (b. 1904): Cuban novelist, whose novel *Los pasos perdidos* (*The Lost Steps*, Victor Gollancz Ltd and Alfred A. Knopf, Inc., 1956) was described by J. B. Priestley as 'one of the major works of our time'. Its successor *El siglo de las luces* (*Explosion in a Cathedral*, Victor Gollancz Ltd, 1963), set in the West Indies in the period of the French Revolution, has the same rich style, but perhaps fails to achieve the mastery of Carpentier's first story of an expedition by sophisticated people into the primeval forest. 'Journey to the Seed' is taken from *Guerra de tiempo*, 1958, a short novel and three stories on the time theme. Carpentier has travelled widely, and at present directs a publishing house in Havana.

ROSARIO CASTELLANOS (b. 1925): Mexican poet and novelist. Her novel *Balún Canán* (*The Nine Guardians*, Faber and Faber Ltd and Vanguard Press, Inc., 1959) tells of her childhood among the Indians of Chiapas province. Her poetry has matured from a gentle lyricism to the powerful symbolism of 'The Foreign Woman'.

ALÍ CHUMACERO (b. 1918): Mexican poet of small output and great concentration. *Palabras en reposo*, 1956, contains his best and most strictly constructed pieces.

JULIO CORTÁZAR (b. 1916): Argentinian novelist and short story writer, who was born and has lived much of his life in Europe. His earlier stories treat the theme of the monster in man. The collection *Bestiario*, 1951, from which the present story has been taken, contains some remarkable and fantastic nightmares. Two further volumes, *Final del juego*, 1956, and *Las armas secretas*, 1959, contain stories of greater length and variety. 'El perseguidor' (The Pursuer) in the latter volume treats of a biographer's possession by his subject, a drunken, drug-taking pioneer of jazz. A selection of his stories has appeared in French (*Les armes secrètes*), and will shortly appear in English. Cortázar's novel *Rayuela*, 1963 (*Hopscotch*, Harvill Press and Pantheon Books, New York, 1966), an anti-novel written in the concentrated style of his shorter work, is a work of absolute mastery.

JOSÉ DONOSO (b. 1925): Chilean novelist and short story writer. His novel *Coronación*, 1957 (*Coronation*, The Bodley Head, Ltd, 1965) contrasts the decay of an aristocratic family in Santiago with the character and vigour of their servants. His second volume of short stories, *El Charleston*, 1960, from which 'Ana María' is taken, treats various urban themes with colloquial directness. A new novel, with the English title *The Footman Snickers*, has just been finished; its setting is a small-town brothel in Chile.

CARLOS DRUMMOND DE ANDRADE (b. 1902): Brazilian poet. With *Alguma poesia*, 1930, he broke completely with prevailing traditions, turning from French models to English. His early work is violent, free in form and social in its overtones. Later, it has grown more ironical and better organized. It is often rhymed and in traditional metres. He sometimes writes almost regular sonnets. He is primarily a realist. 'Time is my material, the present time, living men and the present life,' he said in an interview. He has had great influence on later poets, including João Cabral de Melo Neto.

PABLO ARMANDO FERNÁNDEZ (b. 1930): Cuban poet of many themes and considerable vigour, who has succeeded in *Libro de los héroes*, 1963 (from which the three poems here are taken) in relating the deaths of his friends in the Cuban revolution to the eternal themes of freedom and destiny. His poetry is here much more economical and his imagery more compressed than in *Toda la poesía*, his collection of 1962.

CARLOS FUENTES (b. 1929): Mexican novelist, author of a vast panorama of life in Mexico City, *La región más trasparente*, 1958 (*Where the Air is Clear*, Farrar, Straus & Co., Inc., 1960), and *La muerte de Artemio Cruz*, 1962 (*The Death of Artemio Cruz*, Collins, Sons, and Co. Ltd and Farrar, Straus & Co., 1964), the story of a political boss told in retrospect from his death-bed. Though primarily a novelist, Fuentes began with a volume of short stories, and has published *Aura*, a tale in the tradition of Henry James, as a small book, and a new collection of stories, *Cantar de ciego* (1964).

GABRIEL GARCÍA MÁRQUEZ (b. 1928): Colombian novelist and short story writer. *Los funerales de la mamá grande*, 1962, from which 'The Day after Saturday' is taken, is a collection of short stories of life and character in the backward regions of his country. He had great success with his novel, *La Hojarasca*, 1955, which owes something to Faulkner and Joyce. *El colonel no tiene quien le escriba*, 1961, a masterly short novel of life in a decayed town, has appeared in a French translation, and is about to appear in English. García Márquez lives in Mexico.

ALBERTO GIRRI (b. 1918): Argentinian poet, whose principal theme is solitude and the failure of love. Deriving from surrealism, he has refined his poetry to one of essences. His hermeticism is sometimes obscure, but his line is always attractively hard.

JOÃO GUIMARÃES ROSA (b. 1908): Brazilian novelist and short story writer. His *Grande Sertão: Veredas*, 1956, is a regional novel of the jungle, written in an individual, poetic style. He is a master of language, and an innovator after the manner of James Joyce. He has published two collections of short stories and a book of reportage. 'The Third Bank of the River' has been taken from a periodical. Guimarães Rosa is a doctor by training and a diplomat by profession.

ENRIQUE LIHN (b. 1929): Chilean poet. His third small collection *La pieza oscura*, 1963, from which the present selection is taken, contains a wide variety of poems in a style that has only now attained complete independence. Lihn can be realistic, or write on the theme of historical recurrence, as in 'The Invasion', or on the strangely personal drama of a child lost in a mysterious world. A new collection, *Poesía de paso, la derrota y otros poemas*, won the Casa de las Américas prize in Havana, 1966.

GABRIELA MISTRAL – pseudonym of Lucila Godoy Alcayaga – (1889–1957): Chilean poet and Nobel Prizewinner. She began with the collection *Desolación*, 1922, which contains her best poetry. Her principal theme is of love and the loss of love, and she wrote with rustic simplicity which, at its beginnings, was both affecting and influential.

RICARDO E. MOLINARI (b. 1898): Argentinian poet of great discipline. Beginning with Borges in the *ultraist* movement, he has become more intense and traditional. The finest of his poems are the Odes of *Mundos de la madrugada*, 1943, and subsequent collections, which convey an individual landscape of the desolate South, and a preoccupation with loneliness, loss and the memories of love.

MARCO ANTONIO MONTES DE OCA (b. 1931): Mexican poet of great and plethoric vigour, whose work has gradually attained order and form under the pressure of social and religious conviction. His imagery remains bold and exciting.

VINICIUS DE MORAES (b. 1913): Brazilian poet independent of movements, who has written lyrics for the Bossa nova and the script of the film *Orfeo negro* (*Black Orpheus*), which was taken from one of his plays. He writes in conventional forms, including the sonnet, and is concerned with social problems. He has been spoken of as a modern counterpart of Villon, and has himself proclaimed his admiration for Rimbaud. It is as an independent, with a light and sardonic lyrical gift, that he seems to hold his place in modern poetry.

PABLO NERUDA – pseudonym of Neftalí Ricardo Reyes – (b. 1904): Chilean poet, whose *Veinte poemas de amor y una canción desesperada*, 1924, the direct account of a love affair, has secured him a vast public. The three volumes of *Residencias*, surrealist in an individual way, have been widely translated. His *Canto general*, 1950, attempts to cover the whole story of America, from its unpeopled beginnings to the struggles of dictators and Communists in the present age. Neruda, converted to Communism as a result of the Spanish Civil War, sometimes writes with rhetorical partisanship. The best of the *Canto general*, of which 'Some Animals' is an example, contains his poetry of greatest vision. The earlier *Odas elementales*, 1954, also, like that to the magnolia, transmit a remarkable sense for objects in their visual and tactile aspects. Neruda is most of all a poet of *things*. His later work has been prolific, but somewhat 'manufactured'.

JUAN CARLOS ONETTI (b. 1909): Uruguayan writer of short novels and stories. His habitual themes are urban loneliness and sexual obsession, his moods pessimistic. *El infierno tan temido*, 1962, from which the title story has been taken, contains most of his shorter work. Monotonous and haunted, he sometimes recalls the early Sartre, of whom, however, he is completely independent. His finest novel *El astillero* (1960) is being translated for Charles Scribner's Sons, New York.

JOSÉ EMILIO PACHECO (b. 1939): One of the most promising of the younger Mexican writers. 'The Elements of Night' is the title poem of a small collection of poetry (*Los elementos de la noche*, 1963). El *viento distante*, 1963, contains some stories of great delicacy. He has also written good criticism.

NICANOR PARRA (b. 1914): Chilean poet. Beginning with popular romances, Parra went on to the ironical poetry of *Poemas y antipoemas*,

1956, from which the poems here are taken. Parra is deliberately and ironically commonplace in his images, and flat in his rhythms. His anti-poems are not careless like those of the North American beats, whom he admires. His real attitude is not anti-poetic but anti-rhetorical. His humour is often grim, and his social involvement patent.

OCTAVIO PAZ (b. 1914): Mexican poet of metaphysical profundity, concerned with the contradictions between eternal Being and existence in Time. He has a great lyrical gift, and also a power of symphonic construction, similar to T. S. Eliot. His masterpiece is the cyclical *Piedra de sol*, 1958 (*Sun-Stone*, New Directions). Emerging from surrealism, he retains a profound admiration for André Breton. His social involvement began with the Spanish Civil War. His *Laberinto de la soledad* (*The Labyrinth of Solitude*, Grove Press, Inc., 1962) examines the role of Mexico in history and the importance of its double ancestry and double heritage of civilization, from the Spaniards and the Indians.

CARLOS PELLICER (b. 1899): Mexican poet of light and colour who rejoices in the exuberance of the tropics. His joy of life and his fervent catholicism are translated in pictorial terms, and sensual music. 'Let me for a single moment cease to be cries and colour' – '*Déjame un solo instante/ dejar de ser grito y color*' – he wrote. It would have been impossible.

JUAN RULFO (b. 1918): Mexican novelist, author of one novel, *Pedro Páramo*, 1955 (translation published by Grove Press and John Calder Ltd, 1959), which presents the history of a long-dead political boss with the voice of a ghost fragmentarily talking to ghosts, and one volume of short stories, *El llano en llamas*, 1953. Rulfo's stories describe the violence of the Mexican landscape and the bitter resignation of the Indians. His writing is spare, and his treatment of time tensely original.

JAIME SABINES (b. 1926): Mexican poet. Sober, disillusioned and ironical, Sabines writes objectively of himself, his love, his family and his fear of death, and of the city scene. His values are tactile, his sympathy with the Indian, bewildered by the harsh life of the Capital. He himself comes from Chiapas, and maintains a dogged independence of intellectual society. *Recuento de poemas*, 1962, from which these two poems are taken, contains the whole of his work.

CÉSAR VALLEJO (1892–1938): Peruvian poet and the first to break with symbolism and modernism in the Spanish speaking world. *Trilce*, 1922, from which four poems have been taken, was a violent declaration of independence. The book laments the loss of his mother and brothers and childhood home, his unjust imprisonment and exile that awaited him. He went to

Paris, never to return, and there devoted himself to Marxist propaganda, writing occasional stories, plays and journalism. In 1936, under pressure of his approaching death and the Spanish war, he wrote his *Poemas humanos*, and a group of poems about Spain. These are hastier and harsher than *Trilce*, which contains, among many unsuccessful experiments, poetry that influences poets in all the Spanish-speaking countries. Vallejo is one of the great poets of this century.

C. VASCONCELOS MAIA (b. 1923): Brazilian, born in the south-west of the state of Bahia. Has published four volumes of short stories, *Fora da Vida*, *Contos da Bahia*, *O Cavalo e a Rosa*, and *O Leque de Oxum*, and three books about Bahia called *Agua de Meninos* (with drawings by Caribé), *O Primeiro Misterio* and *Lembranca de Bahia*. He is represented in the principal collections of modern Brazilian short stories, and lives in Salvador da Bahia where he works as a journalist and for the Tourist Department.

Some other books published in the
Writing Today . . . Series are described on the
following pages

The Writing Today . . . Series

An interesting new venture by Penguins which aims to inform the English-speaking reader of new developments in the literature of other countries.

The following volumes are available or in preparation

The New Writing in the U.S.A.*
African Writing Today
Latin American Writing Today
South African Writing Today
German Writing Today

African Writing Today *is described overleaf*

Not for sale in the U.S.A.

African Writing Today

Edited by Ezekiel Mphahlele

African Writing Today provides a cross-section (in translation, where necessary) of recent African work in English, French and Portuguese from the following countries:

Angola, Cameroun, Congo
Dahomey, Gambia, Ghana, Guinea
Ivory Coast, Kenya, Moçambique
Nigeria, Ruanda, Senegal
Sierra Leone, South Africa

DATE DUE

2:40			
3:30			
8:15			
3:45			
MAR 13 71			
DS			
MAR 16 71			
12:30 NOON			
10:20 AM			
8 p.m.			
9 AM Tue			
JUL 5 1983			
NOV 2 0 1989			
GAYLORD			PRINTED IN